Self-Instruction Materials on Narrative Discourse Analysis

SIL International®

Editor-in-Chief
Sue McQuay, Managing Editor

Managing Editor
Eugene Burnham

Proofreader
Eleanor J. McAlpine

Production Staff
Priscilla Higby, Production Manager
Judy Benjamin, Compositor
Barbara Alber, Graphics Designer

Self-Instruction Materials on Narrative Discourse Analysis

Stephen H. Levinsohn

SIL International®
Dallas, Texas

© 2023 by SIL International®
Library of Congress Control Number: 2022943456
ISBN: 978-1-55671-461-0 (pbk)
ISBN: 978-1-55671-496-2 (ePub)

All rights reserved

No part of this publication may be reproduced, stored in a retrieval system, or transmitted in any form or by any means – electronic, mechanical, photocopy, recording, or otherwise – without the express permission of SIL International®. However, short passages, generally understood to be within the limits of fair use, may be quoted without permission.

Copies of this and other publications of SIL International® may be obtained through distributors such as Amazon, Barnes & Noble, other worldwide distributors and, for select volumes, www.sil.org/resources/publications:

SIL International Publications
7500 W. Camp Wisdom Road
Dallas, TX 75236-5629 USA

General inquiry: publications_intl@sil.org
Pending order inquiry: sales_intl@sil.org

Scripture quotations identified as *NEB* are from *The New English Bible*, copyright © 1970, The Delegates of the Oxford University Press and the Syndics of the Cambridge University Press. All rights reserved.

Scripture quotations identified as *NIV* are from the *Holy Bible, New International Version®, NIV®*, © 1973, 1978, 1984, Biblica, Inc.® All rights reserved worldwide. Used by permission.

Scripture quotations identified as *NRSV* are from the *New Revised Standard Version Bible*, copyright © 1989, National Council of the Churches of Christ in the United States of America. Used by permission. All rights reserved.

Scripture quotations identified as *RSV* are from the *Revised Standard Version of the Bible*, copyright © 1946, 1952, and 1971, National Council of the Churches of Christ in the United States of America. Used by permission. All rights reserved.

Scripture quotations identified as *TEV* are from the *Today's English Version*, copyright © 1976, American Bible Society. Used by Permission.

Greek examples and word-by-word translations were adapted from *The New Greek-English Interlinear New Testament* by Brown, Comfort and Douglas, copyright © 1990. Used by permission of Tyndale House Publishers. All rights reserved.

Contents

Tables	**xi**
0 Introduction	**1**
0.1 The nature of text-related explanations	1
0.2 Some key concepts in textlinguistics	2
0.2.1 Choice implies meaning	2
0.2.2 Semantic meaning and pragmatic effects	3
0.2.3 Default versus marked phenomena	4
0.3 Language types	6
0.4 Overview of chapter topics	7
0.5 Assignments and consulting	8
1 Preparation and Charting of Narrative Texts	**9**
1.1 Why analyse texts?	9
1.2 Types of text	11
1.2.1 The number of speakers	11
1.2.2 The text genre	11
1.3 Text selection: What sort of text should I begin with?	12
1.4 Preparing your texts for charting and analysis	13
1.4.1 Editing	13
1.4.2 Controlling the facts	13
1.4.3 Segmenting the text	13
1.4.4 Constituent order and co-occurrence	15
1.5 Displaying a text in chart form	16
1.5.1 The basic chart	16
1.5.2 Conventions for charting	17
Appendix A: Sample Chart for an SV/OV Language	19
Appendix B: Sample Chart for a VS/VO Language	21
2 Articulations of the Sentence, Coherence and Discontinuities	**23**
2.1 Articulations of the sentence	23
2.1.1 Topic-comment articulation	24
2.1.2 Identificational articulation	24
2.1.3 Presentational articulation	25
2.1.4 Event reporting and thetic	25
2.1.5 Final thoughts on sentence articulations	27

2.2 More on focus	27
2.3 Coherence and cohesion	28
2.4 Thematic continuity, discontinuities and segmentation	29
2.4.1 Place	29
2.4.2 Participants	30
2.4.3 Time	30
2.4.4 Action	30
2.5 Segmentation into groupings	33
Appendix C: Bekwarra text	36

3 Points of Departure — 41

3.1 Propositional topic, comment and point of departure	41
3.2 Points of departure involving renewal	47
3.2.1 Renewal by means of a referential point of departure	47
3.2.2 Renewal by means of a situational point of departure	48
3.2.3 Renewal by means of "tail-head linkage"	48
3.3 Potential points of departure that do not begin a sentence	50

4 Focus, Emphasis and Prominence — 53

4.1 Focus versus topic and point of departure	53
4.2 Preferred positions for focal constituents	55
4.2.1 Established/nonestablished	55
4.2.2 Constituent ordering in thetic propositions	56
4.2.3 Preposed focal constituents	56
4.2.4 The dominant focal element	58
4.3 Devices used to give prominence to a focal constituent	59
4.4 Categories of (prominent) focus	60
4.5 Distinguishing points of departure from preposed focal constituents	61
4.6 Thematic prominence	63
4.6.1 Prominent entities	63
4.6.2 Prominent parts of the theme line	64
4.7 Emphatic prominence	64
4.8 Foils	65
4.9 Types of *it*-cleft structures	66

5 The Relative Prominence of the Sentences of a Text — 69

5.1 Foreground and background	69
5.2 Sentences that present background information in narrative	72
5.2.1 Nonevents	72
5.2.2 Secondary events	73
5.2.3 Devices used to background sentences	73
5.2.4 Backgrounding *within* a sentence	75
5.3 Natural prominence: verb semantics and verb aspect	77
5.3.1 Verb types and natural prominence	78
5.3.2 Verbal aspect and background versus foreground	78
5.3.3 Marked uses of aspects	79
5.4 Highlighting of sentences	81
5.4.1 Climaxes	81
5.4.2 Highlighting significant developments and changes of direction	83

6 Nonsubordinating Connectives in Narrative — 87

6.1 The default way of coordinating sentences in narrative	87
6.2 Pragmatic connectives	88
6.3 Connectives that constrain an additive interpretation	89
6.3.1 Ways in which additives involving parallelism between propositions have been found to differ in the same language	90
6.3.2 The varied pragmatic effects that the same additive may convey in different contexts	92

      6.3.3 Default and marked positions for additives   93
  6.4 Connectives that constrain a countering interpretation   94
      6.4.1 Encoding countering relations in specific contexts   94
      6.4.2 Factors that may determine when a countering relation is marked or left implicit   96
      6.4.3 Application to Koine Greek   97
  6.5 Particles that constrain a developmental interpretation   97
      6.5.1 Extract 1: Tyap   98
      6.5.2 Extract 2: Koorete   100
      6.5.3 Extract 3: Koine Greek   101
      6.5.4 Marking new developments   102
      6.5.5 Stories which build up to a moral or other teaching point   104
  6.6 Packaging information in development units   105

7 The Reporting of Conversation in Narrative   109
  7.1 Forms of reporting speeches   109
      7.1.1 Factors that may determine the form of reporting   110
      7.1.2 Extract 1: Goemai   111
  7.2 The speech orienter   112
  7.3 Closed conversations   113
  7.4 The relationship between successive speeches in a reported conversation   114
  7.5 The status of reported speeches in the overall story   114
      7.5.1 Many reported speeches are backgrounded   114
      7.5.2 Many reported speeches are not treated as new developments   115
      7.5.3 Many reported speeches are grouped into couplets   115
      7.5.4 Speeches as theme-line events   116
  7.6 Changes of direction in reported conversations   116
  7.7 References to the speaker and addressee in speech orienters   117
  7.8 Repetition of speech orienters   118
  7.9 The relative status and authority of the participants   119
  7.10 Interpretive-use marker   119

8 Participant Reference   123
  8.1 Introduction of new participants   123
      8.1.1 Major versus minor participants   123
      8.1.2 Introduction to a new versus an existing mental representation   124
      8.1.3 One, a certain   125
      8.1.4 Points of departure and the introduction of a participant   125
      8.1.5 Highlighting the introduction of a participant   126
  8.2 Further reference to activated participants   126
      8.2.1 Givón's Iconicity Principle   127
      8.2.2 Default encoding values for activated subjects   128
      8.2.3 Marked encoding values for activated subjects   130
      8.2.4 Cross-linguistic default encoding values   131
  8.3 NP references to active participants and story development in Biblical Hebrew   132
      8.3.1 Marked encoding of references to subjects in contexts S1 and S2   132
      8.3.2 Marked encoding of references to active participants in other contexts   134
      8.3.3 Conclusion   135
      8.3.4 Implication for translation   135
  Appendix D: Chart for Biblical Hebrew: Genesis 21:33b–22:14   136
  Appendix E: Chart for Tyap   138

9 VIPs, Determiners, Directionals   141
  9.1 VIPs   141
      9.1.1 Two reference strategies   141
      9.1.2 The role of *other* in a reference strategy   142
      9.1.3 Global and local VIPs   142

9.2 Determiners	144
9.2.1 Thematic and athematic determiners	144
9.2.2 Thematic determiners and orientation	145
9.2.3 Other distinctions signalled by determiners	146
9.2.4 The (definite) article	146
9.3 Directional verbs and auxiliaries	148
9.3.1 Orientation	148
9.3.2 Movement	149
9.3.3 Extended senses	149
Appendix F: Demonstratives in Koine Greek	151
Appendix G: Determiners in Languages of the Philippines	154
10 Subordinate Clauses, Especially Relative Clauses	**155**
10.1 Brand-new information and subordinate clauses	155
10.2 Information load	156
10.3 Relative clauses	158
10.3.1 Review of terminology	158
10.3.2 Restrictive and nonrestrictive relative clauses	158
10.3.3 Types of restrictive relative clause	159
10.3.4 Types of nonrestrictive relative clause	159
10.3.5 Which constituents may be relativised?	160
10.3.6 Restrictions on the use of relative clauses in particular languages	161
10.3.7 Relative clauses in Biblical Hebrew	163
10.3.8 Implications for translation	164
References	**165**
Questionnaire: Narrative Text Features	**171**
Index of Languages	**177**
Index of Scripture References	**179**

Tables

Table 1. Basic verb forms in Jóola (without default)	5
Table 2. Basic verb forms in Jóola (with default)	5
Table 3. Contrast of text orientation and organisation in four text genres	11
Table 4. Chart of part of the Bekwarra text	17, 71
Table 5. Dimensions of continuity and discontinuity in narrative	29
Table 6. Common boundary features	33
Table 7. Chart of an Inga folktale	70
Table 8. Constituent order and propositional order correlations	96
Table 9. Propositional order and means of conjoining correlations	96
Table 10. Chart of a Tyap folktale	98
Table 11. Illustration of the affix -ka in storyline development in Inga	103
Table 12. Illustration of constituent order in Gude storyline	103
Table 13. Chart of a Gumawana folktale	112, 115
Table 14. Chart of a Teribe conversation	119
Table 15. Noun phrases in context S1 in Hebrew, Tyap and Greek	133
Table 16. Information load in a Tunebo text	157

0

Introduction

Textlinguistics, or discourse analysis, as it tends to be called in SIL circles, covers a vast domain – a domain so vast that you could spend the whole of your linguistic career studying nothing else. This course does not even start to give you an overview of all the topics that pertain to textlinguistics. Rather, it focuses on a very narrow subset, namely those features that have a direct pay-off for translation of narrative texts from one language to another. This subset has as its origin a list of text-related topics that translation consultants in the Cameroon Branch of SIL International identified in the early 1990s as problem areas when translating into the languages of that country.

This introductory chapter begins by considering the nature of text-related explanations (0.1). It then presents three key concepts that underlie the analysis of texts: choice implies meaning, the difference between semantic meaning and pragmatic effects, and the concept of default versus marked phenomena (0.2). The chapter ends with an overview of the topics covered in subsequent chapters (0.3).

0.1 The nature of text-related explanations

This course concerns the analysis of **narrative texts** (discourses). The *Oxford English Dictionary (OED)* defines **discourse** (text) and **narrative** as follows:

> **Definitions**
> Discourse (text): a connected series of utterances.
> Narrative: a spoken or written account of connected events in order of happening.

The term **utterance** is problematic (see Crystal 1997:405). The *OED* defines it as "an uninterrupted chain of spoken or written words not necessarily corresponding to a single or complete grammatical unit". In punctuated written texts, an utterance typically ends with a period (full stop). In spoken texts, its boundaries are usually characterised by silence and a change of intonation contour. The utterances of a well-told spoken narrative text generally correspond to one or more written sentences, though sentence fragments sometimes make up an utterance.

Textlinguistics (discourse analysis) does not draw its explanations from within the sentence or word (in other words, the factors involved are not syntactic or morphological). Rather, its explanations are **extra-sentential** (from the linguistic and wider context of the utterance). A significant part of textlinguistics involves the study of **information structure**, which concerns "the interaction of sentences and their contexts" (Lambrecht 1994:9).

As I said above, textlinguistics is a vast topic. This course concentrates on those factors that have a direct pay-off for translation. So we will be concerned primarily with the **function** of different forms, constructions, orders, etc. Dooley (1989:1) defines the functional approach to textlinguistics as "an attempt to discover and describe what linguistic structures are used for: the functions they serve, the factors that condition their use".

> This functional approach contrasts with the *structural* one, which is 'an attempt to describe linguistic structure ... essentially for its own sake' (ibid.). At its worst, the structural approach might tell you, for example, that [Koine] Greek clauses manifest all six possible orders of subject (S), object (O) and verb (V) – SVO, SOV, OSV, OVS, VSO, VOS – without ever addressing the question of when to use which. A functional approach, on the other hand, starts from the existence of the six orders (i.e., it presupposes a structural analysis) and concentrates on identifying the factors that determine the selection of one order over against another. (Levinsohn 2000:vii)

Thus, our textlinguistic goal is to discover WHY a particular constituent sometimes begins a clause and at other times does not. It is to discover WHY a connective such as *Then* or *After that* sometimes opens a sentence and at other times does not. It is to discover WHY speech is sometimes reported directly and at other times indirectly. It is to discover WHY successive sentences with the same subject sometimes refer to the subject only with a person marker in the verb and at other times with a pronoun such as *he* or a noun phrase such as *the boy*, etc.

There are some **pitfalls** to avoid when looking for textlinguistic explanations of phenomena. One is that we can become so interested in textlinguistic explanations that we fail to realise that a perfectly good syntactic rule or semantic definition accounts for the feature being analysed. Yes, some linguistic features can only be explained with reference to extra-sentential factors. The textual use of others, though, follows naturally or by extension from a syntactic rule or semantic definition.

A second pitfall is **not relating** textlinguistic observations to a valid syntactic rule or semantic definition. For example, it is common for demonstratives to have both a spatial and a textual usage. Take a language such as Spanish [spa] with three demonstratives, defined spatially as *this (close to the speaker), that (an intermediate distance from the speaker)* and *that-far (far from the speaker)*. An analyst studies the occurrence of these demonstratives in narratives and discovers, perhaps, that *this* always refers to the participant who is the current centre of attention (see ch. 9). *That-far*, in contrast, denotes a participant who is NOT the current centre of attention. These spatial and narrative uses are not distinct, to be described in different parts of a grammar. Rather, the demonstratives have the same function in different contexts. For example, the referent of *this* may always be at the centre of attention, whether spatial (where the speaker is) or textual. Such a unity should then be reflected in their linguistic description.

0.2 Some key concepts in textlinguistics

This section discusses three key concepts that underlie the analysis of texts: choice implies meaning (0.2.1), the difference between semantic meaning and pragmatic effects (0.2.2), and the concept of default versus marked phenomena (0.2.3).

0.2.1 Choice implies meaning

One basic principle of a functional approach to textlinguistics is that choice implies meaning. In most sentences, authors have the option of expressing themselves in more than one way. Are these ways simply 'stylistic variations'? Textlinguistics answers, No! Because there is a choice of ways, the ways differ in significance; there are reasons for the variations.

To illustrate this point, consider the variations mentioned in the previous section.
- A particular constituent sometimes begins a clause and at other times does not. This is not just a question of style; there is a linguistic reason for the change of order (see ch. 3).
- A connective such as *Then* or *After that* sometimes opens a sentence and at other times does not. This is not a question of style; there is a linguistic reason for its presence or absence (see ch. 6).

- The speeches reported in a narrative are sometimes direct and sometimes indirect. This is not a question of style; there is a linguistic reason for the way each speech is reported (see ch. 7).
- Successive sentences with the same subject refer to the subject at times only in the verb and at other times with a pronoun such as *he* or a noun phrase such as *the boy*. This is not a question of style; there is a linguistic reason for choosing one form of reference rather than another (see ch. 8).

The converse of this principle is that, if there is NO choice, there is nothing more to be said. Suppose a language always uses indirect speech when the speaker is reporting what someone said to him or her (e.g. *She told me that I am to go* but not *She told me, 'You are to go'*). In such a language, there is nothing to investigate in that area. In contrast, if the language can report a particular sort of speech either directly or indirectly and there is no grammatical reason for the variation, it is the job of text analysis to discover the significance of selecting the one form of reporting over against the other. 'Optional variation' is not an adequate explanation!

Application to the language you are analysing

Once you have charted a narrative text (see ch. 1), look for features such as the four mentioned above where the author could have expressed him or herself in a different way. Include in your consideration particles that are sometimes present and sometimes absent; if you do not know why they are there (or not there), then use different-coloured highlighters to mark the presence (or the absence) of each one.

Stylistic variation and register

Like 'optional', **stylistic** variation is also a suspect textlinguistic explanation. It is fine to talk about variation **between** storytellers, since individuals clearly have different styles (see Dooley and Levinsohn 2001:11–12). However, to cite 'stylistic variation' as an explanation for the presence versus the absence of features in texts by a **single** storyteller is a cop-out.

It is true that the same individual may use distinct styles or **registers** in different circumstances. I employ one register in a lecture, but a different register in casual conversation (Dooley and Levinsohn 2001:12–13). Furthermore, maturity leads to changes in an individual's style (mostly, because they control a greater variety of features). Nevertheless, when I examined thirty texts given to me over a ten year period by the same mature storyteller in the Inga [inb][1] (Quechuan, Colombia) language, I found great consistency in his use of a number of significant textual features.

Since stylistic variation between storytellers is a fact of life, this has implications for text analysts and translators. As far as possible, we should analyse narratives related by **accomplished** storytellers. We can then have some confidence in the validity of our conclusions. Otherwise, beware! I remember how excited Dr Robert Longacre was when, early in a workshop in 1975–1976, he observed in a Colombian language something comparable to the cyclic style of storytelling characteristic of many languages of Papua New Guinea. This observation never appeared in print, though, because it turned out that the author had never recorded a story before, and he was so nervous that he kept starting it over afresh!

0.2.2 Semantic meaning and pragmatic effects

In common with many other analysts, there is a crucial distinction in my approach to textlinguistics between the inherent or semantic meaning of an expression or construction and the pragmatic effects of using it in a particular context. According to Leech (1983):

- **semantics** is the property of expressions in a given language: *what does expression X mean?*; it is the inherent or natural meaning of the expression.
- **pragmatics** is meaning in relation to the user of the expression: *what does the speaker mean by X?*

To illustrate this distinction between semantic meaning and pragmatic effects, consider the utterance, *The door's open*. Its natural meaning is that a door, known at least to the speaker, is open.

---

[1] ISO 639-3, *Codes for the representation of names of languages*, are incorporated into this volume in square brackets following the language name, when known. For example, Inga [inb], Jóola [dyo], Chichicapan Zapotec [zpv]. For further information see www.ethnologue.com/codes.

This meaning belongs to semantics. However, if someone tells you, *The door's open*, and you are sitting by the door, his or her intention in uttering the expression is probably to get you to get up and close the door. This intended effect belongs to pragmatics.

The pragmatic effects of using an expression vary with the context. Suppose you had knocked on the door of an office and a voice inside calls out, *The door's open*. In that context, the user's intention in uttering the expression would normally be to invite you to enter the office. Whereas the semantic meaning of an expression is more or less invariable, the pragmatic effects of using it vary with the context.

The distinction between semantic meaning and pragmatic effects may usefully be applied to a variety of textual features. Consider the **progressive** construction in English [eng]. It has a semantic meaning of individual instance and incompleteness. For example, *It's raining* refers to an individual instance of the event of raining and portrays the event as not complete. In certain contexts, though, the progressive carries an overtone of insincerity, as in *John is being polite*, in contrast to *John is polite*. Insincerity is not an inherent part of the semantic meaning of the English progressive. Rather, it is one of a number of pragmatic effects that are achieved by using the progressive in different contexts (see Zegarač 1989).[2]

Although pragmatic effects vary with the context, they are not entirely arbitrary; they usually relate to the semantic meaning in some way. For example, overtones of insincerity may well arise from the fact that the progressive refers to an individual instance of an event. *John is being polite* may thus suggest to the hearer that he is not habitually polite and so is putting on an act on this particular occasion.

0.2.3 Default versus marked phenomena

When an analyst seeks to explain some feature, it is important to find an explanation that works both when the feature is present and when it is absent. For example, to really explain why a particular constituent sometimes begins a clause, the proposal should predict not only when it will be there, but also when it will not.

Balancing this requirement is the concept of **markedness**.[3] This says that, when a marked form is used, the meaning associated with the form is conveyed. When the marked form is not used, in contrast, NOTHING is said about the meaning associated with it – the sentence is **not marked** for that feature. In other words, it is not necessarily true that the function of the default form is the opposite of that of the marked form.

The concept of markedness is important not only in phonology and grammar, but also in text-related explanations. The following are some examples.

- Languages have default versus marked orders of constituents in clauses and sentences. Say the default order is SVO. Then the analyst needs to explain the occurrences of OV or VSO order, but not why a sentence has SVO order (see chs. 3–4).
- Languages have a default verb form for presenting the events of a narrative. So the analyst needs to explain the use of OTHER verb forms to present narrative events, but not why the default form occurs in a narrative (see ch. 5).
- Languages have a default way of conjoining the sentences of a narrative. So the analyst needs to explain the use of OTHER forms of conjoining, but not why the default form of conjoining occurs (see ch. 6).
- Languages have a default way of reporting speeches in narrative. So the analyst needs to explain the use of OTHER forms of reporting, but not why the default form of reporting occurs (see ch. 7).
- Languages have a default way of referring to an active participant in specific narrative contexts. So the analyst needs to explain the use of OTHER forms of reference, but not why the default form of reference occurs (see ch. 8).

---

[2] See also 3.3 where the distinction between semantic meaning and pragmatic effects is applied to constituent order, 5.3.3 for its application to verbal aspect, and 6.3.2 for its application to connectives.

[3] See Andrews 1990 for discussion of Markedness Theory.

0.2 Some key concepts in textlinguistics

An instance of mistakenly giving a positive label to a default form

A common mistake, when contrasting a marked form with a default form, is to allocate a positive label not only to the marked form, but also to the default form. Although the label may then describe the **typical** function of the default form, it will not account for all instances of its usage.

I was once shown the following matrix (in French [fra]) for the basic verb forms of Jóola [dyo] (Bak, Senegal):[4]

Table 1. Basic verb forms in Jóola (without default)

Emphasis on:	Aspect	
	Completive	Habitual
verb	completive emphasis on verb	habitual emphasis on verb
noun	completive emphasis on noun	habitual emphasis on noun

The above matrix gives positive labels for both members of each contrasting pair: completive versus habitual, and verb emphasis versus noun emphasis. In neither pair is a default member identified. However, in both pairs, the label for one of the members is too specific, as I now show.

First, consider the "emphasis" parameter (better described as **focus** – see ch. 2):
- When the verb is marked for "noun emphasis", the preposed noun (or other nonverbal constituent) is in focus, as in *[It was]* **John** *I met* (the focal constituent is bolded).
- The grammar claimed that, when the verb is marked for "verb emphasis", the verb itself is in focus, as in *I* **met** *John*. However, examples in natural text show that the same verb forms are used also for sentences such as *I met John* or *I met* **John**.[5]

Thus, the "emphasis" parameter does not distinguish between "noun emphasis" and "verb emphasis", but between a marked form of "emphasis" (focus) and a default form.

Now consider the **aspect** parameter, where it is the "completive" label that is too specific. Jóola verbs in the "completive" aspect TYPICALLY describe past events that have been completed, as in *I met John* and *I have met John*. However, the same verb form is used also for states, as in *She is pretty*, and for comparatives such as *That tree is farther away than this one*, neither of which are completed. In fact, the "completive" aspect portrays events or states as a WHOLE and so is more correctly described as the default, **perfective** aspect (see 5.3.2).

The matrix of basic verb forms in Jóola is therefore as follows:

Table 2. Basic verb forms in Jóola (with default)

Focus:	Aspect	
	Default (perfective)	Marked (habitual)
default	(default)	+ habitual
marked	+ marked focus	+ marked focus + habitual

---

[4] The source is unknown. Please advise if possible.
[5] Such sentences have "predicate focus" (Lambrecht 1994:222–223 – a concept discussed in ch. 2).

0.3 Language types

Dryer (1997) distinguishes languages on the basis of two variables: whether or not the object (O) follows the verb (V) (VO versus OV) and whether or not the subject (S) commonly follows the verb (VS versus SV).[6] A number of discourse features tend to correlate with these variables.

For example, we shall see in 6.4.2 that, when one proposition of a pair is positive and the other negative (e.g. 'Allow the children to come to me; do not prevent them'), many **OV** languages prefer the negative proposition to precede the positive one (e.g. 'Do not prevent the children from coming to me; allow them to come'). Conversely, many **VO** languages prefer the positive proposition to precede the negative one. For example, older translations into English of Philemon 14b–c preserve the negative-positive order of the Greek [grc] (e.g. "in order that your goodness might not be by compulsion but of your own free will" – *RSV*). However, the *NRSV* translation judges the positive-negative order to be more natural: "in order that your good deed might be voluntary and not something forced" (*NIV* is similar).

You may well know already whether the language you are analysing is of the VO or OV type. If the subject sometimes precedes the verb and sometimes follows it, though, it may not be obvious whether it is of the VS or SV type. To establish this, I concentrate on propositions that make a comment about the subject as topic when the subject is a noun or noun phrase (NP). 'Then those people skinned the little donkey' is such a proposition. The NP subject 'those people' is the propositional topic and the rest of the proposition ('skinned the little donkey') makes a comment about 'those people' (see 2.1 for a definition of propositional topic).

I consider a language to be of the **VS** type if it is common in narratives for NP subject-topics to follow the verb (see also Longacre 1995:332). This means that the following sample languages have VS order:

Chichicapan Zapotec [zpv] (Oto-Manguean, Mexico)

lwehgu	*bachyu'xi*	*ra' ni'chi*	*buhrri-i'hn*
then	skinned (V)	PL that (S)	donkey-DIM

'Then those people skinned the little donkey.' (Benton 1989:66)[7]

Sama Bangingih [sse] (alt. Sama Bangingi'; N.W. Austronesian, Philippines)

Magtuwi	*anaggaw*	*si Kuyya'*	*ma si Ba'u'u*
immediately	AP.capture (V)	PM monkey (S)	OBL PM turtle

'Monkey immediately snatched at Turtle.' (Gault 1999:398)[8]

Biblical Hebrew [hbo] (Genesis 22:7a)[9]

wayyō'mer	*yiṣḥāq*	*'el-'abrāhām*	*'ābîw*
& spoke (V)	Isaac (S)	to-Abraham	his.father

'Isaac spoke to Abraham his father'

Koine Greek (Acts 16:36a)

apēngeilen	*de*	*ho desmophulax*	*tous logous*	*toutous*	*pros ton Paulon*
reported (V)	and	the jailer (S)	the words	these	to the Paul

'The jailer reported these words to Paul.'

See chapter 3 for reasons why subjects often precede the verb in VS languages.

---

[6] Chapter 5 of Comrie 1989 discusses ways of defining subject.

[7] Benton uses the following abbreviations: DIM: diminutive; PL: plural.

[8] Gault uses the following abbreviations: AP: antipassive; OBL: oblique; PM: person marker. I follow Gault in defining the subject in N.W. Austronesian languages "syntactically as the primary grammar relation ... regardless of its semantic role" (p. 393). In particular, subject constituents agree with the verb and, in propositions with topic-comment articulation (2.1), are the propositional topic.

[9] English glosses of the Hebrew are based on Green (1986). The symbol '&' represents the conjunction *waw*.

0.4 Overview of chapter topics

This section outlines the contents of the remaining chapters of this course.

Chapter 1 concerns the selection, preparation and charting of narrative texts. It asks why a linguist should analyse texts, rather than relying solely on elicited material to learn about the language under consideration. It identifies those texts that are most suitable for beginning text analysis. It describes how to prepare a text for charting, then presents a method of charting them in a systematic way. A folktale in the Bekwarra [bkv] (Benue-Congo, Nigeria) language with SV/VO default constituent order is used to illustrate charting. This is supplemented by sample charts of an SO/OV language and a VS/VO language.

The major concern of chapters 2–4 is to distinguish **topic**-type information from **focus**-type information. This distinction, which is broadly in line with that of Lambrecht (1994), is important because it helps to explain the ordering of constituents in the sentence and the presence versus absence of certain markers.

Chapter 2 starts by defining and illustrating technical terms such as sentence articulation, topic, comment, focus, presupposition, presentational, event reporting and thetic. After reviewing what is meant by coherence and cohesion, it considers how a coherent narrative may be segmented on the basis of changes or **discontinuities** of time and place, participants and types of action.

Chapter 3 looks at a device that signals such discontinuities, namely the placement at the beginning of a sentence of an adverbial or nominal constituent. Most often, such **points of departure** (Beneš 1962) signal a switch from a corresponding constituent in a previous sentence, though they may mark the renewal of an earlier topic or situation. The implications of NOT beginning a sentence with a point of departure are also examined.

Chapter 4 concentrates on what is **focal** within the sentence. It discusses the preferred positions for focal constituents. It illustrates the devices commonly used to give **prominence** to a focal constituent (sometimes called 'marked' focus). It also considers other forms of default versus marked prominence, including **emphatic** prominence. It introduces the concept of a **foil**, whose function is to set off a later topic or focal constituent by contrast. A final section is devoted to types of *it*-**cleft** (two-part sentences such as *It was you who put the milk in [not me]* with the dummy subject *it*).

Chapter 5 argues that the sentences of a narrative are not of equal importance as far as the author's purpose is concerned. Some only supply **background** information, some present the **body** of the text (the theme-line events, typically using a default form of the verb), and some are **highlighted** because of their special importance. The chapter looks at devices that are used for backgrounding or highlighting, including tense-aspect selection, certain particles, and the use of rhetorical devices that slow down a narrative immediately before a climax or significant development.

Chapter 6 looks at nonsubordinating conjunctions and other **connectives**. It stresses the need to identify the **default** way of coordinating sentences within a narrative and the specific function of each other form of coordination. It insists that each connective **constrains** the hearer to relate what follows to the context in a unique way. The chapter also discusses the different ways in which **additives** and **countering** markers are used, and considers particles that signal new **developments** of the theme line. Finally, it identifies devices that are used as **resumptives**, following a break in the theme line.

Chapter 7 considers the syntactic and text-related factors involved in **reporting speech** in other than the default way (which may be direct, indirect or "semidirect", using a special "logophoric" pronoun to refer to the reported speaker). It discusses the significance of different ways of introducing reported conversations and the **status** of such conversations in a narrative. It lists devices used to signal a **change of direction** within a reported conversation, and describes the functions of **interpretive-use** markers – particles that are used when a speech is being echoed or words are being put in someone else's mouth, to name just two possibilities.

Chapter 8 discusses the significance of different ways of introducing major and minor **participants** at the beginning of a story and to an existing scene. It presents a methodology for identifying the **default** way of referring to active participants in various contexts. It then discusses a number of reasons for using **marked** forms of reference to them. Unexpectedly **heavy** encoding usually follows significant breaks in the story or when the author wishes to highlight the action concerned. **Reduced** forms of encoding are associated with the participant who is the current **centre of attention**.

Chapter 9 shows that, if one participant is selected as the current centre of attention, this is often reflected in the use of **demonstratives**, **pronouns** and **directional** verbs or auxiliaries such as *come* and *go*. The chapter also discusses the presence versus absence of the **definite article** when referring to active participants.

Chapter 10 considers common restrictions on the presentation of **new** information in prenuclear subordinate clauses. It also discusses the role of **relative clauses** in Hebrew and many African languages, and includes a brief discussion of information load.

Supplementary reading

Certain chapters of this course assume that you have already read the corresponding chapters in Dooley and Levinsohn 2001. The chapters concerned are indicated at the end of each chapter under the heading **Additional Reading**.

0.5 Assignments and consulting

In each chapter, you will find paragraphs with the heading **Application to the language you are analysing**. These paragraphs suggest how you should apply what you have read to the analysis of your texts.

Questions may well arise as you try to apply what you have read to your texts. If you would like to direct such questions to me, send an email to stephen_levinsohn@sil.org. If you wish to discuss how to analyse any feature of your texts, I invite you to send me a copy of your charted text(s), together with a free translation (see ch. 1).

You are encouraged to record the results of your research, and a questionnaire is available at the end of the book, which you are encouraged to fill in. Various people will benefit from your recording your findings:

1. you (it is common in workshops to find that consultees have forgotten what they have already discovered about the feature being analysed);
2. your translation consultant (if you have explained how different text-related features function, your consultant may not have to ask you how they function, but will be able to read your description!);
3. people working in related languages (there is no value in rediscovering the wheel!).

1

Preparation and Charting of Narrative Texts

This chapter begins by addressing why a linguist should analyse texts, rather than solely relying on elicited material to learn about the language under consideration (1.1). It then briefly reviews the first section of Dooley and Levinsohn 2001, which is entitled "Types of Text". Section 1.3 indicates which texts are most suitable for beginning text analysis. Section 1.4 describes how to prepare a text for charting, and section 1.5 presents a method of charting them in a systematic way. The opening part of a folktale in Bekwarra, which has SV/VO (Subject-Verb/Verb-Object) constituent order, illustrates this method of charting. Appendices to the chapter present sample charts for discourses in languages with SO/OV and VS/VO constituent order.

1.1 Why analyse texts?

If we rely solely on elicited material to analyse the grammar of a language, we will often be misled.
- Sentences elicited by **translation** from one language to another tend to reflect the first language in a number of ways, especially the order of constituents and the way they are arranged in clauses. Suppose, for example, that you are using a language such as English whose basic constituent order is SVO (subject-verb-object) to elicit sentences in a language whose basic constituent order is SOV. Even if the language you are researching is your own, you will find that the elicited sentences will tend to preserve the SVO order of English.[1]
- When translating from a language that commonly packs a lot of information into each clause to a language that tends to distribute that information over more than one clause, elicited sentences will tend to preserve the heavier information load of the source language (and *vice versa*).
- Similarly, subordinate clauses in a source language will tend to be translated into a receptor language with similar subordinate clauses, even if the result is unnatural. In a workshop in 1998 to draft a comparative grammar of the Chocó languages of Colombia, we found that all the languages but one allowed only subjects and objects to be relativised.[2] When we examined the data from the other language, we realised that all the unexpected relative clauses were word-by-word translations of Spanish relative clauses; they even had Spanish rather than Chocó syntactic structure. (So we discarded them!)

---

[1] The same often happens in translation. For example, recordings in the Inga language of Colombia produced in 1968 by Gospel Recordings faithfully reproduced the SVO and VSO orders found in the Spanish source text, even though Inga is an SV/OV language.

[2] In other words, when a clause modifies a head noun, only the subject or the object of the modifying clause can be replaced by a relative pronoun or similar marker. See ch. 10 for discussion of this restriction.

- We may even elicit nonexistent forms. A linguist analysing a language on the Peru-Colombia border succeeded in filling several notebooks with nonexistent verb paradigms. Because he had used Spanish to elicit sentences such as *Had you asked me, I would have helped*, the native speaker duly came up with a word-by-word equivalent in the language, even though it uses a completely different structure to express the same idea!

A second problem with elicited material is that it is usually obtained without any reference to a specific **context**. There are two major drawbacks with this:

1. The analyst can only surmise any context that the native speaker may supply in order to make sense of the expression that is being elicited. I well remember a student eliciting paradigms during a training course and wondering why the forms he was given were inconsistent. It transpired that, because he was eliciting the expressions one after another, his language teacher linked them so that they would make sense as utterances in sequence, e.g. *I am going to town. You-**also** are going there*.

2. Many features of language cannot be studied in isolation. Here are some examples.
   - From an analysis of isolated sentences, we cannot identify devices that signal backgrounded information or which indicate that a theme line is being resumed.
   - From an analysis of isolated sentences, we cannot identify devices that signal topic continuity or a change of topic.
   - From an analysis of isolated sentences, we cannot identify devices that give prominence to certain events or participants over against others.
   - From an analysis of isolated sentences, we cannot discover the significance of the different ways of linking sentences with their context, such as by means of conjunctions versus subordinate clauses versus simple juxtaposition.

To accomplish any of the above tasks, we need to analyse texts. The same is true for many particles and constructions, and for the range of variations in verb forms and constituent orders which languages display. To distinguish the function of any of these features, we need to analyse texts.

Translation is a **very detailed** task. Every sentence demands a mass of decisions about the details. Translators have to decide which of a set of possible lexical items to use, which tense or aspect is best, whether to use a noun or a pronoun, whether to include this or that particle, etc. Some expatriate members of a translation team are happy to rely on their mother-tongue coworkers to get the details right. The question is: do they? Sadly, the answer may be: no! Here are some examples.

- In a workshop held in 2000 in Cameroon, studies of narratives in a Bushman language revealed that the main events of the stories were presented with the 'narrative' tense. The 'past' tense was used only for events of a background nature. However, the draft of Mark's Gospel in the language had used the 'past' tense to present ALL the events of the Gospel!
- During the 1998 workshop on the Chocó languages of Colombia, we noticed that the tense of subordinated verbs in texts was always 'dependent'. In other words, it was determined with reference to the time of the event described in the main clause, not the time of speaking or writing. However, in the draft translation of *When God looked, it was good* (Genesis 1:10) into one Chocó language, past tense had been used in the subordinate clause (reflecting Spanish). The result was that, whereas the Hebrew indicates that what God had created was good AT THE TIME He looked (present tense), the Chocó draft translation indicated that what God had created was good AFTER He looked!
- I was once asked to visit Panama to find out why an existing translation into the Guaymí [gym] (alt. Ngäbere; Chibchan, Panama) language was considered to be unintelligible. One problem we identified involved conjunctions. Whenever *and* appeared in the source text, the Guaymí translation had also inserted a conjunction. In natural texts in Guaymí, however, conjunctions were only used to mark breaks in the story. The result was that, for example, the story of Zacchaeus in Luke 19:1–10 was divided into 25 paragraphs!

Most of the linguistic problems that we discover in translations result from **mismatches** between the source and receptor languages. Some translators will preserve the forms of the source language even when they make no sense in their home language. For mother-tongue translators, perhaps the most important benefit of studying texts in the source and receptor languages is when we discover **mismatches** between them. We can then replace literal renderings that make the translation unnatural or worse with correct and natural alternatives.

1.2 Types of text

The purpose of this section is to remind you of two dimensions along which texts differ:
- the means of production: the number of speakers who produced the text
- the type of content: the text genre

1.2.1 The number of speakers

> One of the dimensions along which discourses differ involves the number of speakers involved in their production. Some discourses are produced by a single speaker; these are referred to as MONOLOGUES. Other discourses are produced by more than one speaker; these are referred to as DIALOGUES or CONVERSATIONS. (Dooley and Levinsohn 2001:4)

Narratives are typically produced by a single speaker or writer, so this course will be concerned with monologues. However, even spoken monologues may require audience participation. Depending on the culture and circumstances, this may consist of nods and grunts, the repetition of the last words uttered, comments and evaluations of certain utterances, and other ways of encouraging the narrator to continue. Often, this participation is of a very systematic nature and needs to be analysed at an early stage if analysts are ever to successfully be the audience when someone is telling them a story!

1.2.2 The text genre

Earlier, I cited the *OED* definition of narrative: "a spoken or written account of connected events in order of happening". *Narrative* is a text genre, which means that it is "an identifiable category of literary composition" with "several identifiable characteristics ... notably in relation to subject-matter, purpose..., textual structure, form of argumentation, and level of formality" (Crystal 1997:168).

Narrative is one of Longacre's (1996) **broad** text genres. It differs from the **procedural** genre in that it is **agent oriented**. Narratives are concerned with who does what. Procedural texts are concerned primarily with what is done and how it is done, rather than who does it, so are not viewed as agent oriented.

Narrative is differentiated from the **behavioural** and **expository** genres on the basis of text **organisation**. The events of a narrative tend to be organised **chronologically** ("in order of happening" – *OED*). Behavioural texts (ones that call for a change of behaviour, such as exhortations, rebukes and eulogies) are usually organised logically; they concern what the addressees ought to do and why they should do it. Expository texts (budgets, scientific articles, etc.) also tend to be organised logically or **conceptually**.

The following matrix shows how narrative contrasts with the other three broad text genres according to the parameters of text orientation and organisation:

Table 3. Contrast of text orientation and organisation in four text genres

Organisation	+Agent oriented	−Agent oriented
Chronological organisation	narrative	behavioural
Conceptual/logical organisation	behavioural	expository

Application to the language you are analysing

1. Read Dooley and Levinsohn 2001:7–9, which contains further discussion of Longacre's broad categories of genre.
2. Classify the texts in your corpus according to their broad text genre. Discuss with your consultant the genre of any text that does not seem to fit into any of the four genres mentioned in this section.

1.3 Text selection: What sort of text should I begin with?

For beginning text analysis, narrative usually yields the best results and is best understood. The text should have a moderate amount of complexity, since the point of the exercise is to see how complexity is handled. Specifically, it should have two or more major participants, as well as a problem, conflict, or area of tension, along with its resolution. (Dooley and Levinsohn 2001:44)

Ideally, none of the major participants in such narratives should be the storyteller. This is because the centre of attention in autobiographical material is almost invariably the speaker or writer, and one of the reasons for analysing narratives is to find out how they indicate and change the centre of attention (see ch. 9). So an ideal sort of text for beginning analysis is a **third**-person narrative with two or more major participants interacting, such as an eyewitness account of an argument, a fight or a debate.

In many cultures, the easiest narratives to obtain are traditional **folktales** such as animal stories. As well as making good material for reading books, they can be very valuable for text analysis. They have certain drawbacks, however. For example, certain verb forms or other features may be peculiar to folktales (e.g. the opening *Once upon a time* in English). The means of tracking the participants in a folktale may not be typical of other types of narrative, either, as the participants are too well known. We have even found that, in some languages, direct reporting of speeches by the participants is the norm in animal folktales, whereas indirect reporting is the norm in other forms of narrative (see ch. 7). So, include some folktales in your corpus, but obtain other sorts of narrative, as well.

Procedural texts are of limited value for text analysis, as they are organised in a very stereotyped way. They typically use a specific verb form (e.g. the imperative or infinitive). They may employ a specific way of referring to the person who is to carry out the procedure (e.g. *you*, an impersonal *we* or *one*). They tend also to have a specific way of marking the end of each stage in the procedure (e.g. *Having finished* ...). To discover what characterises procedures in the language you are analysing, you will want to include a few procedural texts in your corpus, but not too many!

Behavioural texts are good to analyse, once narrative is understood. They are characterised by certain systematic changes with respect to narrative, such as a different distribution of verb forms and connectives. I recommend that you undertake a full analysis of narrative and **then** turn your attention to behavioural texts.[3]

So a beginning corpus for a workshop to analyse mainly narrative texts might consist of the following:
- three traditional folktales;
- three or four third-person eyewitness accounts (including the report of a debate – see 7.5.4);
- a couple of texts on the history of the language group; and
- one or two autobiographical accounts.

It is important that you record **how** you obtained each text in your corpus, as this often affects how the text begins and whether the participants in it are treated as new or as already known (see ch. 8). For example, if you request, *Tell me a story*, the first sentence of the story will probably specify who or what it is about. In contrast, *Tell me the story about Dog, Hare and their pups* allows the narrator to begin with the first event of the story (e.g. *Once Dog and Hare entered into an agreement*).

---

[3] See also Levinsohn 2015.

Application to the language you are analysing

Select from your corpus a third-person narrative with two or more major participants interacting.

1.4 Preparing your texts for charting and analysis

This section concerns the editing of texts, the need to control the facts they convey, and the segmentation of an edited, interlinear text prior to charting it. It also discusses what you will need to know about the normal order and co-occurrence of constituents before setting up the basic chart.

1.4.1 Editing

> According to Grimes (1975:33), 'the texts that yield the most consistent analysis are edited texts'. These will approximate what might be thought of as the text analyst's version of competence (accepted uses of the resources of the language), as contrasted with performance (including incidental mistakes, infelicitous choices, etc.). Although editing generally implies that the text is in written form, it could be one that was originally recorded, then transcribed. The editing should be done by a member of the language community (by the original author of the text, if possible) to preserve the author's mental representation and stylistic preferences …
>
> Ideally, the text should be by a person who has 'a reputation for consistently producing the kind of discourse that other people want to listen to' (loc. cit.). This will also help insure that the text is well formed. (Dooley and Levinsohn 2001:44)

A **well-formed** text is one that a native speaker considers to be grammatically correct and acceptable. Typically, half the sentences in an unrehearsed discourse in English are incomplete or ungrammatical, and the same is likely to be true of texts in other languages. So, if the text to be charted was originally **recorded**, check that it has been transcribed correctly and that the transcription includes indications of the pauses and intonation contours used. Make sure, too, that a native speaker has checked the transcription. Similarly, if the text was originally produced in **written** form, then check that it has been carefully read both by and to a native speaker.

Note any changes that are suggested in the process of editing, but do not completely discard the original, as proposed changes are not always 'correct'. This may be because the editor may not have understood the intent of the original speaker, or because problems arose when hearing the sentence in isolation that disappear as soon as its context is supplied.

1.4.2 Controlling the facts

This section is addressed specifically to analysts who are NOT analysing texts in their mother tongue.

> Before charting the text, you need to 'control the facts of the discourse', i.e., 'know who did what to whom, and, as far as possible, what relation one action has to the other actions in its immediate context' (Longacre and Levinsohn 1978:111). This means that you should have a fairly complete picture of the text world, and of the external contextualization as well. For this, you should get a free translation of the story and then ask specific questions. As a side benefit of this process, you will gain cultural insights. (Dooley and Levinsohn 2001:44)

When asking questions about a narrative, be concerned especially with **implicit** information. If a participant is identified only by a pronoun or verb affix, for instance, verify the intended referent. So, if the sentence reads, *He hit him*, ask, *Who hit him?* and *Whom did he hit?*

1.4.3 Segmenting the text

Once the text has been edited and a word-by-word or morpheme-by-morpheme gloss added, it is time to segment it in preparation for charting. The following glossed text is the opening part of a folktale in

Bekwarra (see Stanford 1967:310ff.). Periods represent sentence breaks. The abbreviations used are: 3: 3rd person, p: plural, s: singular. A free translation of the passage follows.

únyang	*kìn*	*ùbuhó*	*àhe*	*n'-anyamchù*	*e-ngwìà*	*iyim*
time	one	dog	3s	with-hare	p-entered	agreement

abe	*e-dè*	*è-káá*	*èbwa*	*íbere*	*ja*	*e-dè*	*è-káá*	*ùngwa*	*úbuhó*	*ja*
3p	p-said	p-fry	children	their	eat	p-said	p-fry	child	of.dog	eat

ùbuhó	*a-dè*	*ímin*	*ì-yi*	*apètèré-apètèré*	*k'-ìrìchì*
dog	s-said	his	s-has	infection	in-eye

è-tyàng	*k'-ímin*	*ì-kpèrè*	*ukpang*
p-leave	to-his	s-be.well	before/first

é-kung	*ang'-ányamchù*	*kung*	*kaa*	*ji*	*ang'-úbuhó*	*á-bé*	*ka*	*kpèrè*
p-took	that-of.hare	took	fried	ate	that-of.dog	s-came	then	was.well

'Once upon a time, Dog and Hare made an agreement. They said, "Let's fry our children and eat them." They said, "Let's fry Dog's child and eat it." Dog said, "Mine has an eye infection. Let's leave it to become well first." They took Hare's, fried it, and ate it. Dog's then became well.'

The first task in segmentation is to mark tentative **divisions** of the story into sentences, clauses and phrases. Use your previous knowledge of the language and of typological principles to decide where the breaks occur. I usually insert three slashes to indicate sentence breaks (///), two slashes for clause breaks (//) and a single slash to separate phrasal constituents (/).

The second task is to **number** the sentences consecutively (NOT the clauses, as the basic units of a text are sentences). Insert matching numbers in the free translation.

The third task (which you can do as you divide the clauses into phrasal constituents) is to give simple **labels** to the constituents. For the Bekwarra text, I have used the following labels (in order of appearance): T: time, S: subject, V: verb (phrase), O: object, L: location.[4] I have also indicated the function of the subordinate clause in the fourth line (Purp: purpose; [...] indicates its extent).

The opening part of the Bekwarra glossed text now looks like this:[5]

	T		S			V	O
1	*únyang*	*kìn /*	*ùbuhó*	*àhe*	*n'-anyamchù /*	*e-ngwìà /*	*iyim ///*
	time	one	dog	3s	with-hare	p-entered	agreement

	S	V	V	O		V		V	V	O		V
2	*abe /*	*e-dè //*	*è-káá /*	*èbwa*	*íbere //*	*ja ///*	(3)	*e-dè //*	*è-káá /*	*ùngwa*	*úbuhó //*	*ja ///*
	3p	p-said	p-fry	children	their	eat		p-said	p-fry	child	of.dog	eat

	S	V	S	V	O	L
4	*ùbuhó /*	*a-dè //*	*ímin /*	*ì-yi /*	*apètèré-apètèré /*	*k'-ìrìchì ///*
	dog	s-said	his	s-has	infection	in-eye

[4] If the language you are analysing is syntactically ergative (see Comrie 1989:70ff.), you may wish to use the labels ERG 'ergative' and ABS 'absolutive' instead of S and O.

[5] These divisions reflect some previous knowledge of the language, such as the fact that *kin* 'one' modifies the preceding noun (line 1), that *bé* 'came' is functioning as an auxiliary, and that *ka* 'then' is also part of the verb phrase (sentence 7).

	V	Purp [S	V	T]
5	è-tyàng //	k'-ímin /	ì-kpèrè /	ukpang ///
	p-leave	to-his	s-be.well	before/first

	V	O	V	V	V	S	V		
6	é-kung /	ang'-ányamchù //	kung //	kaa //	ji /// (7)	ang'-úbuhó /	á-bé	ka	kpèrè ///
	p-took	that-of.hare	took	fried	ate	that-of.dog	s-came	then	was.well

'1. Once upon a time, Dog and Hare made an agreement. 2. They said, "Let's fry our children and eat them." 3. They said, "Let's fry Dog's child and eat it." 4. Dog said, "Mine has an eye infection. 5. Let's leave it to become well first." 6. They took Hare's, fried it, and ate it. 7. Dog's then became well.'

1.4.4 Constituent order and co-occurrence

In order to decide on the number, order and size of columns to use in your chart, you need to know the following information about the language you are analysing:
- What is the most common order of phrasal constituents in the clause? It might be S-V-IO-O-Adjunct, for instance.
- What combinations of constituents occur in your texts? You might find that no more than three constituents follow the verb, for instance.
- Are sentence introducers usually very short (e.g. conjunctions such as *Then* and *So*) or are they generally more complex (e.g. *After that, Because of this*)?
- Do sentence introducers and prenuclear adverbial constituents (e.g. *the next day*) often co-occur?

You probably know the answer to most of these questions already. If you are unsure of any of them, then make a list of the different orders and combinations of constituents that occur in your texts.

The following is a list of the different orders and combinations of constituents in the opening part of the Bekwarra text (2R, 3R, 4R refer to the reported speeches which are the complement of *say* verbs):

1	T	S	V	O		
2		S	V		[Reported Speech]	(also 4)
2R			V	O		(also 3R, 6)
3			V		[Reported Speech]	
4R		S	V	O	L	
5			V	Purp		
5(Purp)		S	V	T		
7		S	V			

The above orders and combinations of constituents may be summarised as:

    T S V O Adjunct.[6]

---

[6] In fact, further orders and combinations are found in later sentences of the Bekwarra text; a sentence introducer and a prenuclear adverbial constituent co-occur, and the object may be followed by **two** adjuncts.

Application to the language you are analysing

1. If you are in a position to do so, check that the first narrative you have selected for charting (see the Application at the end of 1.3) is well formed and that you control the facts. Obtain a free translation of the text.
2. In a glossed copy of the narrative, mark tentative divisions into sentences, clauses and phrases. Number the sentences consecutively and give simple labels to the constituents.
3. Answer the questions posed immediately below the heading of this section (1.4.4).

1.5 Displaying a text in chart form

The kind of chart proposed in this section displays similar syntactic constituents in the same column and enables the analyst to look at different features of the language in turn. It is a useful display not only for text analysis, but also for basic syntactic analysis. Such a display is not busywork; without it, you are likely to discover far less than you will by using it!

I first describe the setting up of the basic chart and then set out the conventions for charting (see also Dooley and Levinsohn 2001:44–47). The Bekwarra text is again used for illustration.

1.5.1 The basic chart

First, turn an A4 or 8½" x 11" sheet **sideways.** If you will be charting on a computer, format the page to **landscape** orientation. Do NOT be tempted to use wider paper. If the chart is too wide, the eye cannot take in the whole page at once, and it will be more difficult to observe textual patterns.

Now divide the sheet into columns: first, a narrow column for the sentence number (Ref), then three or four main columns, as follows:

- Column 1: for sentence introducers (connectives).
- Column 2: for prenuclear constituents.

Note: If sentence introducers and prenuclear constituents seldom occur together in the same sentence (see your answer to the question above about their co-occurrence), then combine these two columns.

- Column 3: a very broad column for the nuclear predication itself, as it will have three to five subcolumns (see below).
- Column 4: for postnuclear adjuncts and right-dislocated constituents that follow the nuclear predication.

The relative size of the columns will depend on the characteristics of the language. For example, if most sentence introducers are simple conjunctions, column 1 will be very narrow. However, if they tend to be more complex, then column 1 will need to be wider (see your answer to the question above about sentence introducers).

Now divide column 3 into three to five subcolumns and select appropriate subcolumns for the nuclear subject and verb so that the most common order of constituents within the clause is reflected. The column labelled '(O)' (object) may also be used for complements and other nuclear constituents.

Applying the above guidelines to the opening part of the Bekwarra text leads to the following decisions:

- Combine columns 1 and 2, since sentence introducers and prenuclear constituents do not co-occur.
- Divide column 3 into three subcolumns: S-V-(O).

The result is the following division of the page into columns and subcolumns. (Because there are so few columns, it is not necessary to use landscape orientation.):

Ref.	Columns 1 & 2	Column 3			Column 4
	Pre-S	S	V	(O)	Adjunct

1.5.2 Conventions for charting

As you insert the text into the chart you have prepared, here are some conventions you should follow (reproduced from Dooley and Levinsohn 2001:46):

1. Start a new line for every new clause[7] and label it. See sentence 2 of the chart (below) of the Bekwarra text; the three clauses are charted on separate lines (labelled 2a, 2b, 2c).
2. Put a line across the table before every new sentence.[8]
3. If a consultant is likely to be helping you with text analysis, include the word-by-word (and where relevant, morpheme-by-morpheme) gloss in a language that the consultant understands.
4. Do not rearrange the order of constituents or hide an unusual order by moving down the page.
   - If a constituent is in an 'unusual' position, put 'POSTVERB', 'PREVERB', etc., in the appropriate column, but record the constituent itself in its actual place of occurrence (see p. 18).
   - Move down the page when the constituent includes a clause and/or is too long to fit in the correct column. See sentence 1 of the chart below; it was necessary to use two lines to accommodate the complex subject *ùbuhó àhe n'-anyamchù* 'dog 3s with-hare'.
5. Mark implicit constituents (especially subjects, plus objects of transitive verbs) by a dash: ——. See sentence 6 of the chart below for some examples.
6. For reported speech, use a different colour or type of underlining. See sentences 2–5 of the chart below.

The following is a chart of the opening part of the Bekwarra text, following the above conventions. (If needed, see appendices A and B in this chapter for sample charts for an SV/OV language and a VS/VO language.)

Table 4. Chart of part of the Bekwarra text

Ref.	Pre-S	S	V	(O)	Adjunct
1	*únyang kìn* time one	*ùbuhó àhe* dog 3s *n'-anyamchù* with-hare	*e-ngwìà* p-entered	*iyìm* agreement	
2a		*abe* 3p	*e-dè* p-said		
2b		....	*è-káá* p-fry	*èbwa íbere* children their	
2c		....	*ja* eat	....	
3a		——	*e-dè* p-said		
3b		....	*è-káá* p-fry	*ùngwa úbuhó* child of.dog	
3c		....	*ja* eat	....	

---

[7] Unless it is a relative clause that is embedded in another clause constituent; see clause 29c.
[8] I view a sentence as a main CLAUSE together with those clauses that are subordinate to it. Very often, as a result, each sentence will contain only one main clause.

Table 4, continued

Ref.	Pre-S	S	V	(O)	Adjunct
4a		ùbuhó dog	a-dè s-said		
4b		ímin his	ì-yi s-has	apètèré-apètèré infection	k'-ìrìchì in-eye
5a		....	è-tyàng p-leave		
5b	k'- to	ímin his	ì-kpèrè s-be.well		ukpang before/first
6a		——	é-kung p-took	áng'-ányamchù that-of.hare	
6b		——	kung took	——	
6c		——	kaa fried	——	
6d		——	ji ate	——	
7		áng'-úbuhó that-of.dog	á-bé ka kpèrè s-came then was.well		

The following is an instance (from the last sentence of the Bekwarra text, shown in appendix C in ch. 2) where a constituent is in an 'unusual' position (see point 4 of 1.5.2 Conventions for charting). The object (O) has been preposed, so it is recorded in its actual place of occurrence, but [PREVERB] has been inserted in the O column.

29a		èkáànì elders	e-kà kung p-then took		
29b		....	dè said	he 3sO	dèè (say)
29c	[ipì àwo ó-ji kwom (O)] place.where you you-ate T		h'-ó-fià kwom FOCUS-you-pay T	[PREVERB]	

You may wish to indicate in some way that a subordinate clause is functioning as an adjunct in its matrix clause. Two ways to do this are illustrated with sentence 5 of the Bekwarra text.

(a) Record the subordinate clause in the Adjunct column (which will need to be wide):

5		....	è-tyàng p-leave		k'-ímin ì-kpèrè ukpang to-his s-be.well before/first

(b) Display the subordinate clause in the nuclear subcolumns, but enclose it in square brackets and also indicate its position and function in the Adjunct column of the matrix clause in square brackets:

Table 4, continued

Ref.	Pre-S	S	V	(O)	Adjunct
5a		....	è-tyàng p-leave		[PURP: 5b]
5b	[k'- to	ímin his	ì-kpèrè s-be.well		ukpang] before/first

Application to the language you are analysing

1. Decide what columns and subcolumns you need for your basic chart.
2. Start inserting the text you have selected into your chart, following the conventions for charting given above.
3. When you have completed two pages of your chart, ask your consultant to check it. Note: The first page or two of your first narrative may need to be charted several times to find the optimal way to allocate columns.

Suggested reading

The following chapters of Dooley and Levinsohn 2001 relate to the topics covered in this chapter: 1–4 (Types of Text) and 8.1 (What kind of text should I begin with?), 8.2 (The basic chart) and 8.3 (Conventions for charting).

Appendix A: Sample Chart for an SV/OV Language

The next page presents a sample chart in the Dungra Bhil [duh] (Indo-Aryan, India) language.[9] The body of the chart has seven columns, as clause or sentence introducers (conjunctions) and prenuclear constituents often co-occur, since they have been combined into one column. However, the last column ('Post-V') is seldom needed, since nearly all the sentences end with a verb. Two columns occur between the subject (S) and the verb (V), into which objects and adjuncts have been placed in their order of occurrence.

The following abbreviations are used in the chart:
ACC accusative; FUT future; OB oblique; INF infinitive; POS possessive.

The following is a free translation of the extract:

'1. Oh, my children, you are not to drink liquor. 2. Liquor is like a poison. 3. (If) you see the eyes of a person who drinks liquor, his eyes look completely red. 4. And, (If) you see his life, (if) he drinks liquor at one go, then he will acquire a desire for liquor; 5. and, whatever work he may do, he will drink liquor with it (that will be completed in liquor drinking). 6. Then what will his wife and children do? 7. They will die of hunger; 8. and no one will give him any money because people will say to him, "You're a drunkard."'

---

[9] I am grateful to Sunil and Maya Mathew (p.c.) for providing this hortatory text, which was given by a man from Mathwad village.

Ref.	Conjunctions	Prenuclear	S		V	Post-V
1		o ma-a pujra oh my oh.children (VOCATIVE)	tumi you	horu liquor	ma pi-ha don't drink-be.PLURAL	
2			horu to liquor PARTICLE	ek dʒer hudu one poison like	hoje. be	
3a		horu pi-nara mahõ-õ dʑua liquor drink-AGENT man-POS eye.OB	tumi you	[PREPOSED O]	pala, see	
3b				tija-a dʑua he-pos eye.OB	dekh-a. see-PASSIVE	
4a	ono &	tija-a dʒĩgi he-POS life	tumi you	[PREPOSED O] ekdom rata rata complete red red	pala, see	
4b			tuʔu he	ek vaʔa horu one time liquor	pit-neje, drink-COMPLETIVE	
4c	tahã then			tija-ha him-ACC	nag-e. feel-FUT	
5a	ono &		tuʔu he	tija-a phaje dʒetihi modʒuri he-POS with how.much work	koʔ-e, do-FUT	
5b			—	tetaha horu that.much liquor	pi dʒa-je. drink go-FUT	
6	tahã then	tuʔu tija-a bujeẽ ono pujre he he-POS lady & children	kihĩ what		koʔ-eʔ do-FUT	
7			—	phuko hunger.OB	moʔ-e die-FUT	
8a	ono &	tija-ha him-ACC	koɖa no.one	pojsa money	naj ap-e NEG give-FUT	
8b	kihĩke because		[tuʔu he	daruɟiu drunkard	hojel be	
8c		[8b] ehnoho this.way	maʔhe people	tija-ha him-ACC	[LEFT DISLOC]	ko-je. say-FUT

Appendix B: Sample Chart for a VS/VO Language

The next page presents a sample chart of the first part of a folktale in the Southeastern Nochixtlán Mixtec [mxy] (alt. Santo Domingo Nuxáa Mixtec; Oto-Manguean, Mexico) language. The author was Rodolfo N. Miguel (Miguel López 1998). The text was transcribed and translated by Inga McKendry.

The following abbreviations are used in the chart:

EMPH emphatic; F feminine; HAB habitual; IMPF imperfective; M masculine; PF perfective; PL plural; 1 1st person; 2fam 2nd person familiar; 3 3rd person.

The following is a free translation of the extract:

'1 (Title). The animal that thought it was really brave. 2. The sheep were very happy; they were eating grass on the mountain. 3. Their owner was whistling because he was happy, too, that his sheep were grazing peacefully. 4. Suddenly, sheep belonging to a different person appeared and one of them, a ram, said "Hello, lass." 5. "Hello, brother," said a ewe. 6. (The ram replied,) "What are you doing grazing on my territory?"'

Ref.	Conjunctions	Prenuclear	Verb	Subject	Object	
1		ti 3animal	ʃé-tee IMPF-make.brave	βee-ti self-3animal		
2a			kuðíí-ini IMPF-be.happy	tʃikaʃi sheep		
2b			ʃeʃi' IMPF.eat	ti 3animal	ite kʷi grass green	iⁿ-ti PL-3animal	iⁿ tʃinuu one mountain
3a	te and		ʃita' ðutu IMPF.sing whistle	asto'o ti owner 3animal		
3b	tʃi because	ta'aⁿ ðe also 3m	kuðíí-ini IMPF-be.happy	ʃi 3general		tuku also
3c	xa that	iyo βii very peacefully	ʃinee HAB.graze	tʃikaʃi ðe sheep 3m		[PREPOSED Manner]
4a	te and	uuⁿ-niⁿ suddenly	niⁿ-kákú_nuu PF-appear	tʃikaʃi iⁿnka ka ayivi sheep another person		
4b	te and		niⁿ-ka'aⁿ PF-speak	iiⁿ ti one 3animal		
4c		βa'a_tikuu noⁿ lia hello 2famM lass	niⁿ-ka'aⁿ PF-speak	iiⁿ karneru one ram		
5a		βa'a_tikuu naⁿ_kʷa'a hello 2famF brother	niⁿ-ka'aⁿ PF-speak	iiⁿ ti di'i one female		
6a		naikuu ja what that	ʃede' do	noⁿ 2famM	[PREPOSED O]	
6b			kaneé IMPF.graze	noⁿ 2famM		kuu nuuⁿ ʒu'uⁿ niⁿ EMPH on land 1

2

Articulations of the Sentence, Coherence and Discontinuities

This chapter begins by defining a number of technical terms that will be needed during this course. You will be introduced to the idea that clauses and sentences are **articulated** in various ways. You will meet the terms **topic**, **comment**, **identificational**, **focus**, **presupposition**, **presentational**, **event reporting** and **thetic**. You will then review the concepts of **coherence** and **cohesion**. Finally, you will consider how a text may be **segmented** on the basis of **discontinuities** of situation, action and participants, or topic. A chart of the complete text in Bekwarra is found in appendix C.

2.1 Articulations of the sentence

The information conveyed by a clause or sentence may be presented in several different ways. Consider the following three sentences:

1a *Dog and Hare made an agreement.*[1]

1b *It was Dog and Hare who made an agreement.*

1c *Once there were a Dog and a Hare [who made an agreement].*

All three sentences convey the same information, in that they all talk about *Dog and Hare* and describe something that they did (*made an agreement*). However, this information is not presented in the same way by each to the hearer. In technical jargon, the three sentences have different **articulations**.

> **Definition**
> Sentence ARTICULATION: the way that the information in a clause or sentence is presented.

We can see that the information in sentences 1a and 1b is presented in different ways if we formulate questions that might have 1a and 1b as (long) answers. A reduced form of 1a responds to a question about what Dog and Hare did:

1a' *What did Dog and Hare do? They made an agreement.*

---
[1] Chapter 3 discusses sentence-initial adverbials such as *One time* in *One time Dog and Hare made an agreement.*

In contrast, a reduced form of 1b responds to a question about who made an agreement:

1b′   *Who was it who made an agreement? It was Dog and Hare.*

Sentences 1a–1c above illustrate the three principal articulations that Andrews (1985:77–80) distinguishes: topic-comment (1a), 'identificational' (Lambrecht 1994:122) (1b), and presentational (the first clause of 1c). We now consider them in turn.

2.1.1 Topic-comment articulation

In sentence 1a (repeated below), the speaker says something about Dog and Hare. We therefore call *Dog and Hare* the **topic** of the sentence, whereas *made an agreement* is a **comment** about that topic. Sentence 1a thus has *topic-comment* articulation.

1a   TOPIC   COMMENT

    Dog and Hare   *made an agreement.*

> **Definition**
> (Propositional) TOPIC: "A referent is interpreted as the topic of a proposition if in a given situation the proposition is construed as being about this referent, i.e. as expressing information which is relevant to and which increases the addressee's knowledge of this referent" (Lambrecht 1994:131).
> COMMENT: information about the topic.

Here are three useful observations to remember about (propositional) topics:
- The topic is usually the subject of the clause or sentence.
- The topic must be either already established in the text or easily related to one that is already established (Lambrecht 1994:164).[2]
- Care must be taken not to confuse the term '(propositional) topic' with the topic (hereafter, the theme) of a paragraph or longer stretch of speech or writing.

2.1.2 Identificational articulation

For sentence 1b (repeated below) to be used correctly, the speaker and hearer must already know that some participants have made an agreement. The speaker then identifies that it was Dog and Hare who did so. *Dog and Hare* are the **focus** of the sentence, whereas *(someone) made an agreement* is the **presupposition**.[3]

1b   FOCUS   PRESUPPOSITION

    It was Dog and Hare   *who made an agreement.*

> **Definitions**
> PRESUPPOSITION: a proposition that, except for one element, is assumed to be known.
> FOCUS: the element that needs to be identified in the presupposed proposition (see further below).

---

[2] Dog and Hare commonly feature in Bekwarra folktales, so are assumed to be known to the hearer ("under certain conditions topics may be interpretable as current even though they haven't been brought up in the current discourse" – Lambrecht 1994:164). Otherwise, the story would probably have begun with a presentational sentence such as 1c. See further discussion in 2.1.3.

[3] Andrews uses the terms "focus-presupposition" for identificational articulation.

2.1.3 Presentational articulation

When a clause or sentence has *presentational articulation*, it introduces an "entity" (Lambrecht 1994:144), which may be animate (2a below) or inanimate (2b). Both use a verb of existence to introduce the entity. One is introduced at the beginning of a story (2a), the other to an existing story (2b):

2a *Once there lived a dog and a hare.*

2b *Now some water jars were there.*

In 2a, a dog and a hare are presented without saying anything about them in that clause. The same is true of the *water jars* of 2b. Such clauses or sentences have presentational articulation because they do not make a comment about an established topical subject.

> **Definition**
> PRESENTATIONAL: A clause or sentence has presentational articulation if it introduces a new entity into a text without linking its introduction "to an already established topic or to some presupposed proposition" (Lambrecht 1994:144).[4]

We now return to sentence 1c: *Once there were a Dog and a Hare who made an agreement*. This sentence consists of two clauses. The first (*Once there were a Dog and a Hare*) has presentational articulation, because it introduces *Dog* and *Hare* to the story. The second (*who made an agreement*) has topic-comment articulation, because it makes a comment about them (Lambrecht 1994:129). In other words, the sentence as a whole combines presentational and topic-comment articulation.

A word like **one** or **certain** modifies the subject of some sentences:

3 *A certain man had two sons.* (Luke 15:11)

Such sentences combine presentational and topic-comment articulation in a single clause. *A certain man* introduces a participant to the story, while the rest of the clause makes a comment about him.

2.1.4 Event reporting and thetic

Lambrecht uses the term **event reporting** for clauses or sentences of "an 'all-new' character" (1994:144) that report an event. Such sentences might respond to a question like *What's happening?* Examples:

4a *It's raining.*

4b *There's going to be a fight.*

> **Definition**
> EVENT REPORTING: An event-reporting sentence is one that introduces a new event into a text without linking its introduction to an established topical subject or to some presupposed proposition.

Event-reporting sentences are similar to those with presentational articulation, in that both introduce a new element into the text "without linking this element either to an already established topic or to some presupposed proposition. ... The difference between the presentational and the event-reporting type is that in presentational sentences proper the newly introduced element is an ENTITY ... while in event-reporting sentences it is an EVENT, which necessarily involves an entity" (Lambrecht 1994:144). Lambrecht uses the term **thetic** to designate the category that includes both presentational and event-reporting sentences.

> **Definition**
> THETIC: A thetic sentence is one that introduces a new element (be it an entity or an event) into a text without linking its introduction to an established topical subject or to some presupposed proposition.

---

[4] In this context, Lambrecht uses 'established topic' to mean an established **subject** as topic.

Now consider example 5:

5   *Then an angel of the Lord appeared to him.* (Luke 1:11)

Lambrecht considers sentences such as (5) to be thetic in English, even though the experiencer *him* (Zechariah) has "topic status" (1994:145). This is because there is a strong correlation in English between subject and topic. When an English sentence has topic-comment articulation, the subject never carries the primary stress. When the subject is accented, then the sentence has identificational articulation (as in 1b) or is thetic (5).

In languages where the correlation between subject and topic is less strong than in English, sentences like (5) may well have topic-comment articulation. Such would be the case in many N.W. Austronesian languages. In the Tombonuo [txa] (Malayo-Polynesian; Sabah) language, for instance, the third-person pronoun *him* (3s) would be an experiential or referential topic (REF), and *an angel of the Lord* would be an "oblique core argument" (Van Valin 2005:7) marked by the genitive case suffix (GEN):

5' *Then appeared*-REF / *3s* / *an angel of the Lord*-GEN.

A subject-as-experiencer in English has to be expressed in a different case in some languages. For example, the topic-comment clause 'she has lost a ring' becomes 'a ring is lost to her' in Inga, which is thetic in Lambrecht's system. It may prove useful to set up a distinct articulation type for clauses and sentences in which a constituent with "topic status" is not the subject.[5]

Cross-linguistically, event-reporting sentences are very infrequent in narrative texts. This is because the introduction of nearly every new event in a narrative is linked "either to an already established topic or to some presupposed proposition" (Lambrecht 1994:144). Often, the only exceptions are temporal expressions such as *It became day* or *An interval of about three hours passed* (Acts 5:7).

Review questions

1. What are the three principal articulations of the sentence, according to Andrews?
2. Label the type of articulation of the following sentences from Greek and Bekwarra:
   a) *At Joppa there was a certain disciple named Tabitha.* (Acts 9:36)
   b) *Dog's (child) then became well.* (Bekwarra 7)
   c) *What happened that you refuse to fry it?* (Bekwarra 13)
3. What is a thetic sentence? What two types of thetic sentence does Lambrecht distinguish, and how do they differ from each other?
4. Why are event-reporting sentences very infrequent in narrative texts?[6]

---

[5] A term which would be consistent with Lambrecht's terminology might be 'experiencer predicate focus'.

[6] **Suggested answers**:

1. The three principal articulations of the sentence, according to Andrews, are topic-comment, identificational, and presentational.
2. a) *At Joppa there was a certain disciple named Tabitha* has presentational articulation; the sentence introduces the entity *a certain disciple named Tabitha* into the story without linking its introduction to an established topic or to some presupposed proposition. (The status of the sentence-initial adverbial *At Joppa* is discussed in ch. 3.)
   b) *Dog's (child) then became well* has topic-comment articulation; *became well is a comment about the topic Dog's (child).*
   c) *What happened that you refuse to fry it?* has identificational articulation. The proposition *Something happened that you refuse to fry it* is assumed to be known; the focus is on *what*.
3. A thetic sentence is one that introduces a new element into the text without linking its introduction to an established topic or to some presupposed proposition. Lambrecht distinguishes presentational from event-reporting sentences. The difference between them is that in presentational sentences the newly introduced element is an ENTITY, while in event-reporting sentences it is an EVENT.
4. Event-reporting sentences are very infrequent in narrative texts because the introduction of nearly every new element in a narrative is linked either to an established topic or to some presupposed proposition.

Application to the language you are analysing

Identify the articulation of each clause and sentence of the narrative text that you have charted.

(To avoid complications, ignore any reported speeches in your text.)

Note: In many narratives, most if not all of the clauses and sentences may have topic-comment articulation.

2.1.5 Final thoughts on sentence articulations

You may be wondering why it is useful to identify the articulation of the clauses and sentences of your texts. One reason is that the distinction between topic-comment and other forms of articulation is typically marked in a systematic way (see Lambrecht 1994:234–235). For example, the following features indicate that the subject is NOT the topic of a topic-comment sentence in the language concerned:

- **primary accent** on the subject in English;
- the subject **after the verb** in Bantu and many other languages (Lambrecht 2000:634ff.); and
- the **prominence particle** *e* after the subject in Byali [beh] (Gur, Benin) (Berthelette 2004).

In addition, we shall see in the next section that the focus of a sentence is directly linked to its articulation, and in chapter 4, we will find that the order of constituents in a sentence may depend on its articulation and focus.

2.2 More on focus

The focus of a sentence with identificational articulation was defined in 2.1.2 as the element that was lacking in the presupposed proposition. Topic-comment sentences and thetic sentences also have one or more focal constituents, so a more general definition of focus is needed that can be applied to any clause or sentence.

The following are general definitions of the FOCUS of a clause or sentence:[7]

- "the information ... that is assumed by the speaker not to be shared by him [or her] and the hearer" (Jackendoff 1972:230).
- "that part which indicates what the speaker intends as the most important ... change to be made in the hearer's mental representation" (Dooley and Levinsohn 2001:62).

Most clauses and sentences with topic-comment articulation have **predicate focus** (Lambrecht 1994:222). The focus of a topic-comment sentence is all the nonestablished information in the comment (unless otherwise marked – see ch. 4).

Sentences with identificational articulation have **narrow focus** (Van Valin 2005:71). In information questions, the focus is the **constituent** that is being questioned. Similarly, the corresponding constituent in the answer is the focus:

FOCUS	PRESUPPOSITION		FOCUS	PRESUPPOSITION
Who	*made an agreement?*	—	*Dog and Hare*	*did.*

A subset of sentences with topic-comment articulation also has narrow focus. Typically they are sentences with "copular predicates" (Lambrecht 1994:123) such as *Now the names of the twelve apostles are* **these** (Matthew 10:2) or *So they are no longer* **two**, *but* **one** *flesh* (Matthew 19:6).[8]

Thetic clauses and sentences have **sentence focus**. Typically, the focus of thetic sentences is the element being presented. In Luke 1:11, for example, the focus is *an angel of the Lord (appeared)*.

---

[7] See Lambrecht 1994:213 for a more formal definition of focus.
[8] See Bailey 2009, 3.3.2.2.

Review questions

1. Match the following articulations and the type of focus typically associated with them:

a. topic-comment	i. narrow focus
b. identificational	ii. sentence focus
c. thetic	iii. predicate focus

2. What is the focus of the following sentences?
   a. *At Joppa there was a certain disciple named Tabitha.* (Acts 9:36)
   b. *They said to fry their children and eat them.* (Bekwarra 2)
   c. *Dog's then became well [lit. came then was.well].* (Bekwarra 7 – the reported speech of sentence 5 read, *Let's leave it to become well [lit. be well] first.*)[9]

Application to the language you are analysing

Identify the focus of all the sentences in the narrative you have charted that do NOT have topic-comment articulation. (Again, to avoid complications, ignore any reported speeches in your text.)

In addition, identify the focus of the first five sentences that have topic-comment articulation.

2.3 Coherence and cohesion

If you have not already read chapters 5 and 6 of Dooley and Levinsohn 2001 on coherence and cohesion, you should now do so!

Review questions

1. What does it mean to say that a text is coherent?
2. What is meant by cohesion?
3. Point out four signals of cohesion in sentence 2 of the Bekwarra text (p: plural, 3: 3rd person)

   (1 *Once upon a time Dog and Hare made an agreement.*)
   2 abe   e-dè   è-káá   èbwa   íbere   ja
       3p   p-said   p-fry   children   their   eat
       'They said to fry their children and eat them.'[10]

---

[9] **Suggested answers:**
1. a. Most topic-comment sentences have iii. predicate focus.
    b. Identificational sentences have i. narrow focus.
    c. Thetic sentences have ii. sentence focus.
2. a. The focus of *At Joppa there was a certain disciple named Tabitha* is the new entity that is being introduced: *a certain disciple named Tabitha*.
    b. The focus of *They said to fry their children and eat them* is all the nonestablished information in the comment: *said to fry their children and eat them*.
    c. The focus of *Dog's then became well* is *then (be)came* (*be well* was established in sent. 5).

[10] **Suggested answers:**
1. "A text is said to be coherent if, for a certain hearer on a certain hearing/reading, he or she is able to fit its different elements into a single overall mental representation" (Dooley and Levinsohn 2001:23).
2. Cohesion is "the use of linguistic means to signal coherence. ... Signals of cohesion indicate how the part of the text with which they occur links up conceptually with some other part." (Dooley and Levinsohn 2001:27)
3. Four signals of cohesion in sentence 2 of the Bekwarra text are:
   a) the pronoun *abe* 'they', which shows that the subject of sentence 2 is the same as that of sentence 1;
   b) the pronoun *íbere* 'their', which shows that the possessor of 'children' is the same as the subject of the sentence;

2.4 Thematic continuity, discontinuities and segmentation

We start, then, with the assumption that the texts we analyse are basically coherent. As each new sentence of the text is presented, hearers/readers who are reasonably conversant with the world-view of the author can relate the information in it to the mental model that they have formed from hearing/reading what has already been presented in the text.[11]

Nevertheless, the sentences of such a text do not form a simple string. Rather, groupings of sentences seem to belong together over against other groupings of sentences, and groupings of groupings of sentences seem to belong together over against other groupings of groupings of sentences. We usually refer to groupings of sentences as paragraphs, and groupings of groupings of sentences as sections, chapters or, in narrative, episodes.

Question

Look at sentences 1–9 of the Bekwarra text. Which sentences appear to group together over against another group, so that the nine sentences form two groupings?[12]

While editors often do not agree where one group of sentences ends and another begins, consciously or unconsciously they use as a basis for their segmentation changes "in scene, time, character configuration, event structure, and the like" (Chafe 1987:43). Givón (1984:245) formalises these changes for narrative as **discontinuities** of place, time, participants and action. Table 5 (based on Givón 1984:245) indicates how continuity and discontinuity are manifested along each of these dimensions.

Table 5. Dimensions of continuity and discontinuity in narrative

Dimension	Continuity	Discontinuity
Place	same place or (for motion) continuous change	discrete* change of place
Time	events separated by at most only small forward gaps	large forward gap or events out of order
Participants	same cast or gradual change of cast	discrete* change of cast
Action	all material of the same type: event, nonevent, reported conversation, etc.; events are in sequence	change from one type of material to another and/or the event is NOT the next in sequence

*The term 'discrete' is used in linguistics when elements have "definable boundaries, with no gradation or continuity between them" (Crystal 1997:120). The following paragraphs discuss when changes of place or in the cast of participants are discrete, and when they are not.

2.4.1 Place

A discrete change of place may be discerned when one group of sentences describes events in one place while the next group switches to events in another place. Acts 9:36–43 is set in Joppa, for instance, whereas Acts 10:1 is set in Caesarea. There is "no gradation or continuity between" Joppa and Caesarea, so there is a discontinuity of place at the beginning of chapter 10.

9:43 *And it happened that he [Peter] stayed in Joppa for some time with a certain Simon, a tanner.*
10:1 *Now a certain man in Caesarea named Cornelius ...*

---

c) ellision of the subjects of 'fry' and 'eat', which shows that the subject of the sentence remains unchanged;
d) ellision of the object of 'eat', which shows that the object of 'eat' is the same as the object of 'fry'.

[11] Much of the following material is taken from Levinsohn 2000:3–5. The Greek text has been omitted.
[12] **Suggested answer**: Sentences 1–6 appear to group together over against sentences 7–9.

In contrast, when the description of a **journey** occurs between the presentation of events in the place where the journey begins and the place where it ends, NO discrete change of place may be discerned. For example, in the parable of the Prodigal Son (Luke 15:11–13), verses 11–12 are set at the father's house while 13bff. are set in a distant country. Nevertheless, because 13a describes the younger son's journey from his father's house to the distant country, there is no discontinuity of place at the beginning of 13.

11 *A certain man had two sons. (12) And the younger of them said to his father, 'Father, give me the share of the property that will belong to me.' So he divided his property between them.*

13a *A few days later the younger son, having gathered all he had, travelled to a distant country*

13b *and there he squandered his property in dissolute living.*

2.4.2 Participants

Discontinuities of participants also involve discrete changes of cast. For instance, in Acts 10:1 (cited above), the previous scene involved the apostle Peter and some disciples in Joppa (Acts 9:36–43). Chapter 10 begins with an interaction between the centurion Cornelius, an angel and members of Cornelius' household. The cast of participants in the two scenes is completely different (discrete), so participant discontinuity occurs.

In contrast, there is no discrete change of cast in Luke 15:11–13 (above). The younger son leaves his father and brother behind and eventually interacts with a citizen of the country to which he has gone. However, he himself is active in both locations, so there is no discontinuity of participants.

2.4.3 Time

Discontinuities of time occur when there are "large forward gaps" and when events are "out of order". These are illustrated in turn.

Large forward gaps. There is a discontinuity of time at Luke 15:13a (repeated below), since the events described in that sentence occur *a few days later* than those of 12. *A few days later* constitutes a large forward gap.

11 *A certain man had two sons. (12) And the younger of them said to his father, 'Father, give me the share of the property that will belong to me.' So he divided his property between them.*

13a *A few days later the younger son, having gathered all he had, travelled to a distant country*

Out of order. When events are out of order, the term **flashback** is used, since a flashback is "set in a time earlier than the main action" (*OED*). Mark 6:17 is an instance of a flashback, since Herod's arrest of John takes place prior to his hearing of Jesus performing miracles.

16 *But when Herod heard of it [Jesus' miracles], he said, 'John, whom I beheaded, has been raised.'*

17 *For Herod himself had sent men who arrested John ...*

2.4.4 Action

Discontinuities of action may involve changes in the type of action described or failure to move the narrative forward to the next action in sequence. These are discussed in turn.

Changes in the type of action described. The following paragraphs illustrate two instances involving a change in the type of action described:
- a shift from the description of events to nonevents
- a shift from speaking to doing: the reporting of a conversation or long speech to actions resulting from that conversation or speech.

We shall see in chapter 3 that languages tend to mark the presence of an **action discontinuity** in both of these circumstances. Note, however, that a shift from action to reported speech does NOT normally constitute a discontinuity of action.

2.4 Thematic continuity, discontinuities and segmentation

A shift from the description of events to **nonevents** is illustrated in Acts 19:14. The action described in 15 resumes the sequence of foreground events that was interrupted by the nonevent material of 14. So a discontinuity of action occurs at 14.

13 *Then some of the itinerant Jewish exorcists undertook to pronounce the name of the Lord Jesus over those who had evil spirits ...*

14 *There were seven sons of a Jewish high priest named Sceva who were doing this.*

15 *But in answer, the evil spirit said to them ...*

A shift from speaking to doing (the reporting of a **conversation or long speech** to actions resulting from that conversation or speech) is illustrated in Matthew 7:28. The previous three chapters (5:3–7:27) recount the Sermon on the Mount.

28 *When Jesus had finished these sayings, the crowds were astounded at his teaching ...*

Failure to move the narrative forward to the next action in sequence. This factor is described as an action discontinuity because Givón (1983:8) defines **continuity of action** as follows:

> [A]ction continuity pertains primarily to temporal sequentiality within [a] thematic paragraph ... [A]ctions are given primarily in the natural sequential order in which they actually occurred and most commonly there is small if any temporal gap ... between one action and the next.

It follows from the above definition that action discontinuities are to be discerned when a sentence describes an event that fails to move the narrative forward to the next action in sequence. The following paragraphs illustrate two circumstances when this happens:
- when simultaneous events are involved
- when restatements are involved.

We shall again see in chapter 3 that languages tend to mark the presence of a discontinuity in both of these circumstances.

In an action discontinuity involving **simultaneous events**, the second event takes place at the same time as the first. It is not the next in sequence. In Acts 12:5, for example, the prayers of the church for Peter (5b) are simultaneous with him being kept in jail (5a):

5a *Peter was being kept in prison,*

5b *but the church was praying fervently to God for him.*

Note 1. Simultaneous events typically are presented with imperfective aspect (see 5.3.2). This is reflected in the English glosses of Acts 12:5 (above) *was being kept* and *was praying*.

Note 2. Sentences describing simultaneous events or restating a proposition usually belong to the **same** thematic grouping. Such action discontinuities tend not to form the basis for a new thematic grouping.

Matthew 25:15 is an example of an action discontinuity involving a generic-specific **restatement**. The event of verse 15 is not in sequence with that of 14b; rather, it is a specific instance of that event.

14a *For it is as if a man, going on a journey, summoned his slaves*

14b *and entrusted his property to them;*

15 *to one he gave five talents ...*

Review questions

1. What are the four **dimensions** of continuity and discontinuity in narrative, according to Givón?
2. What type of discontinuity does a **flashback** display?

3. Why does the description of **simultaneous events** and **restatements** involve discontinuities of action, according to Givón's definition of action continuity?[13]

We said earlier that the sentences of a narrative are segmented into paragraphs, episodes and chapters on the basis of changes or discontinuities in four dimensions: time, place, participants and action. Dooley and Levinsohn (2001:37) put it like this:

> In narrative, then, the speaker typically begins a new thematic grouping when there is a significant discontinuity in at least one of these four dimensions. Within a thematic grouping, there is usually continuity along all four dimensions. One can think of a new thematic grouping resulting when the speaker leaves one section of the mental representation and moves on to, or perhaps creates, another.

Earlier, I asked you to divide sentences 1–9 of the Bekwarra text into two groupings and suggested that 1–6 appear to group together over against 7–9. We now examine this suggestion by considering the continuity or discontinuity of the four dimensions.

First of all, consider the free translation into English of sentences 1–6:

1   Once upon a time Dog and Hare made an agreement.
2   They said, 'Let's fry our children and eat them'.
3   They said, 'Let's fry Dog's child and eat it'.
4   Dog said, 'Mine has an eye infection. (5) Let's leave it to become well first.'
6   They took Hare's, fried it and ate it.

Note the continuity in sentences 1–6 in three of the four dimensions:
- There is continuity of time, because the events are separated by at most only small forward gaps.
- There is continuity of place, because the events all take place in the same (unspecified) location.
- There is continuity of participants, because the same cast is involved throughout.

Question

Two discontinuities of action occur in sentences 1–6. What are they?[14]

Now consider sentences 6–10.

6   They took Hare's, fried it and ate it.
7   Dog's then became well.
8   They said, 'Let's fry Dog's and eat it'.
9   Dog ran off, gathered them together, went and hid them in a broom, twisted it together, threw it into the yard and set off for his farm.
10 So one morning Hare went off and had a discussion with Dog.

---

[13] **Suggested answers**:
1. The four dimensions of continuity and discontinuity in narrative, according to Givón, are time, place, participants and action.
2. A flashback displays discontinuity of time, since the events concerned are out of sequential order.
3. The description of simultaneous events and restatements involves discontinuities of action, according to Givón's definition, because the events concerned fail to move the narrative forward to the next action in temporal sequence.

[14] **Suggested answer:**
- There is a discontinuity of action between sentences 1 and 2, because sentence 2 fails to move the narrative forward to the next action in sequence. Rather, it states the specific agreement that Dog and Hare entered into, so is a **restatement** of 1. (This discontinuity is reflected in Bekwarra by the independent pronoun *abe* at the beginning of 2.)
- There is a discontinuity of action at sentence 6. Sentences 2–5 describe a reported conversation, whereas 6 **shifts** to an action resulting from that conversation. (This discontinuity is not marked in Bekwarra, because sentences 1–6 set the scene for the rest of the story – see ch. 6.)

Questions

1. In which dimension is there almost certainly discontinuity between sentences 6 and 7?
2. Is there a discontinuity of place between sentences 8 and 9?
3. The discontinuity of time between sentences 9 and 10 is signalled by *one morning*. But is there also a discontinuity of **place** between 9 and 10?[15]

Concluding remarks about Givón's thematic dimensions

Givón's thematic dimensions in narrative may be generalised for other text genres as three parameters:
- **situation**: continuity or discontinuities of time, place, conditions, circumstances and assumptions (typically associated with adverbials – see chapter 3)
- **reference**: continuity or discontinuities of participants and themes (most often associated with nominals – chapter 3)
- **action**: as continuity or discontinuities related to moving the narrative forward, but only for texts that are organised chronologically (see 1.2.2).

So, when we approach a text, we assume it is coherent. Within this coherent text, though, we may find discontinuities of situation, reference and action. Every language has devices both for indicating discontinuities and for maintaining the overall coherence of the text. Chapter 3 considers one such device.

2.5 Segmentation into groupings

This section concerns surface features found in narrative texts which may help the hearer or reader to recognise the boundaries of groupings. For fuller discussion of such "boundary features", see Levinsohn 2000:271–284 (on Greek) and chapter 8 of my course on non-narrative texts (Levinsohn 2015).

Table 6 (based on Dooley and Levinsohn 2001:40, but with the word "hesitation" omitted) gives an overview of common boundary features in narratives. It also indicates in which chapter of the current course they will be discussed.

Table 6. Common boundary features

Initial in a grouping, it is common to find
- a prenuclear expression, especially one of time, place or topic (see ch. 3);
- a "reorientation" particle such as *Well* or *Now* (Carlson 1994) or the absence of the normal particle (see ch. 6);
- certain sentence connectives (e.g. *Then, So*), or the absence of the normal connective (see ch. 6);
- active participants referred to by full noun phrases instead of pronouns or implicitly (see ch. 8).

Initial or final in a grouping, it is common to find
- changes in the tense-aspect of verbs (e.g. other than the default form for narrative – see ch. 5);
- a summary (e.g. *That's what they did*) or evaluation of the last events described (e.g. *So that was exciting*).

Between groupings in an *oral* text, it is common to find
- a pause or break in timing, followed by
- a change in the pitch of the intonation contour. Typically, the previous contour will have drifted downwards, whereas the new contour resumes a higher pitch range.

---

[15] **Suggested answers**:
1. There is almost certainly a discontinuity of time between sentences 6 and 7; *Then* suggests a "large forward gap".
2. No, there is no discontinuity of place between sentences 8 and 9 because the journey between the place of the conversation and Dog's farm is described in 9.
3. Yes, sentence 9 ends up at Dog's farm, whereas sentence 10 starts elsewhere.

The following potential boundary features from table 6 are found in the **Bekwarra** text (see appendix C):
- the prenuclear time phrase *ichìè kìn* 'one sun' in sentence 10
- the particle *ka* 'then' in the verb column of sentences 7, 10, 28 and 29
- the connective *nánáánáng* at the beginning of sentence 10
- a quasi-summary in sentence 15: *e-kàng ngángáángá* 'They talked on and on like that'.

These potential boundary features lead to the following observations about the structure of the Bekwarra text:
- We have already noted (footnote 15) a discontinuity of time at sentence 7 (expressed in the English version of the text by the connective *then*, which translates the Bekwarra verb phrase particle *ka*).
- The presence of three boundary features in sentence 10 (a prenuclear time phrase, a sentence connective and the particle *ka*) suggests a major division of the narrative at this point.
- Sentence 15 marks the end of the conversation between Dog and Hare. The following sentence appears to begin a new episode, as Hare goes to the elders with a complaint against Dog.
- The presence of *ka* in sentence 28 corresponds to a shift from reported conversation (20–27) to the concluding event of 28 (a discontinuity of action – see 2.4.4).
- Sentence 29 presents the moral of the story, so could well be a separate unit of the folktale. The presence of *ka* may well signal this (see further in ch. 6).

The above surface features suggest that the Bekwarra text has the following structure:

1–6	Opening exchange between Dog & Hare, leading to Hare's pup being eaten
7–9	Second exchange between Dog & Hare, leading to Dog hiding his pup
10–15	Third exchange between Dog & Hare, in which Dog denies that they had agreed to eat their pups
16–28	Dog before the elders, including the event (28) that results from the conversation between them
29	The elders pronounce the moral of the story

Application to the language you are analysing

1. In the narrative text that you have charted, look for places where there appear to be discontinuities (as defined in table 5) of time, place, cast of participants and action. You may wish to display your findings in a table similar to the one presented on p. 48 of Dooley and Levinsohn 2001.
2. Look for formal boundary features from the list in table 6 that occur at these or other places in the text.
3. Do the same for other texts.

Note 1. For the purposes of text analysis, treat the sentences of your narrative as indivisible units (unless the language you are analysing expresses complete episodes in single sentences). Do NOT look for discontinuities between the individual clauses of a sentence!

Note 2. Treat reported speeches that extend over more than one sentence as a single unit when analysing the structure of a narrative (see "Review questions" above where sentences 4–5 of the Bekwarra text were handled as a single unit).

Note 3. "Although the presence of a surface feature can be taken as supporting evidence for a paragraph or section boundary, it must be emphasised that the presence of such a feature is seldom a sufficient criterion on which to base a boundary. Rather, if one of the reasons for the presence of a certain feature is because of a boundary between units, almost invariably there will be other reasons why that feature might be present." (Levinsohn 2000:271)

The topic of segmentation and boundary features will be taken up in later chapters. Significant boundaries between groupings are characterised by the CLUSTERING of boundary features (as in sentence 10 of the Bekwarra text).

Note 4. You will learn in chapter 3 that languages have means of downplaying the significance of individual discontinuities, to keep them from contributing to the segmentation of the text.

Suggested reading

The following chapters of Dooley and Levinsohn 2001 relate to the topics covered in this chapter: 5 (Coherence), 6 (Cohesion), 7 (Thematic groupings & thematic discontinuities) and 8.4 (Indicating thematic groupings).

Appendix C: Bekwarra text

Abbreviations: 3: 3rd. person; O: object; p: plural; Q: polar question marker; s: singular; TR: terminated; SPACER: see 5.2.3–5.2.4.

Ref.	Pre-S	S	V	(O)	Adjunct
1	únyang kìn time one	ùbuhó àhe dog 3s n'-anyamchù with-hare	e-ngwìà p-entered	iyìm agreement	
2a		abe 3p	e-dè p-said		
2b		....	è-káá p-fry	èbwa íbere children their	
2c		....	ja eat	....	
3a		——	e-dè p-said		
3b		....	è-káá p-fry	ùngwa úbuhó child of.dog	
3c		....	ja eat	——	
4a		ùbuhó dog	a-dè s-said		
4b		ímin his	ì-yi s-has	apètèré-apètèré infection	k'-ìrìchì in-eye
5a		....	è-tyàng p-leave		[Purp: 5b]
5b	[k'- to	ímin his	ì-kpèrè s-be.well		ukpang] before/first
6a		——	é-kung p-took	áng'-ányamchù that-of.hare	
6b		——	kung kaa ji took fried ate	——	
7		áng'-úbuhó that-of.dog	á-bé ka kpèrè s-came then was.well		
8a		——	e-dè p-said		
8b		....	è-kúng p-take	áng'-úbuhó that-of.dog	

Appendix C: Bekwarra text

Ref.	Pre-S	S	V	(O)	Adjunct	
8c		....	kaà ja fry eat	....		
9a		ùbuhó dog	ì-bwà nòkpó s-runs goes.away			
9b		———	báng gathers	abe 3p		
9c		———	ya nyèrè ha goes hides puts	———	k'-ìrìgwìè in-broom	
9d		———	kùng nìbì tyàng takes twists throws	———	ká k'-ùfànúko there in-yard	
9e		———	nùò sets.out		ímin k'-ùtyén his to-farm	
10a	nánáánáng ichìè kìn so sun one	anyamchù hare	a-kà nòkpó s-then went.away			
10b			dè said	abe 3p	n'-ùbuhó ìhà with-dog two	
11a		———	a-dè s-said	———		
11b		ùbuhó dog	ì-wám s-remove	ùngwa ímin child his		
11c		....	kaà fry	kìn one	[Purp: 11d]	
11d	[k'- to	abe 3p	è-ji p-eat	.......]		
12		ùbuhó dog	á-chwen s-refused			
13a		———	a-dè s-said			
13b		ìbang what	h'-a-sì FOCUS-s-did			
13c		ng'-ámín -3s	á-chwen s-refused		dèè (say)	
13d		....	i-káà s-fries	....	re not	
14a		———	a-dè s-said			

Ref.	Pre-S	S	V	(O)	Adjunct	
14b		àhe n'-ámín 3s with-3s	e-ngwìà p-entered	iyìm ùngwan àjini agreement child eating		re not
15		—	e-kàng p-spoke		ngángáángá thus (repeated)	
16a		anyamchù hare	a-nòkpó s-went.away			
16b		—	ye kuo went called	ùbuhó dog	ùchi lawsuit	
16c					k'-àbìa ékáànì at-feet of.elders	
17		—	á-ye s-went		yè kin from here	
18a		—	é-kuo p-called	anyamchù hare		
18b		—	bé chi came sat			áná SPACER
19a		—	é-kuo p-called	ùbuhó dog		
19b		—	bé chi came sat			áná SPACER
20a		—	é-bii p-asked	ùbuhó dog	dèè (say)	
20b		abe n'-anyamchù 3p with-hare	e-ngwìà p-entered	iyìm èbwan àjini agreement children eating	bu à indeed Q	
21a		ùbuhó dog	á-chi s-sat		ngá there	
21b		—	nè looked.at	he 3sO	chùù k'-àchì carefully in-face	
21c					ékáànì of.elders	áná SPACER
22		—	á-kung bàng s-took agreed			
23a		—	a-dè s-said			
23b		abe 3p	e-ngwìà p-entered	iyìm èbwan àjini agreement children eating		
24a		—	e-dè p-said			

Appendix C: Bekwarra text

Ref.	Pre-S	S	V	(O)	Adjunct	
24b		....	é-kaa p-fried	áng'-ányamchù that-of.hare		
24c		....	ji mìà ngin ate finished complete	....		
25a		....	e-já p-eat	áng'-ámín that-of.3s		à Q
25b	hàà or	....	e-já p-eat	....		re not
26		———	á-chi wòm s-sat quietly			
27a		———	e-dè p-said	he 3sO		dèè (say)
27b	gb'- if	ámín 3s	a-ngwìà s-entered	iyìm èbwan àjini n'-anyamchù agreement children eating with-hare		
27c		ámín 3s	ì-bang s-gather	èbwa ámín children of.3s	[Purp: 27e]	
27d		....	kaa fry	....		
27e	[k'-abe n'-anyamchù to-3p with-hare		è-ji p-eat	———]		
28a		———	a-kà kung s-then took	ùngwa ímin child his		
28b		———	wam kaa removed fried	———	[Purp: 28c]	
28c	[k'-abe n'-anyamchù to-3p with-hare		è-ji p-eat	———]		
29a		èkáànì elders	e-kà kung dè p-then too said	he 3sO		dèè (say)
29b	[ipì àwo ó-ji kwom (O)] place.where you you-ate TR		h'-ó-fìà kwom focus-you-pay tr	[PREVERB]		

Free translation of Bekwarra text

1. Once upon a time Dog and Hare made an agreement.
2. They said, "Let's fry our children and eat them."
3. They said (i.e. It was said to Dog), "Let's fry Dog's child and eat it."
4. Dog said, "Mine has an eye infection. (5) Let's leave it to become well first."
6. They took Hare's, fried it and ate it.
7. Dog's then became well.

8. They said (i.e. It was said to Dog), "Let's fry Dog's and eat it."
9. Dog ran off, gathered them [the pups] together, went and hid them in a broom, twisted it together, threw it into the yard and set off for his farm.
10. So one morning Hare went off and had a discussion with Dog.
11. He told Dog to fry one child of his for them to eat.
12. Dog refused.
13. He said, "What happened that you refuse to fry it?"
14. He said, "I did not make an agreement with you to eat our children."
15. They talked on and on like that.
16. Hare went off and issued a summons against Dog in the presence of the elders.
17. He went from here.
18. So Hare was called and came and sat, (19) Dog was called and came and sat, (20) then Dog was asked whether he and Hare had indeed made an agreement to eat their children.
21. Dog sat there looking at him carefully before the elders, (22) then agreed.
23. He said that they had made an agreement to eat their children.
24. They said, "Since you have finished frying and eating Hare's, (25) are people going to get to eat yours or not?"
26. He sat in silence.
27. They told him that, since he had made an agreement with Hare about eating children, he should gather his children and fry them for Hare and himself to eat.
28. So he took one of his children and fried it for Hare and himself to eat.
29. The elders told him, "What you have eaten, you must pay in full."

3

Points of Departure

This chapter looks at a device that signals discontinuities of situation, of reference, and sometimes of action, namely the placement of a situational or referential constituent at the beginning of a sentence. In linguistic circles, such a constituent is often said to be **topicalised**. However, because of the potential for confusion between this term and 'topic', I will say that such constituents establish **points of departure**.[1]

Section 3.1 examines the significance of points of departure. Most points of departure imply a **switch** to the initial constituent from a corresponding constituent in a previous clause or sentence. However, certain points of departure **renew** an earlier point of departure or propositional topic (3.2). Section 3.3 examines the implications of **not** starting a sentence with a potential point of departure.

3.1 Propositional topic, comment and point of departure

We saw in chapter 2 that a well-formed text is coherent. Within such a text, discontinuities of situation (time and place in narrative), reference (participants and themes) and action underlie the segmentation of the text into groupings of sentences (paragraphs, sections, episodes).

One device that is used at points of discontinuity is the placement at the beginning of the sentence of an appropriate constituent. This device, as will be seen below, indicates both the nature of the discontinuity and the relationship of what follows to the context.

We saw in 2.1.1 that, in a sentence with topic-comment articulation, the speaker talks about something – the propositional topic – and makes a comment about that topic. Examples:

TOPIC	COMMENT	
Hare	*went off and had a discussion with Dog.*	(see Bekwarra 10)
The younger son	*set off for a distant country.*	(see Luke 15:13a)[2]

A problem arises, however, if an analyst tries to divide all sentences with topic-comment articulation into just a topic and a comment. If *Hare went off and had a discussion with Dog* is preceded by the temporal phrase *one morning*, I still consider *Hare* to be the propositional topic. Consequently, following the Prague School linguist Beneš, I divide the sentence into three functional parts (not counting the conjunction):

	POINT OF DEPARTURE	TOPIC	COMMENT	
So	*one morning*	*Hare*	*went off and had a discussion with Dog.*	(Bekwarra 10)

---

[1] Buth (1999:101) prefers the term "contextualizing constituent".
[2] Much of this chapter is based on Levinsohn 2000:7–15 (citations in Greek have been omitted).

Question

How does the sentence *Not long after that, the younger son ... set off for a distant country* (Luke 15:13a) divide into point of departure, topic and comment?[3]

Some linguists who have described the function of points of departure concentrate on what follows them in the discourse. Thus, Chafe (1976:50) says that such constituents set "a spatial, temporal or individual domain within which the main predication holds". In other words, a point of departure establishes a setting for what follows.

Other linguists, however, recognise that points of departure are as much backward- as forward-looking (see, for example, Givón 1990:847). In other words, such constituents have a **bi-directional** function:

- to serve as a starting point for the communication, and
- to provide the primary basis for relating a sentence to its context or mental representation.

This insight should probably be credited to Beneš. In 1962, he referred to such a constituent as the "basis" which, "serving as a point of departure for the communication, is directly linked to the context" (as translated by Garvin 1963:508).

For example, in Bekwarra sentence 10, the initial phrase *one morning* has a bi-directional function. It looks forward, serving as a temporal starting point for what follows. It also looks backward, indicating that the communication is to be related to the context primarily on the basis of time, involving a "switch" (Andrews 1985:78) from the temporal setting of the events of sentences 7–9.

Question

What is the bi-directional function of the initial phrase *A few days later* in Luke 15:13a (see 2.4.3)?[4]

> **Definition**
>
> The term POINT OF DEPARTURE designates an element that is placed at the beginning of a ... sentence with a dual function.
>
> 1. It establishes a starting point for the communication; and
> 2. It "cohesively anchors the subsequent clause(s) to something which is already in the context (i.e. to something accessible in the hearer's mental representation)" (Dooley and Levinsohn 2001:68).

Note that conjunctions such as *so* (Bekwarra 10) are ignored when identifying the initial element of a clause or sentence.

As the above definition implies, points of departure "make reference to something which is currently accessible to the hearer, so as to anchor the clause at that place in the mental representation" (Dooley and Levinsohn 2001:69).[5]

In narrative, points of departure relate events to their context on the basis of time, place or reference (participants or themes). In behavioural texts (some of which are found in reported speeches in narrative), constituents expressing condition, reason, purpose and other situational relations may also be placed initially in the sentence to serve as points of departure. The following sections illustrate situational points of departure. They will be followed by discussion of referential points of departure.[6]

---

[3] **Suggested answer:**
Point of departure: *Not long after*; topic: *the younger son*; comment: *set off for a distant country*.

[4] **Suggested answer:**
The initial phrase *not long after* in Luke 15:13a looks forward, serving as a temporal starting point for what follows. It also looks backward, indicating that the communication is to be related to the context primarily on the basis of time, involving a switch from the temporal setting of the previous events to *not long after* that time.

[5] For a simiilar claim about propositional topics, see Lambrecht 1994:164 and the end of 2.1.1.

[6] For discussion of points of departure in English, see Levinsohn 1992.

3.1 Propositional topic, comment and point of departure 43

Situational points of departure

We now look at a variety of mostly adverbial phrases and clauses that begin sentences. In each case, they set a situational point of departure for the communication. (Remember: To be a point of departure, the constituent must be **initial** in its sentence. In this and all subsequent examples, the point of departure is <u>underlined</u>.)

As we saw above, a **temporal** point of departure is used in Bekwarra 10, namely the phrase *ichiè kìn* 'one sun'. This phrase establishes the temporal setting for what follows. It also indicates that the primary basis for relating the communication to the context is by a switch from the time of the events of sentences 7–9 to a later time (p: plural; s: singular; 3: 3rd person).

9   ùbuhó   i-bwà   nòkpó   báng   abe   ya   nyèrè   ha   k'-irìgwiè
    dog   s-runs   goes away gathers   3p   goes   hides   puts   in-broom

    kùng   nìbì   tyàng   ká   k'-ùfànúko   nùò   ímin   k'-ùtyén
    takes   twists   throws   there   in-yard   sets out his   to-farm

'Dog ran off, gathered them together, went and hid them in a broom, twisted it together, threw it into the yard and set off for his farm.'

10 nánáánáng   <u>ichiè</u> <u>kìn</u>   anyamchù   a-kà   nòkpó   dè   abe   n'-ùbuhó   ihà
    so   sun   one   hare   s-then   went away   said   3p   with-dog   two

'So <u>one morning</u> Hare went off and had a discussion with Dog.'

Matthew 6:2 opens with a temporal point of departure which is an adverbial **clause**. This signals that the primary basis for relating the communication to the context is by a switch from the habitual practice of *your piety* (1) to the practice of a specific type of piety.

1 *Beware of practising your piety before others in order to be seen by them; for then you have no reward from your Father in heaven.*

2 *So, <u>whenever you give alms</u>, do not sound a trumpet before you ...!*

A **spatial** point of departure (i.e. one involving a discontinuity of place) occurs in Acts 9:36a. Here, the initial adverbial phrase *At Joppa* establishes the spatial setting. It also indicates that the primary basis for relating the communication to the context is by a switch from Lydda and Sharon to Joppa.

35 *And all the residents of Lydda and Sharon saw Aeneas and they turned to the Lord.*

36a *Now <u>at Joppa</u> there was a disciple named Tabitha.*

Acts 14:26 exemplifies a spatial point of departure in the context of a **travelogue**. Here, the initial adverbial phrase *from there*, which refers back to the goal of the previous stage of the journey, establishes the point of departure for the next stage. It also indicates that the primary basis for relating what follows to the context is by a switch from the starting point of the previous journey (Perga).

25 *and, having spoken the word in Perga, they went down to Attalia.*

26 *And <u>from there they</u> sailed back to Antioch ...*

Matthew 6:14 and 15 begin with adverbial clauses of **condition**.[7] The petition of 12 becomes the point of departure in 14 for the assertion that will be true if the condition is fulfilled (discussed in 3.2.3). The opposite condition is the point of departure for 15. In this particular passage, the switch between these two points of departure has the effect of **contrasting** the consequences of fulfilling the two conditions; contrast is a special case of switch.

---

[7] On initial *if* clauses in English, see Ramsey 1987:385.

12   And forgive us our debts, as we also have forgiven our debtors ...
14   For *if you forgive men when they sin against you*, your heavenly Father will also forgive you;
15   but *if you do not forgive men their sins*, neither will your Father forgive your sins.

Revelation 3:16 begins with an adverbial clause of **reason** to establish a point of departure for what follows. It also relates the communication to the context by a switch from the wish that the addressees be either cold or hot (15b) to the opposite.

15a   I know your works, that you are neither cold nor hot.
15b   I wish that you were either cold or hot.
16   So, *because you are lukewarm, and neither cold nor hot*, I am about to spew you out of my mouth.

Ephesians 6:21 begins with an adverbial clause of **purpose** (introduced in Greek by *hina* 'so that') to establish a point of departure for what follows. It also relates the communication to the context by a switch from the purpose clause that immediately precedes it in 20.[8]

19   (Pray) also for me, so that (hina) a message may be given to me when I speak, to make known with boldness the mystery of the gospel, (20) for which I am an ambassador in chains, so that (hina) I may declare it boldly, as I must speak.
21   *So that (hina) you also may know how I am and what I am doing*, Tychicus ... will tell you everything ...

Finally, John 15:4b begins with an adverbial clause of **comparison** to establish a point of departure for what follows. It also relates the following assertion about *you* back to the figure of 2b by a switch from branches that bear fruit to those that cannot unless they abide in the vine.

2b   and every branch that bears fruit he prunes to make it bear more fruit.
3   You have already been cleansed (pruned) by the word that I have spoken to you. (4a) Abide in me as I abide in you.
4b   *Just as the branch cannot bear fruit by itself unless it abides in the vine*, neither can you unless you abide in me.

Question

In the following excerpt from Dorothy Sayers' short story *Talboys* (2018:416), what is the primary basis for relating sentence b to sentence a?

a   At the back, trained against the wall, stood the peach tree, on which one great, solitary fruit glowed rosily among the dark leafage.
b   Across the bed ran a double line of small footprints.[9]

Note: In some languages, the equivalent of a situational point of departure may be an independent clause. In the following extract from a text in the Gumawana [gvs] (Malayo-Polynesian, Papua New Guinea) language, for instance, the expression translated 'the next morning' is literally 'the village dawned' (Olson 2014:228).

Vanuwo	*i-tomo*	*idi*	*kiyama*	*si-kabi-di,*	*si-na,*	*idi*	*oga*	*si-tala.*
village	3s-dawn	their	axe	3p-get-3p	3p-go	their	canoe	3p-cut

'*The next morning* they got their axes, went and cut their canoes.'

---

[8] On initial purpose clauses in English, see Thompson 1985.

[9] **Suggested answer:**
The primary basis for relating sentence b to sentence a is spatial, involving a switch from *At the back, trained against the wall* to *Across the bed*.

Referential points of departure

Some referential points of departure are prepositional or postpositional phrases (e.g. *Concerning X, As for Y*) which establish the **theme** for a paragraph or longer section. They typically relate the communication to the context by a switch from a previous paragraph theme.

1 Corinthians 8:1 provides an example. The initial prepositional phrase *concerning food sacrificed to idols* establishes the theme for the chapter. It also relates what follows to the context by a switch from the theme of the previous section (which began with *concerning virgins* – 7:25).

1   Now <u>*concerning food sacrificed to idols,*</u> *we know that we all possess knowledge.*

Referential points of departure may also be **nominal** constituents. In such instances, the point of departure may also be the subject and propositional topic of a topic-comment sentence.

In Acts 20:6a, for example, the initial subject *we* is both the point of departure and the propositional topic of the sentence. Koine Greek is a VS/VO language, and the initial position of the subject in the sentence indicates that the basis for relating what follows to the context is by a switch from the activities of *these men* to *we*. The switch has the effect of contrasting the activities of the two groups (compare Matthew 6:15 above).[10]

5   <u>*These men,*</u> *going before us, awaited us in Troas.*

6a PT OF DEPARTURE/TOPIC   COMMENT

   <u>*We,*</u>   *however,*   *sailed from Philippi after the days of Unleavened Bread*

Note that *we* is a point of departure in Koine Greek because the default position of the subject is after the verb. **Subject-initial languages** typically use a **spacer** (Dooley 1990:477) or **left dislocation** to separate the subject from the rest of the sentence and indicate that it is a point of departure.[11]

Spacers

> Spacers tend to be short expressions with little or no stress, whose lexical meaning has sentence scope ... They may have a default grammatical position in the sentence ... but alternatively can be placed between constituents with distinct discourse-pragmatic roles. (Dooley and Levinsohn 2001:73)[12]

In the above translation into English of Acts 20:6a, *however* functions as a spacer. Its default grammatical position is at the beginning of the sentence. When it occurs after the subject, it separates it from the rest of the sentence and signals that it is also a point of departure.

Left dislocation

Left-dislocated points of departure are separated from the rest of the sentence by a **pause** (or a comma, in written material). Typically, a pronominal **trace** of the left-dislocated constituent occurs in its usual position in the clause (e.g. <u>*Moi,*</u> *je* ... '<u>Me</u>, I ...' – French).[13]

In the following example from Gude [gde] (autonym Gudé; Chadic, Cameroon dialect) (Perrin n.d.), *gyaagya* 'cock' is left-dislocated and a pronominal trace (*ci*) occurs in its usual position later in

---

[10] When a referent is contrasted with another one, Givón (1990:705) talks of "contrastive topicalization" and "Y-movement".

[11] As an alternative to a point of departure, some languages use a 'thematic' pronoun or demonstrative – see ch. 9. In pro-drop languages such as Spanish, the presence of a personal pronoun as subject may also be the equivalent of a point of departure.

[12] Taglicht (1984:82) uses the term **partition**: "*too* ... has its normal, unmarked place ... at the end of the sentence. When it stands anywhere else it functions as a 'partition'." For example, it stands "between the marked theme [i.e. point of departure] and the textual element that follows it". See also chapter 4.

[13] The Semeur translation of Acts 20:6a begins, <u>*Quant à nous,*</u> *nous nous sommes embarqués* ... ('<u>As for us</u>, we ...').

the sentence. This makes 'cock' the point of departure for the communication (NOM: marker of nominal points of departure):

a   *'He said to Cock, "Get up; let's go to my in-laws!"'*

b

Asee,	*má*	*gyaagya,*	mararaŋəkii	nə	*ci*
now	NOM	cock	crafty	be	3s

'NOW <u>Cock</u>, he was crafty.'

Occasionally, **two** points of departure begin a sentence, one situational and one referential. The first one will indicate the primary basis for relating the sentence to its context.

In Romans 11:30, for instance, the referential point of departure *you* indicates that the primary basis for relating the sentence to its context is by a switch from *all Israel* (26). This is followed by the situational point of departure *at one time*, which marks a secondary switch from the present setting of 28.

26   *And so all Israel will be saved … (28) As regards the gospel they are enemies of God for your sake; but as regards election, they are beloved, for the sake of their ancestors; (29) for the gifts and the calling of God are irrevocable.*

30   *For just as <u>you</u>, <u>at one time</u>, were disobedient to God …*

Questions

Read the following excerpt from Dorothy Sayers' short story *Talboys* (2018:418), then answer the questions that follow it.

a   *One man climbed to the top [of the ladder] and took the peaches,*

b   *while the other, I think, stood at the foot to keep guard and receive the fruit in a bag or basket or something.*

1. What is the basis for relating part b of the above sentence to part a? (Ignore the subordinator *while*.)
2. How is the point of departure indicated in b?[14]

Now for some definitions of terms that we have been using! They are taken from Crystal (1997).

Definitions

- **Preposing**: "the MOVEMENT of a CONSTITUENT to a POSITION earlier in the SENTENCE". Preposing may be for a number of reasons (see ch. 4). The term "preposing" itself does not indicate the function of such movement.
- **Topicalisation** "takes place when a CONSTITUENT is moved to the front of a sentence, so that it functions as" a point of departure.[15]
- **Left dislocation**: "a type of SENTENCE in which one of the CONSTITUENTS appears in INITIAL position and its CANONICAL position is filled by a PRONOUN or a full LEXICAL NOUN PHRASE with the same REFERENCE, e.g. ***John***, *I like him/the old chap*."

  The converse of left dislocation is:
- **Right dislocation**: "a type of SENTENCE in which one of the CONSTITUENTS appears in FINAL position and its CANONICAL position is filled by a PRONOUN with the same REFERENCE, e.g. … *He's always late, **that chap**.*"

---

[14] Suggested answers:
1. The basis for relating part b to part a is referential; there is a switch of attention from *one man* to *the other*.
2. The placement of *I think* between the subject and the remainder of the sentence indicates that the subject also functions as a point of departure. In other words, *I think* functions as a spacer.

[15] Especially in SV/OV languages, constituents may also be topicalised to conform to the Principle of Natural Information Flow, which is discussed in 4.2.1.

> The converse of preposing is:
> - **Postposing**: "the MOVEMENT of a CONSTITUENT to a POSITION later in the SENTENCE". In the Greek of James 2:2, for instance, the subject is moved to a position after the adjunct: *For if comes into your assembly **a person with gold rings** ...*
>
>   Like preposing, postposing may be for a number of reasons (see ch. 4). The term "postposing" itself does not indicate the function of such movement.

3.2 Points of departure involving renewal

So far, we have only looked at points of departure which relate to the context by a switch from a corresponding constituent. However, points of departure may also relate to the context by **renewal**.[16] In other words, the point of departure renews a previous point of departure or topic.

For instance, Luke 2:36 first introduces Anna, then makes some comments about her as topic. The initial constituent of 36b (*this* [*fem.*]) refers again to her, so (since Koine Greek is a VS/VO language) is a point of departure involving renewal.

36a *There was also a prophetess, Anna, the daughter of Phanuel, of the tribe of Asher.*

36b <u>*This (fem.)*</u> *was very old; she had lived with her husband seven years after their marriage,*

The referents of points of departure involving renewal typically feature in the immediate context. Consequently, such points of departure often employ a "reduced" form (Werth 1984:9), i.e. a pronoun (Luke 2:36) or, if situational, a pronominal adverb such as *there* or *thus*.

In narrative, the majority of referential points of departure involving renewal introduce **background** material (see ch. 5). Consider Mark 6:17 (a flashback – see ch. 2):

16 *But when Herod heard of it [Jesus performing miracles], he said, 'John, whom I beheaded, has been raised'.*

17 *For <u>Herod himself</u> had given orders to have John arrested ...*

The initial constituent of Mark 6:17 (above) refers to the topic of the previous sentence, namely Herod, so is a point of departure involving renewal. (Note that Herod is the topic of the previous **narrative** clauses, but not of the reported speech which intervenes. Reported speeches may be viewed as the complements of speech verbs, and are embedded in the overall structure of the narrative, rather than being part of the narrative structure itself.)

The following sections consider renewal by means of referential points of departure (3.2.1), situational points of departure (3.2.2), and "tail-head linkage" (Loos 1963; Thompson and Longacre 1985:209–213) (3.2.3).

3.2.1 Renewal by means of a referential point of departure

Mark 6:17 (above) illustrated the use of a referential point of departure involving renewal to introduce background material in narrative. If successive sentences begin with the **same** referential point of departure, then each introduces a **different** background comment.

This is illustrated in Luke 2:36b and 37. We have already seen that the background comment of 36b begins with a point of departure involving renewal whose referent is Anna. In 37, the initial constituent *she* again refers to Anna, so is a further point of departure involving renewal that introduces a different comment about her. (Remember that both points of departure are also the propositional topic of their respective sentences.)

36a *There was also a prophetess, Anna, the daughter of Phanuel, of the tribe of Asher.*

36b <u>*This (fem.)*</u> *was very old; she had lived with her husband seven years after their marriage,*

37 *and <u>she</u> then, as a widow until she was eighty-four, never left the temple ...*

---

[16] Andrews (1985:78) refers to such points of departure as "expected topics".

A referential point of departure involving renewal occasionally introduces a **foreground** event. Such is the case in Luke 22:41. Following Jesus' instruction to the disciples to pray (40), the initial pronoun *he* ensures that attention remains on Jesus, rather than on the disciples' response to his instruction. This effect might be captured in English by a translation such as "He himself withdrew …" (*NEB*, rather than "Then he" – *NRSV*).

40   *Having come to the place, he said to them, 'Pray that you may not come into the time of trial'.*

41a <u>*He himself*</u> *withdrew about a stone's throw beyond them*

3.2.2 Renewal by means of a situational point of departure

One reason for using a situational point of departure involving renewal is to introduce **different episodes** that occur in the same general setting (compare the renewal of referential points of departure to present different comments about the same referent). For example, Mark 12:38 begins with a situational constituent that repeats the setting for the previous episode, and an episode on a different topic follows.

35   *Jesus was saying, while teaching in the temple, 'How can the scribes say that the Christ is the son of David? … (37) David himself calls him Lord; so how can he be his son?' And the large crowd was listening to him with delight.*

38   *And,* <u>*as he taught*</u>*, he said, 'Watch out for the teachers of the law …'*

Sentence 3 of the following extract from a folktale in the Tsuvadi [tvd] (autonym Tsùvádí; Kainji, Nigeria) begins with a situational point of departure by renewal: *When he arrived* (see sent. 2). This point of departure is followed by **background material** that was true at the same time as the event of 2. There is a discontinuity of action with respect to the event of 2, since 3 does not describe the next event in sequence (see 2.4.4 – IMPF: imperfective).[17]

1   'He said, "Come, let's go to the bush!"'

2   <u>ana</u>   <u>u-ráwa</u>   u-zúwa   akala   danduruwa   rikicim
    when   3s-arrived   3s-met   bean-cakes   (HAUSA LOAN WORD)   all over

    '<u>When he arrived</u>, he saw bean-cakes all over [the tree].'

3   <u>ana</u>   <u>u-ráwa</u>   uëanga   u-tsi-tyó   hosilo
    when   3s-arrived   tree   3s-IMPF-go home   God

    '<u>When he arrived</u>, the tree was going home to God.'

4   'He said, "Come back, tree …"'

3.2.3 Renewal by means of "tail-head linkage"

Tail-head linkage involves "the repetition in a subordinate clause, at the beginning (the 'head') of a new sentence, of at least the main verb of the previous sentence (the tail)" (Dooley and Levinsohn 2001:16).[18] The subject of the clauses concerned usually remains the same, too. Such subordinate clauses may often be interpreted as points of departure involving renewal.

---

[17] The first clause of Num. 5:18 (*& the priest shall cause the woman to stand before YHWH*) is a repetition of 16b. This independent clause is the equivalent in Hebrew of an initial adverbial constituent that renews the setting for the previous paragraph to introduce a different point.

[18] Neither 'head' nor 'tail' have their usual linguistic meaning here. In particular, 'head' does not refer to grammatical head. Often, a semantic equivalent of the main verb is used at the beginning of the new sentence (e.g. **said** … *When he* **spoke** *thus*).

The aspect of the head may be perfective, imperfective or completive. I now discuss in turn tail-head linkage with each of these aspects.[19]

Perfective heads are often used as a SLOWING-DOWN device, immediately before the description of CLIMACTIC material, "to highlight what follows because of its importance for the story" (Mfonyam 1994:195). Revelation 5:8 begins with a subordinate clause that repeats the final main verb of 7. The effect is to slow down the narrative and thus highlight the event that follows.[20]

7   *He came and took [the scroll] from the right hand of the one who was seated on the throne.*

8   *When he took the scroll, the four living creatures and the 24 elders fell before the Lamb ...*

However, in ORAL narratives in some languages, perfective heads may simply ASSOCIATE events together. This usage of tail-head linkage is seldom acceptable in written texts.[21]

Imperfective heads indicate that the event described in the previous sentence was not completed before the next event took place (e.g. *He spoke to them. While he was speaking* ...). Imperfective heads are often followed by the description of a SIGNIFICANT DEVELOPMENT such as the (re)introduction of a major participant. This is illustrated in Acts 4:1.

3:12   *On seeing this, Peter addressed the people, '[12b–26].'*

4:1   *While they were speaking to the people, the priests, the captain of the temple, and the Sadducees came to them ... (3) and arrested them ...*

Completive heads (with a morpheme or word such as *finish* – e.g. *After you finish cooking it*) are often used in procedural texts to introduce the next STEP in the procedure being described. In narratives, they may mark the beginning of a NEW EPISODE, since they summarise a complex set of events presented (or implied) in the previous unit. Luke 7:1 begins with a completive head.

6:20a   *And he, looking up at his disciples, said, '[20b–49].'*

7:1   *After he had finished all his sayings in the hearing of the people, he entered Capernaum.*

Like other points of departure involving renewal, tail-head linkage may introduce nonevents or other BACKGROUND material. See, for example, sentence b of the following extract from a text in the Shekacho [moy] (Omotic, Ethiopia) language.

a   *When the Gospel first arrived among the Shekacho, a problem for believers was created.*

b   ***When this problem was created,** it was 1983.*

Tail-head linkage is employed also as a RESUMPTIVE device, following assertions concerning a different theme (e.g. the description of events concerning a different participant). For example, Matthew 6:14 resumes the theme of 12, following the petitions of 13 on another theme:

12   *And forgive us our debts, as we also have forgiven our debtors.*

13   *And do not bring us to the time of trial, but rescue us from the evil one.*

14   *For if you forgive men when they sin against you, your heavenly Father will also forgive you;*

Questions

1. What do referential points of departure involving renewal most often introduce in narratives?
2. When a situational point of departure repeats the setting of the previous episode, what does this often indicate?

---

[19] The meaning of the terms perfective and imperfective is reviewed at the beginning of 5.3.2.

[20] See Num. 5:27 for the equivalent of tail-head linkage in Hebrew, involving the repetition of the previous **proposition** (*he shall cause the woman to drink the water*) in an independent clause.

[21] In some languages of Papua and Papua New Guinea, it is normal even in written texts to use what Vries (2005) calls 'chained' tail-head linkage to associate events together. The head will usually be perfective, but may be completive.

3. What does "tail-head linkage" involve?
4. Read the following extract from the Bekwarra text, then answer the question that follows it (3sO: 3rd person singular object).

23	a-dè	abe	e-ngwìà	iyìm	èbwan	àjini.
	3s-said	3p	3p-entered	agreement	children	eating

'He said that they had made an agreement to eat their children.'

24 *'They asked, <u>since they had finished frying and eating Hare's</u>, (25) whether people would get to eat his or not.'*

26 *'He sat in silence.'*

27	e-dè	he	dèè	<u>gb'-ámín</u>	<u>a-ngwìà</u>	<u>iyìm</u>	<u>èbwan</u>	<u>àjini</u>	<u>n'-anyamchù</u>
	3p-said	3sO	saying	if-3s	3s-entered	agreement	children	eating	with-hare

'They told him that, <u>since he had made an agreement with Hare about eating children</u>, he should gather his children and fry them for Hare and himself to eat.'

What appears to be the function of the tail-head linkage between sentences 23 and 27?[22]

Application to the language you are analysing

1. List all the examples of situational points of departure that occur in your texts. Put any points of departure that involve renewal in a separate list, and describe their function(s). (Remember: to be a point of departure, the constituent must be **initial** in its sentence. And remember: conjunctions such as 'so' are NOT points of departure.)
2. Do the same for the referential points of departure that occur in your texts.
3. If you work in a subject-initial language, how does the language indicate when a subject is also a point of departure? Is the same device used for nominal constituents functioning as objects?
4. List all the examples of tail-head linkage that occur in your texts and classify them according to their aspect (perfective, imperfective, completive). Describe the function(s) of each.

3.3 Potential points of departure that do not begin a sentence

In all languages in which adverbial constituents (and nominal constituents, where applicable) have the option of beginning a sentence or of occurring later in the sentence, a corollary follows from the principle that points of departure indicate the primary basis for relating the sentence to its context. Thus, if a potential point of departure would NOT indicate the primary basis for relating the sentence to its context, then it will NOT be placed initial in the sentence.

This is illustrated in Acts 20:6a (repeated below), which contains the temporal phrase *after the days of Unleavened Bread*.[23] The fact that the initial constituent is the subject, and not the temporal

---

[22] **Suggested answers:**
1. In narrative, referential points of departure involving renewal most often introduce background comments.
2. When a situational point of departure repeats the setting of the previous episode, this often indicates that a **different episode** occurred in the same general setting as the first episode. Alternatively, it may introduce **background material**.
3. Tail-head linkage involves the repetition, in a subordinate clause at the beginning of a new sentence, of at least the main verb of the previous sentence.
4. The tail-head linkage between sentences 23 and 27 appears NOT to be a resumptive device, since the intervening assertions are on the same topic. It is probably a SLOWING-DOWN device, to highlight the elders' judgement ('he should gather his children and fry them for Hare and himself to eat').

[23] As in many other languages, it is unusual in Koine Greek for references to a point in time NOT to be initial in the sentence. In Acts, for instance, only 13 out of 81 such expressions do not begin sentences.

3.3 Potential points of departure that do not begin a sentence 51

expression, indicates that the sentence is to be related to its context primarily on the basis of a switch of attention from one participant to another, rather than a change of time.

5   *These men, going before us, awaited us in Troas.*

6a *We, however, sailed from Philippi after the days of Unleavened Bread*

1 Corinthians 11:25 is similar. The second part of Paul's account of the Lord's supper is to be related to the first primarily on the basis of a switch from *the bread* to *the cup*. Contrast the *NIV* translation "In the same way, after supper he took the cup", which relates the two parts primarily on the basis of a switch of time from *when he had given thanks* (24) to *after supper*.[24]

23 *The Lord Jesus on the night when he was betrayed took a loaf of bread,* (24) *and when he had given thanks, broke it and said, 'This is my body that is for you. Do this in remembrance of me.'*

25 *Similarly also with the cup, after supper ...*

If NO potential point of departure begins a sentence, then the pragmatic effect is often to convey **continuity** with the context. Points of departure signal discontinuities of situation, reference and, sometimes, action. Consequently, the absence of a point of departure means that no such discontinuity has been indicated **by this means**. (This does not stop a discontinuity being signalled by some other means.)

Acts 5:21 is an instance in which no adverbial or nominal constituent begins the sentence.[25] If the sentence had started with the temporal phrase *about dawn*, then the primary basis for relating the sentence to its context would have been through a switch to a new temporal setting. This might have raised the question as to why the apostles waited till morning to obey the angel's command. The fact that neither this nor any other potential point of departure is initial has the pragmatic effect of conveying continuity with the context, in this case with the command of 20. This relationship of command and appropriate response takes precedence over the change of temporal setting.[26]

19 *An angel of the Lord ... said,* (20) *'Go, stand and speak in the temple ...'*

21 *(On) hearing this, they entered the temple courts about dawn and began teaching.*

In a story in the Lower Tanudan Kalinga [kml] (Malayo-Polynesian, Philippines) language, the temporal phrase *the next day* follows the verb. This has the pragmatic effect of conveying continuity with the previous sentences: the two halves of the coconut shell were placed at the base of some reeds to look for evidence that it would be good to live there (1–2) and the evidence was forthcoming (3). The relationship of stimulus and desired response takes precedence over the change of temporal setting.

1   *When they had cleared (a place for a house), they put together two halves of a coconut shell and placed it at the base of some reeds.*

2   *They did like this to see if those who would live there would have a good way of living.*

3   *They saw, then, the next day, many ants in the coconut shell (and) said, 'It's good because there are many ant eggs'.*

Review questions

1. If a potential point of departure is not placed initial in the sentence, what does this indicate?
2. In the following extract from a story in Tula [tul] (Adamawa-Ubangi, Nigeria), *that day* (sent. b) refers to the same day as *one day* in sentence a. What would be the effect of beginning sentence b with *that day*? What is the effect of placing it after the verb?

---

[24] I am interpreting *similarly* as a conjunction. See Romans 11:30 (discussed in 3.1) for the possibility of two points of departure occurring in the same sentence.

For an example in Hebrew of a potential point of departure that does not begin a sentence, see Exodus 7:7 (& *Moses* = *80 years* & *Aaron* = *83 years* **when they spoke to Pharaoh**).

[25] Prenuclear participial clauses in Greek are not to be interpreted as points of departure (see Levinsohn 2000:187).

[26] The *TEV* captures this effect by beginning 21, "The apostles obeyed". *NIV*, in contrast, begins the sentence "At dawn".

a   <u>One day</u> he lacked wine and was lying sick.
b   *This man went out that day* ...[27]

Application to the language you are analysing

Look for any instances in your texts in which a potential point of departure is not in fact preposed. For each instance, give a reason why preposing did not occur (e.g. because it was not the primary basis for relating the sentence to its context and/or to preserve continuity with the context).

Suggested reading

Chapter 11 of Dooley and Levinsohn 2001, especially section 11.4, relates to the topics covered in this chapter.

---

[27] **Suggested answers:**
1. If a potential point of departure is not placed initial in the sentence, this indicates that it is not the primary basis for relating the sentence to its context.
2. The effect of beginning sentence b with *that day* would be to signal a discontinuity. Since *that day* would then be a point of departure involving renewal, this would probably mean that the speaker was introducing a different episode that took place at the same general time. By placing *that day* after the verb, the speaker preserves continuity between sentences a and b. This suggests that the event described in sentence b is the result of the one described in sentence a.

4

Focus, Emphasis and Prominence

Chapters 2 and 3 looked at one type of constituent that is placed at the beginning of a sentence: the point of departure for the communication. This chapter looks at the ordering of other constituents of sentences. Key concepts are **focus**, **emphasis** and **prominence** in general.

In common parlance, "emphasis" denotes any kind of **prominence**. However, Kathleen Callow (1974:50) uses emphasis in a narrower sense. For her, prominence is the general term for "any device whatever which gives certain events, participants, or objects more significance than others in the same context". I follow Callow (p. 52) in distinguishing focal and thematic prominence:

- **focal** prominence (some device is used to give prominence to a focal constituent – see 4.3)
- **thematic** prominence (prominence is given to "what I'm talking about" – see 4.6).

For Callow, **emphatic** prominence (to express strong feelings about an item or to indicate that what follows is unexpected) is a separate category from focal or thematic prominence. Since both focal and thematic constituents may be emphasised, though, I prefer to think of emphasis proper as a reason for giving prominence to a constituent (see 4.7).

This chapter begins with a review of the technical terms focus, topic and point of departure (4.1). Section 4.2 recognises two preferred positions of focal constituents: late in the sentence, following established information, and preposed (following the point of departure, if present). The devices used to give prominence to a focal constituent are then considered (4.3), after which Dik's categories of focus are presented (4.4). Section 4.5 addresses the issue of how to distinguish points of departure from preposed focal constituents. Section 4.6 concerns instances when prominence is given not to non-established focal constituents, but to established thematic ones, while section 4.7 deals with emphatic prominence (as defined above). Section 4.8 introduces the concept of a *foil*: a constituent that serves to set off a later constituent by contrast. The final section (4.9) presents the four types of *it*-cleft construction identified for English by Delin (1989), which may have correlates in other languages.

4.1 Focus versus topic and point of departure

Two general definitions of the focus of an utterance were given in 2.2:
- "the information ... that is assumed by the speaker not to be shared by him [or her] and the hearer" (Jackendoff 1972:230).
- "that part which indicates what the speaker intends as the most important ... change to be made in the hearer's mental representation" (Dooley and Levinsohn 2001:62).

Section 2.2 also stated that utterances with topic-comment articulation have **predicate** focus (Lambrecht 1994:222). The focus of such utterances is all the nonestablished information in the comment (predicate – unless marked to the contrary – see 4.2.4).

Consider the translation into English of sentence 10 of the Bekwarra text:

[9 *Dog ran off, gathered them together, went and hid them in a broom, twisted it together, threw it into the yard and set off for his farm.*]

10   POINT OF DEPARTURE   TOPIC   COMMENT
   So   one morning   Hare   went off and had a discussion with Dog.

I argued in 3.1 that sentence 10 has topic-comment articulation; *Hare* is topic and *went off and had a discussion with Dog* is the comment about Hare. An adverbial point of departure, *One morning*, precedes the topic. The focus of the sentence is all the nonestablished information in the comment.[1] From sentence 9, it appears that the only piece of established information in the comment is *Dog*. This means that *went off and had a discussion with* is the focus of sentence 10.

Notice that, in the above description, the topic and the focus of sentence 10 are **different** constituents. Topic and focus are NOT synonyms in linguistic parlance! In a certain sense, they are opposites.

Most of the time, the following correlation holds:

Topic	correlates with	established
Focus	correlates with	not established

More exactly, propositional topics – and points of departure – differ from focal constituents in that:

- a propositional topic or point of departure must either be already established in the text or be easily related to one that is already established (Lambrecht 1994:164), whereas
- information that is focal either has NOT been established in the text (it is 'new') or needs to be RE-established (see the Engenni example in 4.2.3).

If we apply this distinction to sentence 10 of the Bekwarra text, we find the following:

- The point of departure *one morning* is to be related to the time that has already been established in the text. It is understood to mean 'one morning after the events of sentence 9'.
- The topic *Hare* is a participant who has already been established in the text.
- The focal information of the comment *went off and had a discussion with* is information that has NOT already been established in the text.

Review questions

1. What technical term does Callow (and this course) prefer instead of "emphasis"?
2. I am sometimes told, "This point of departure is focal." What is wrong with this statement?[2]

---

[1] It is wrong to equate nonestablished ('new') information with the focus of an utterance. Nevertheless, if there IS nonestablished information in the utterance, the focus will be on some or all of that nonestablished information.

[2] **Suggested answers**:
1. Callow (and this course) use the technical term **prominence** to refer to "to any device whatever which gives certain events, participants, or objects more significance than others in the same context".
2. Points of departure relate to established information, whereas focal constituents usually relate to nonestablished information. Therefore the two terms cannot be applied to the same constituent. What the quoted speaker usually means is, "This point of departure has been given **prominence**" – see 4.6.

4.2 Preferred positions for focal constituents

This section considers the tendency for focal constituents to occur in one of two places:
- late in the sentence, following established information (4.2.1–4.2.2)[3]
- preposed (following the point of departure, if present – 4.2.3).

Comments in which established information precedes nonestablished information are presented in 4.2.1. Section 4.2.2 discusses the position of focal constituents in thetic propositions. A final section (4.2.4) considers when it is useful to identify among the constituents of the comment about a topic a "dominant focal element" (Heimerdinger 1999:167).

4.2.1 Established/nonestablished

Section 4.1 stated that the focus of a topic-comment proposition is all the nonestablished information in the comment (unless marked to the contrary). Many comments about a topic contain both established and nonestablished information (see Bekwarra, sent. 10 in 4.1). In such comments, provided the syntax of the language permits it, the order of constituents tends to conform to the "**Principle of Natural Information Flow**" (Comrie 1989:127–128). When this principle is followed, nonverbal constituents that convey ESTABLISHED information precede those that convey new or NONESTABLISHED information.

Consider the following pair of sentences in English:

		established	nonestablished
a	John gave	the knife	to a boy.
b	John gave	the boy	a knife.

The above sentences show that English syntax allows direct and indirect objects to occur in either order. Firbas (1964:115) points out that, if one object presents established information and the other, nonestablished information, then the established information normally precedes the nonestablished information. In other words, the default order of objects in English conforms to the Principle of Natural Information Flow.[4]

In many languages, arguments (subject, objects and adjectival complements) tend to precede adjuncts. For example, the default order in Koine Greek and Biblical Hebrew is:

     < - - typically ESTABLISHED - - >   < typically NONESTABLISHED >

     verb – pronominals – subject nominal   – other arguments – adjuncts.

However, if the adjunct conveys established information and the argument, nonestablished information, then the argument tends to follow the adjunct (provided the syntax of the language permits such an order). In other words, the argument-adjunct ordering principle is violated in such languages in order to conform to the Principle of Natural Information Flow.

The following sentences from Greek and Hebrew illustrate this:[5]

(Revelation 12:15)		V	S	ADJUNCT	ADJUNCT	ARGUMENT (O)
	&	spewed	the serpent	from its mouth	after the woman	water like a river

---

[3] "[M]any languages have a clearly defined unmarked focus position in the clause; in verb-final languages, it is normally the immediately preverbal position" (Van Valin and Polla 1997:209).

[4] The Principle of Natural Information Flow is grammaticalised in Romance languages in the placement of pronominal objects (established information) before the verb (which, under such circumstances, usually conveys nonestablished information). Compare French *Ils suivirent **Jean*** ('They followed **John**') with *Ils le suivirent* ('They followed **him**').

[5] In many OV languages, the tendency to order nonverbal constituents so that established information precedes nonestablished information is very strong.

(Deuteronomy 4:26)	V	PRONOMINAL	ADJUNCT	ARGUMENT (O)
	I call to witness	*against you*	*this day*	*heaven & earth*
				(see Heimerdinger 1999:174)

4.2.2 Constituent ordering in thetic propositions

It is common for thetic propositions with presentational articulation to place the entity being presented (the focal constituent) towards the end, as the following English sentence shows:

(Luke 4:33)	PT OF DEPARTURE	FOCUS
	In the synagogue was	*a man having the spirit of an unclean demon.*

English sometimes uses the dummy subject **there** so that the entity being presented is at the end:

(Acts 9:10)   *There was   a certain disciple in Damascus named Ananias.*

Preverbal subjects that are focal in English take primary accent. However, many other VO languages typically place focal subjects after the verb (see Lambrecht 1994:319 for a comparison of English and Italian). The ordering of constituents in the French example below conforms to the Principle of Natural Information Flow (4.2.1).

(Luke 1:11)[6]	(English)	FOCUS
		An angel of the Lord appeared to him.
	(French)	FOCUS
		Lui apparut un ange du Seigneur.

Similarly, many OV languages place focal subjects immediately before the verb and after other nonverbal constituents. Again, such ordering conforms to the Principle of Natural Information Flow. The following example from a speech in Dungra Bhil presents the need for a road.

				FOCUS	
sahibe,	*amaa*	*gamo*	*me*	*rohu*	*nahi*
sir	our	village	in	road	not (is)

'Sir, there is no road in our village.'

4.2.3 Preposed focal constituents

The option exists in many languages for focal constituents to be placed either late in the sentence or preposed (following the point of departure, if present). In Koine Greek, for example, the default position for most focal constituents is late in the sentence. Preposing a focal constituent (which often violates the Principle of Natural Information Flow – 4.2.1) appears to give it contrastive or emphatic **prominence** (see below and 4.7, as well as Levinsohn 2000:32–40).

The following sentence from a folktale in Gumawana illustrates these two focal positions (Olson 2014:226). In clause a, the locative adjunct occurs in its normal position after the verb. In clause b, however, it is preposed for contrastive prominence, and the Principle of a Natural Information Flow is violated:[7]

a	*Kitava*	*tomota*	*madaboki-di*	*si-kaiyaka*	*negwasa*	*kiki-na*
	Kitava	people	all-3p	3p-live	sea	next.to-3s

---

[6] See 2.1.4 for discussion of why this proposition is thetic in many languages.
[7] The following abbreviations are used: DET: determiner; LOC: locative; PN: pronoun; TR: transitive marker; 3p, 3s: 3rd person plural, singular.

4.2 Preferred positions for focal constituents

b	go	kina	Gumasai-ya-na	**koya**	yatanai-na	goi	ina	vada	i-yowo.
	SPACER	3s.pn	Gumasai-DET-3s	mountain	on.top-3s	LOC	his	house	3s-build.TR

'Although all of the Kitava people live beside the sea, Gumasai built his house on top of the mountain.'

Kiss (1998:271) points out that, in some languages (though not VS/VO languages such as Koine Greek or Biblical Hebrew), the two positions for focal constituents are associated with **semantically different types** of focus:

- "information focus, the carrier of new information, involving no syntactic reordering" (Lambrecht's predicate focus)
- "identificational focus", often involving preposing (Van Valin's narrow focus)

For instance, in the following exchange in a teachers' common room (see Delin 1989), speaker B uses a cleft sentence[8] to identify and focus on speaker A as the person who put milk in the coffee:

Speaker A: *You've put milk in my coffee.*

Speaker B: *It was **you** who put the milk in.*

The following pair of sentences occurs in a folktale in Engenni [enn] (Benue-Congo, Nigeria). Tortoise owes a debt to another animal, but does not repay it. The lender comes to Tortoise's compound to collect the debt, but Tortoise's wife says he is not there. The lender becomes so angry that he picks up what he thinks is the grinding stone and throws it away. In reality, however, he has thrown Tortoise away. Having related this fact (sent. a), the storyteller re-identifies Tortoise as the entity that the lender threw rather than the grinding stone (sent. b). He does so by preposing the reference to Tortoise (an instance of refocusing an established constituent):

a   *He threw Tortoise into the compound.*

b   ***Tortoise** he threw.*

Simon Dik's template applied to preverbal constituents in VS/VO languages

Dik (1989:363) proposed a template for explaining variations in constituent order that is particularly applicable to VS/VO languages such as Biblical Hebrew, Koine Greek, Oto-Manguean languages of Mexico and N.W. Austronesian languages of the Philippines (see 0.3).[9]

The template is: **P1   P2   V   X**, where

- position P1 can be occupied by one or more points of departure (Dik calls them "TOPIC constituents");
- position P2 can be occupied by a FOCUS constituent (to give it contrastive or emphatic prominence).

In the following Hebrew example (Genesis 4:1a), the preverbal subject as topic *hā'ādām* 'the man' is a referential point of departure that signals a switch of attention from the previous topic ('the LORD God' – 3:23–24). In Dik's terminology, this subject occupies the P1 position:

1a   P1

	wəhā'ādām	*yāda'*	*'et-aḥwwâ 'ištô*
	& the man	knew	OBJ-Eve his wife

'Adam lay with his wife Eve.' (OBJ: definite object marker)

In the following Chichicapan Zapotec (Oto-Manguean) example, a locative constituent occupies the P2 position to give it contrastive prominence:

---

[8] Crystal (1997:63) defines a cleft sentence as "a CONSTRUCTION where a single CLAUSE has been divided into two separate sections, each with its own VERB".

[9] Dik's template, which has P0 instead of P2, also explains why topical subjects in many Bantu languages precede the verb, whereas nontopical subjects follow it.

P2

guriin	*nehza*	hasta	guzaa'hahn
different	way	until	I.will.go

'I will go a **different** way.'

Finally, in the following Greek example (James 2:18b–c), both preverbal positions are occupied. The pronouns for 'you' and 'I' occupy the P1 position (to contrast the two topics). In turn, the words for 'faith' and 'works' occupy the P2 position (to give focal prominence to the contrasting comments about the topics).

	P1	P2	
18b	<u>Su</u>	**pistin**	echeis
	you	faith	you have
18c	<u>kagō</u>	**erga**	echō
	and I	works	I have

(But someone will say,) 'You have faith and I have works …'

4.2.4 The dominant focal element

Firbas (1964:114) argues that, if a focal domain contains more than one constituent, one of the constituents will be more important than the rest. He calls this constituent the "rheme" (see also Perrin 1994:232–233). Heimerdinger (1999:167) refers to the rheme as "the dominant focal element (DFE)". Consider the following pair of sentences:

Speaker A: *What did Gary do?*
Speaker B: *He went to the theatre.*

> Speaker B's reply has "the focus domain extending over several constituents. One element of the predicate is more important than the other one … The denotatum of the NP *theatre* is the element which makes the answer informative; it constitutes the point of the assertion." (Heimerdinger 1999:167)

In other words, Heimerdinger considers *theatre* to be the DFE.

In some languages, the identification of a DFE among the constituents of the comment can be of great value in explaining variations in constituent order or the position of a prominence-marking particle (as in Inga – see Levinsohn 1975). In others, there seems to be little value in identifying a DFE. I suggest the following criteria for deciding whether or not to identify a DFE:

- If the order of constituents in the comment about a topic is **default**, then there is no great value in attempting to identify a DFE.
- If the order of constituents in the comment is **marked**, or if a particle is **not** in its default position, then the marked order or position may be identifying and giving prominence to the DFE.

In Koine Greek, for example, the default position of pronominal constituents of the comment about a topic is immediately after the verb (Levinsohn 2000:29). When a pronominal constituent of the comment follows a nominal adjunct, the order of constituents is marked and the pronominal constituent is often the DFE. In participial clause b of 1 Peter 1:4 below, for instance, none of the information about the inheritance is established, so the whole of the comment constitutes the focus. However, the pronominal adjunct *for you* follows the nominal adjunct *in heavens*. This marked order of constituents identifies *for you* as the DFE and gives it prominence:

a   *To an inheritance imperishable and undefiled and unfading,*
b   *having been kept in [the] heavens* **for you**
c   *who are being protected …*

The default position of the English particle *too* is at the end of the sentence. Taglicht (1984:82) claims that, when it occurs elsewhere, it functions as a **spacer** (3.1),[10] separating the DFE from the rest of the comment about the topic and giving prominence to it. He cites the following example, in which the DFE is the object of *admired*:

They admired, **too,** **Michelangelo's 'Last Judgement'**.

Review questions

1. What are the two preferred positions in the sentence for focal constituents?
2. When the comment about a topic contains both established and nonestablished information, in which order do they occur if they conform to the Principle of Natural Information Flow?
3. What does DFE stand for? Under what circumstances might it be useful to identify a DFE?[11]

4.3 Devices used to give prominence to a focal constituent

When a constituent is marked for prominence, the hearer's attention is drawn to it. In a topic-comment proposition with default constituent order, no special prominence is given to the focal constituents of the comment. However, we saw in 4.2.4 that an author may employ marked constituent order (including moving a particle from its default position) in order to give prominence to the **DFE**.

The same contrast is found with questions with identificational articulation. The question may give no special prominence to the focal question word (**narrow** focus), but the option exists of using a device such as a cleft construction in order to give it special prominence:

Default prominence: *What did John buy?*
Marked prominence: *What was it that John bought?*

This section considers the devices that languages commonly use to give prominence to a focal constituent. They are the following:[12]

- **phonological** features such as a change from the default position of primary accent.
- a change of **tone**. See Aaron 1999:16–18 on the role of tone in marking different types of contrastive focus in Obolo [ann] (Benue-Congo, Nigeria).
- **marked** constituent order. In languages that prepose question words, this includes the preposing of focal constituents. In languages that do NOT normally prepose question words (so that *John bought what?* is the normal order if the language is SV/VO), this includes the preposing of non-focal constituents – see below for some examples from Mambila [mcu] (Bantoid, Cameroon).
- *be* verbs. See below for an example in Koorete [kqy] (Omotic, Ethiopia).
- relative pronouns, demonstratives or other **spacers** which separate the focal constituent from the rest of the proposition (see 4.2.4 on the use of English *too* as a spacer). English cleft sentences use a relative pronoun (e.g. *who, that*) as well as a *be* verb to give prominence to the focal constituent: *What **was** it **that** John bought?*

---

[10] Taglicht's term for spacer is "partition". Spacers separate information of differing importance; the same device may separate points of departure **and** focal constituents from the rest of the communication in which they appear.
[11] **Suggested answers:**
1. The two preferred positions in the sentences for focal constituents are:
   - late in the sentence, following established information
   - preposed (following the point of departure, if present).
2. When the comment about a topic contains both established and nonestablished information, the established material precedes the nonestablished material if they conform to the Principle of Natural Information Flow.
3. DFE stands for 'dominant focal element'. It might be useful to identify a DFE if the order of constituents in the comment about a topic is marked, or if a particle is not in its default position.

[12] When a focal constituent is given prominence by the use of some marking device, this is often referred to as **marked** focus (e.g. in Crozier 1984).

- characteristic **affixation** or a **particle** associated with either the focal constituent or the verb. See below for examples from Mambila and Koine Greek.

Consider the following sentences from Mambila, which illustrate the preposing of **nonfocal** constituents in order to give prominence to the focal constituent, as well as the use of a characteristic **particle** to give prominence to the subject or verb:[13]

		Order of constituents in Mambila	Meaning in English
a	(default order)	*I buy* PAST *cloth yesterday.*	*I bought cloth yesterday.*
b	(*cloth* is prominent)	*I yesterday buy* PAST *cloth.*	*It was* **cloth** *that I bought yesterday.*
c	(*yesterday* is prominent)	*I cloth buy* PAST *yesterday.*	*It was* **yesterday** *that I bought the cloth.*
d	(*I* is prominent)	*I yesterday cloth buy* PAST SFOC.	*It was* **I** *who bought the cloth yesterday.*
e	(*buy* is prominent)	*I cloth this buy* PAST VFOC.	*I* **bought** *this cloth.*

Sentence a (above) has default constituent order; a comment (*bought cloth yesterday*) is made about the topic *I*. In sentences b and c, *yesterday* and *cloth* respectively are preposed, in order to give extra prominence to the focal constituent at the end of the sentence. In sentence d, both *yesterday* and *cloth* are preposed, and the subject-focus particle (SFOC) ends the sentence to give prominence to the subject. Sentence e is similar, except that the verb-focus particle (VFOC) ends the sentence to give prominence to the verb.

The following extract from a folktale in the Koorete (SV/OV) language[14] illustrates the use of *kko* '**be**' to give prominence to the DFE. The nonestablished information is 'throw off a cliff', but *kko* is attached to 'from a cliff' to give extra prominence to this constituent:

a 'It was then that his brothers thought, "What shall we do to this Buxho?"'

b *Gaaganna-***kko** *nu* *dafe* *hidi* *uydo.*
   cliff.from-be we throw saying said.

   'and they decided, "We'll throw him **off a cliff**."'

In the following thetic sentence in Koine Greek (Matthew 1:20), *idou* 'behold' gives prominence to the entity (the angel) that is being introduced to the story:

(*As he was considering this,*) *behold an angel of the Lord appeared to him in a dream ...*

4.4 Categories of (prominent) focus

If the language you are analysing uses more than one device to give prominence to a focal constituent, a number of factors may determine which device is selected. One device may give prominence to the **DFE**. Another may give prominence to the focal constituent in an identificational (**narrow** focus) construction. Another may mark **contrastive** focus. Yet another may give **emphatic** prominence to a constituent (see 4.7).[15]

Application to the language you are analysing

1. Review the list of devices that languages commonly use to give prominence to a focal constituent (4.3).
2. List the devices you have found in your texts that give prominence to a focal constituent.

---

[13] See Perrin 1994:233–236 for the Mambila text and for the circumstances under which each sentence might be used.
[14] SIL linguist Lydia Hoeft (p.c.) obtained, glossed and charted the text from which this extract is taken.
[15] A focal constituent may also be given prominence to provide a **foil** for a later contrasting constituent – see 4.8.

3. Determine which of the devices in your list are used in an identificational (narrow focus) construction, for contrastive focus and, where relevant, to give prominence to the DFE.[16]

If you have carried out the above application and are still unable to distinguish the function of certain prominence-giving devices, you might want to consider the focal distinctions that Dik *et al* (1981:60) have proposed (see also Vallejos 2009:404). (I do NOT recommend that you classify prominent focal constituents into Dik et al.'s categories unless you need to!) They proposed the following categories of focus (many of which are specific instances of Kiss's identificational focus):

selective	e.g. (A: *Did John buy coffee or rice?*)	B: *He bought **coffee**.*
replacing	e.g. (A: *John went to London.*)	B: *No [he didn't go to **London**,*] he went to **New York**.*
expanding	e.g. (A: *John bought coffee.*)	B. *John not only bought **coffee**,* he also bought rice.*
restricting	e.g. (A: *John bought coffee and rice.*)	B: *No [he didn't buy **coffee**,*] he only bought **rice**.*
parallel	e.g.	*JOHN** bought a **bike**, but PETER** a **car**.*

*See 4.8 (Foils) on the prominence of these focal constituents.

**See 4.6.1 (Prominent entities) on the prominence of these propositional topics.

4.5 Distinguishing points of departure from preposed focal constituents

If the language you are analysing has the option of preposing focal constituents, this means that both focal constituents and points of departure can occur at the beginning of a sentence. How are they to be distinguished?

1. If the text you are analysing is **oral**, you will find that preposed focal constituents typically carry the primary accent, whereas points of departure (PT-DEP) do not. Read the following pair of sentences aloud and see where the primary accent falls in English:

   a. (FOCAL) *From the top of a cliff we'll throw him!* (see the Koorete example in 4.3)

   b. (PT-DEP) *From the top of the cliff we descended 100 metres.*

2. Section 4.1 stated that focal constituents differ from propositional topics and points of departure in that:
   - a propositional topic or point of departure must either be already established in the text or be easily related to material that is already established (Lambrecht 1994:164), whereas
   - focal information either has NOT been established in the text or needs to be RE-established.

This difference is illustrated by the following sentences from a folktale in the Kouya [kyf] (Kru, Côte d'Ivoire) language. Both sentences begin with a left-dislocated constituent. The context for sentence a shows that *God* is an established participant, so the reference to him is interpreted as a point of departure. In sentence b, the information *the illnesses that strike people* has not previously been established in the text, so *these* is interpreted as focal.

a *Spider went on high to God's place.*

   ESTABLISHED

   *God, he   is **truly on high**.*

b *God arrived at the village with his children.*

   < - - - - - - - NONESTABLISHED - - - - - >   ESTABLISHED

   *The illnesses that strike people: **these**   are his children.*

---

[16] See 4.7 for questions about marking emphatic prominence.

3. The presence versus absence of a **definite article** or **anaphoric demonstrative** often helps in the identification of established versus nonestablished information. Sentence b of the following extract from the Gumawana folktale (Olson 2014:232) contains two references to a cave. The first is suffixed with the determiner *-ya* (DET), which can be used when the entity is established or accessible information, whereas the second does not have *ya*. This confirms that the first constituent is a point of departure, whereas the second is focal.

a   *When he [Gumasai] came down (the tree), he went into the bush to a cave, entered it and remained (in it).*

b   ESTABLISHED   < - -NONESTABLISHED- - >

*Ego tukubu-**ya**-na   dokanikani ina   tukubu-Ø   Gumasai   i-kaiyaka   sinae-na.*

now cave-DET-3s   giant   his   cave   Gumasai   3s-remain   inside-3s

'As for the cave, it was a giant's cave that Gumasai was inside.'

(In other words, 'Now the cave that Gumasai was inside was a giant's cave.')

4. In many languages, **left-dislocated** constituents are usually points of departure.[17] The only exceptions seem to be when the left-dislocated constituent is nonestablished information which is followed immediately by a so-called "emphatic" demonstrative (see 4.6.1), whose referent is the same as that of the left-dislocated constituent (as in sentence b of the Bété example above).

In the following pair of sentences in Ndyuka [djk] (alt. Aukan; Atlantic Creole, Suriname), both of the initial constituents are introduced with the verb *na* 'be'. The initial constituent in sentence a is left-dislocated; it has its own intonation contour and a pronominal trace occurs later in the sentence, so it is interpreted as a point of departure. The initial constituent in sentence b is included in the same intonation contour as the rest of the sentence and is not followed by a pronominal trace, so it is interpreted as a preposed focal constituent.

a   (PT-DEP)   <u>*na Jack*</u> /   *Charlie hit him.*   *Jack was hit by Charlie.*

b   (FOCAL)   **na Jack**   *Charlie hit.*   *It was Jack whom Charlie hit.*

5. The **relative order** of other constituents may change when a focal constituent is preposed. This is illustrated from the following sentences in Koine Greek. As noted earlier, the default position for a pronominal constituent of the comment in Greek is immediately after the verb, as in Matthew 5:22. However, when a focal constituent is preposed, it is common for any pronominal constituent of the presupposition to immediately precede the verb, as in Galatians 5:7.[18]

Matthew 5:22 (PT-DEP)   *I*   &   *I.say   to.you ...*   *I, however, say to you:*

Galatians 5:7 (FOCAL)   **who**   *you   hindered ...*   *Who hindered you (from being persuaded by the truth)?*

Review questions

1. If a prenuclear constituent of an oral sentence carries primary accent, is it likely to be a point of departure or focal?
2. If a prenuclear constituent conveys nonestablished information, is it likely to be a point of departure or focal?

---

[17] However, in at least some Indo-Aryan languages, the referent of a left-dislocated constituent conveys nonestablished **focal** information.

[18] When the pronominal is preposed, the Principle of Natural Information Flow is clearly violated. The pragmatic effect is probably to increase the prominence that is given to the preposed focal constituent.

3. If a prenuclear constituent includes a definite article or anaphoric demonstrative, is it likely to be a point of departure or focal?
4. If a prenuclear constituent is left-dislocated, is it likely to be a point of departure or focal?[19]

Application to the language you are analysing

If the language has the option of preposing focal constituents and you are uncertain whether certain prenuclear constituents in your texts are points of departure or focal, use the above pointers to determine the function of each.

4.6 Thematic prominence

When a constituent is marked for prominence, the hearer's attention is drawn to it. So far, we have only looked at instances in which attention has been drawn to focal constituents. In such examples, attention has typically been drawn to nonestablished information. However, attention may also be drawn to topics and points of departure, which convey or relate to **established** information. Such prominence may be called **thematic** prominence.

Callow (1974:50) defines thematic prominence as "what I'm talking about", and says that it operates at more than one level. This section concerns two levels of thematic prominence: prominence given to entities such as participants or props (4.6.1) and prominence given to parts of the theme line (4.6.2).

4.6.1 Prominent entities

Prominence may be given to an entity **after** it has been introduced, to draw attention to it: "Pay attention to the person or object about which I'm speaking!" A thematically prominent entity will have a significant role to play in the subsequent discourse.[20]

So-called "emphatic" **pronouns** are often used to give thematic prominence to their referent (see Lowe 1998:36). This is illustrated in a folktale in the Dogosé/Khissé [dos] (Gur, Burkina Faso) language. Various animals arrive at a gathering and speak. After their introduction, further reference to each is made with a default pronoun. When Elephant arrives, however, the next reference to him uses an "emphatic" (in other words, thematic) pronoun. This gives prominence to Elephant and implies that he will be the participant around whom the following events are organised:

Elephant arrived where the other animals were. **He** (thematic pronoun) *said ...*

It is common for one set of **demonstratives** to be used to give thematic prominence to their referent because of his/her/its significant role in the subsequent discourse (see ch. 9).[21]

Now consider the following sentence, which appeared in 4.4 as an instance of Dik's category of parallel focus:

*JOHN bought a **bike**, but PETER a **car**.*

In the above sentence, *bike* and *car* are parallel focal constituents, and are marked in oral speech with a distinctive accent. The propositional topics *John* and *Peter* also carry a distinctive accent to mark them as **parallel topics**. This appears to be another type of thematic prominence.

---

[19] **Suggested answers:**
1. If a prenuclear constituent of an oral sentence carries primary accent, it is likely to be focal.
2. If a prenuclear constituent conveys nonestablished information, it is likely to be focal.
3. If a prenuclear constituent includes a definite article or anaphoric demonstrative, it is likely to be a point of departure.
4. If a prenuclear constituent is left-dislocated, it is likely to be a point of departure (unless it is followed immediately by a so-called "emphatic" demonstrative whose referent is the same as that of the left-dislocated constituent).

[20] Section 8.1.5 discusses devices used to highlight the **introduction** of a participant.

[21] The language may have more than one set of pronouns or demonstratives: a thematic set and a default or even an athematic set. Alternatively, the contrast may simply be between the presence and the absence of the thematic pronoun or demonstrative.

4.6.2 Prominent parts of the theme line

Prominence may be given to a point of departure or connective when it introduces a significant event of the theme line. The effect of marking either as prominent is to highlight the material that follows.

Some of the devices used to give prominence to a focal constituent (4.3) may also be employed to give prominence to a point of departure or connective. This is illustrated from folktales in Koorete. The same marker *kko* 'be' that is used to give prominence to the DFE may also be attached to a point of departure (sent. a) or a connective (sent. b). The effect, in both cases, is to highlight the next events because of their significance. What happened when the child arrived at the shop (a) and when the traders came (b) is crucial to the outcome of the story.

a *A few days later-**kko** (i.e. It was a few days later that) they sent the child to a shop.*

b *He took the skin, dried it, climbed a tree under which people take a rest, and settled down.*

  *Then-**kko** (i.e. It was then that) many traders came ...*

Review questions

1. How does thematic prominence differ from focal prominence?
2. What is a common function of so-called "emphatic" pronouns?
3. When a marker of prominence is attached to a point of departure or a connective, what does it typically do?[22]

Application to the language you are analysing

1. Examine your texts to see whether any markers of prominence are attached to topics or points of departure (constituents that convey or relate to established information).
2. Determine the function of each occurrence in your texts of any so-called "emphatic" or other marked pronouns (e.g. 'long' forms).

4.7 Emphatic prominence

This section uses the term **emphasis** not as a synonym for prominence (see the introduction to this chapter), but in a similar way to Callow (1974). Emphatic prominence is used to convey heightened emotion, as when a speaker feels strongly about something or considers that an event is unexpected. Emphatic prominence may be given to a constituent of a sentence or to a whole sentence.

Constituents of a sentence that are given emphatic prominence are usually **focal**. Such prominence may be achieved by the addition of an **emphatic marker** such as *even* or *right*, as in:

*They were skinning it **right** on the kitchen table!*

In **oral** material, focal constituents may be given emphatic prominence by special phonological features such as pitch (raised or lowered), heavy stress, and vowel lengthening (e.g. *gooooool* 'goal' [Spanish], *jusqu'àààà* 'until' [some African French dialects]). Think how you would pronounce *They were skinning it right on the kitchen table!* if you were a cook sharing the horror of such a discovery with a friend.

Some forms of **repetition** are for emphasis. In both oral and written material in the Bafut [bfd] (Grassfields, Cameroon) language, repetition of the verb emphasises the action (Mfonyam

---

[22] **Suggested answers:**
1. Focal prominence typically gives prominence to nonestablished information. Thematic prominence gives prominence to some aspect of "what I am talking about", such as an established referent.
2. A common function of so-called "emphatic" pronouns is to give thematic prominence to their referent.
3. When a marker of prominence is attached to a point of departure or a connective, it typically highlights the material that follows.

1994:204–206): *He cries cries* 'He really cries'. Similarly, in Hebrew, repetition of the verb in the "infinitive absolute" form emphasises the action, as the following example from Genesis 2:17b shows:

17b   *for <u>on.the.day you.eat from.it</u> **to.die you.will.die*** (i.e. *you will **surely** die*).

Changes in constituent **order** may also give emphatic prominence to a focal constituent. In the Greek of Galatians 2:11a, for example, the focal constituent *kata proso:pon* 'to face' is preposed for emphatic prominence, to show the intensity of the opposition:

(Galatians 2:11a)   *(But when Cephas came to Antioch), **to face** him*[23] *I.opposed* ('I opposed him to his face').

Especially in written material, English expresses emphasis with **emotive** adverbs and adjectives. In the following examples, the emphasised constituent is NOT focal:

a   ***Scathingly*** *he replied ...*
b   *And that **poor** man went away.*

Most of the above devices emphasise a constituent within a sentence. Within the overall story, the speaker may emphasise certain **events** because he or she judges them to be unexpected. A couple of devices used in English to do this are the introduction into the text of a rhetorical question (sent. a) or "collateral information" (sent. b) (see Grimes 1975:64), which tells what did not happen as a basis for what did happen:

a   *And what do you think happened then?*
b   *But he didn't throw it! No, he slipped it into his pocket ...*

Application to the language you are analysing

List the devices used in your texts for emphatic prominence. Which ones give emphatic prominence to a focal constituent? To a nonfocal constituent? To an event?

4.8 Foils

The *OED* defines a foil as "anything that serves to set off another thing distinctly or to advantage by contrast".[24] The concept of a foil is useful for explaining some unusual intonation patterns and otherwise unexplained instances of prominence.

Consider the following pairs of sentences (cited in 4.4 in connection with three of Dik's categories of focus):

- **replacing**   e.g. (A: *John went to London.*)   B: *No, he didn't go to **London**, he went to **New York**.*
- **expanding**   e.g. (A: *John bought coffee.*)   B: *John not only bought **coffee**, he also bought **rice**.*
   restricting   e.g. (A: *John bought coffee and rice.*)   B: *No, he didn't buy **coffee**, he only bought **rice**.*
•

In each of speaker B's replies, the constituent to be corrected (*London, coffee, coffee*) is pronounced with a special intonation which anticipates the second, contrasting constituent. It is this first constituent which I designate the **foil** for the second, because it serves to set off the second constituent "to advantage by contrast".

It is common for the foil for a following **focal** constituent to be marked as prominent. The context for the following extract from a Yoruba [yor] (Benue-Congo, Nigeria) folktale is that Buffalo was so

---
[23] See 4.5 (point 5) on the tendency in Koine Greek for pronominal constituents of the comment to precede the verb when a focal constituent is preposed.
[24] Whereas a foil is a **constituent** that serves to set off a later constituent to advantage by contrast, a **counterpoint** is a contrasting idea or **proposition** that serves to set off the thesis proposition by contrast (see Levinsohn 2015, 3.3).

exhausted from his race with Frog that, when he entered the river, he drowned. When Frog speaks about this, he first uses a cleft sentence (in Yoruba as well as in the translation into English) to give prominence to the focal foil (*water*) (sent. a). This has the effect of setting off to advantage by contrast the **following** focal constituent (*I frog* – in sent. b):

	FOIL	PRESUPPOSITION
a	Was it **water**	*that you heard that it caused him to die?*
	REPLACING FOCUS	
b	*It was* **I frog**	*that killed him.*

In the following sentence in Koine Greek, the focal foil (*by works of law*) is preposed to give it prominence. This again has the effect of setting off by contrast the following focal constituent (*by hearing with faith*):

(Galatians 3:2b)	FOIL	PRESUPPOSITION	REPLACING FOCUS
	By works of law	*you received the Spirit*	**or by hearing with faith**?

A prominent **thematic** constituent may be the foil for a corresponding constituent. This is illustrated in the following extract from a travelogue in Inga:

> When a group including the speaker flew in one morning to Cali airport, we found that there was no room for us on the connecting flight. The ladies in the group were able to get seats on the mid-day flight, but the speaker and I had to wait till 5 p.m.

In sentence b, the prominence marker (PROM) is attached to the topic (*the ladies*). This has the effect of setting off by contrast the topic of the following sentence, *we*, which is thematic (the topic the speaker is really interested in; PD: marker of a point of departure).

a	*After that we went to Cali.*	
	PT-DEP	FOIL/TOPIC	COMMENT
b	*From.there*-PD,	the ladies-**PROM**	*left first for Bogotá* **at noon**.
	PT-DEP/TOPIC		COMMENT
c	*We*-PD		*waited* **until 5 p.m.**

Review questions

1. What is the function of a foil in a text?
2. How does a foil differ from a constituent given prominence to bring out a contrast?[25]

Application to the language you are analysing

Note any devices used in your texts to indicate that a particular constituent is functioning as a foil to set off a later constituent to advantage by contrast.

4.9 Types of *it*-cleft structures

It is often assumed that cleft sentences (or their equivalents) always have identificational articulation, with the focal constituent in the first part of the structure. The following exchange (repeated from 4.2.3) is typical of how cleft sentences are expected to function (the structure is called an "*it*-cleft" because of the dummy subject *it* in English):

---

[25] **Suggested answers**:
1. The function of a foil in a text is to set off a later constituent to advantage by contrast.
2. A foil sets off a **later** constituent to advantage by contrast. A constituent with contrastive prominence contrasts with an **earlier** constituent.

4.9 Types of it-*cleft structures* 67

1. (1st part: primary accent)

   Speaker A: *You've put milk in my coffee.*
   Speaker B: *It was **you** who put the milk in.*

Delin (1989) shows that in fact there are four types of *it*-cleft sentences in English. Her distinctions concern whether primary accent falls on the first or the second part of the structure, and whether the other part carries secondary accent or not. Primary accent always falls on the focal part of the structure. Secondary accent occurs when the other part also contains nonestablished information.

Exchanges (2)–(4), like (1), were recorded in a Scottish teachers' common room. They illustrate the other three types of *it*-cleft that Delin identified (**bold**: primary accent; UPPER CASE: secondary accent):

2. (1st part: primary accent; 2nd part: secondary accent)

   Speaker A: *This coffee's really yukky.*
   Speaker B: *It was **you** who put the MILK in.*

3. (2nd part: primary accent) (prominent point of departure by renewal – see 4.6.2)

   Speaker A: *And does the head know?*
   Speaker B: *It was <u>the head</u> who **arranged** it.*

4. (1st part: secondary accent; 2nd part: primary accent) (prominent point of departure involving switch)

   Speaker A: *Did the student really make this error?*
   Speaker B: *No, it's just <u>ME</u> that can't **type** properly.*

It-cleft constructions like (3) or (4) are often used to create the expectation that something of particular importance is to follow (see the Koorete examples in 4.6.2). In the following extract from an autobiographical text in the Khoekhoe [naq] (formerly known as Hottentot; Khoe, Namibia) language, the first part of the *it*-cleft sentence involves tail-head linkage with the context (see 3.2.3), in order to highlight what is described in the second part of the sentence:

So I went to live in the forest. It was <u>while I was living in the forest</u> that I heard of ...

Application to the language you are analysing

Identify the markers or structures that have a comparable function to cleft sentences in English. Check whether or not the focal constituent always occurs in the first part of the structure, and whether or not nonestablished information can also be presented in the second part.

Suggested reading

Chapter 11 of Dooley and Levinsohn 2001 relates to the topics covered in this chapter. For background reading, you may also wish to look at chapters 9 and 10.

5

The Relative Prominence of the Sentences of a Text

The primary concern of this chapter is NOT about classifying information as foreground or background. Rather, it is concerned with how certain material may be **backgrounded** with respect to other material and how certain material may be **highlighted** with respect to other material. In other words, it is concerned with devices that make material **less** prominent or **more** prominent.[1] Section 5.1 is therefore devoted to a few observations about foreground and background.

Section 5.2 concerns sentences that present background information in narrative texts and distinguishes between nonevents, which are automatically viewed as background information in narratives, and events which are backgrounded because they are of secondary importance. Devices used to background sentences and clauses are also discussed.

Section 5.3 describes correlations between the particular verb type or verbal aspect selected and background versus foreground information. It then considers the implications of using a marked aspect. Finally, devices used to highlight information are presented in 5.4.

5.1 Foreground and background

Callow (1974:52–53) relates foreground in a discourse to **thematic** information: "this is what I'm talking about" (see 4.6.2). Thematic material "carries the discourse forward, contributes to the progression of the narrative or argument ... [and] develops the theme of the discourse".[2] In contrast, nonthematic or background material "serves as a commentary on the theme, but does not itself contribute directly to the progression of the theme ... [it] fills out the theme but does not develop it".

Section 1.2 defined **narrative** in contrast to other discourse genres as agent oriented with its events organised chronologically. Consequently, the theme line for narrative is made up of events that are performed in chronological sequence by agents. Nonevent material is classified as background material in narrative (see 5.2).

In **behavioural** discourses such as parts of the Epistles, exhortations directed to the readers or addressees typically make up the theme line. Such discourses differ from narrative in that the theme line is generally not organised chronologically.

The problem is that one genre is frequently embedded in another. For example, the Epistle to the Galatians contains an embedded narrative (Galatians 1:13–2:14). Similarly, all the Gospel writers have probably arranged their narrative episodes with the goal of influencing their readers. Consequently, "material which might have a background function in narrative may be thematic in ... other types of

---

[1] I hesitate to use the term "foregrounded" because Heimerdinger (1999) identifies it with "foreground". See also footnote 6.

[2] Section 5.1 is based on Levinsohn 2000:169.

discourse" (Callow 1974:56). So, in John's Gospel, a conclusion such as John 20:31 (*But these are written so that you may believe that Jesus is the Messiah …*) is background information as far as the immediately preceding narrative is concerned. However, it is to be interpreted as thematically prominent for the behavioural theme line that unites the narratives of the Gospel.

Thus, the same material may be viewed as background in one genre and as foreground in another. However, there are devices that authors can use to indicate that certain material is backgrounded in relation to other material. Similarly, there are devices that they can use to highlight other material. Consequently, this chapter will concentrate on such devices.

Nevertheless, whatever the genre, certain types of material are NOT thematic. Such is the case with Greek sentences introduced with *gar* 'for'. In all genres, the function of these sentences is to strengthen immediately preceding material (though they can themselves be strengthened and, if the subsequent argument builds upon them, form part of some other theme line).

Background, foreground and highlighting in an Inga folktale

The above discussion assumes that the sentences of a text are not all of equal importance, as far as the author's purpose is concerned. Some present foreground information; others only supply background information. In addition, some information may be highlighted because of its special importance (see the discussion of prominence in 4.6.2).

To see how this works in practice, consider the following chart, which contains a free translation of a short folktale in the San Andrés dialect of Inga, told by Lázaro Mojomboy Pujimoy (see Levinsohn and Avendaño 1982):

Table 7. Chart of an Inga folktale

Ref.	Prenuclear	Nucleus	Postnuclear
1		A serpent used to appear in Sun Pool.	
2		That one used to wait each Sunday at the edge of the pool	for a person to go & be given to it.
3		They used to send someone who didn't go to Mass	to be handed over to the serpent.
4		That one was eating so many people	that the people were already few.
5	Then	they sent a youth	to be handed over.
6		He went with a machete.	
7		That one came & churned up the water	to swallow the youth.
8	When it came & churned [it] up,	he, cutting off its neck with that machete, killed [it].	

Questions

1. Which sentence of the folktale appears to present the **climax** of the story? (The *OED* defines climax as "the event or point of greatest intensity or interest; a culmination or apex".)
2. All the sentences of this folktale describe events, but some can be considered to set the scene for others? Which sent*ences appear to set the scene and so can be labelled* **background**?[3]

Your answers to the above questions reflected your instinct about what constituted the climax of the folktale and which information set the scene for other events. Fortunately, we do not have to rely in this case on our instinct. This is because the Inga author used devices that show which event is the climax and which events form the background for others. These devices are as follows:

- The climax is introduced by **tail-head linkage** (3.2.3). The main verb of sentence 7 (*came and churned up*) is repeated at the beginning of sentence 8 (*When it came and churned up*).

---
[3] **Suggested answers:**
1. Sentence 8 presents the climax of the story.
2. Because sentences 1–4 describe events that used to happen habitually, they appear to set the scene for the events of sentences 5–8 and so can be labelled background.

- Ingas of the San Andrés dialect identify the events which form the background by using the past tense marker *-rka*. This is attached to the verbs of sentences 1–4 and 7 (5.4.1 explains why sent. 7 is backgrounded). In contrast, the verbs of sentences 5, 6 and 8 are unmarked for tense.

This leads to an important cross-linguistic observation. Typically, the body of a text (e.g. the theme-line events of a narrative) is **unmarked** or minimally marked. Rather, events are presented in a **marked** way to **background** them. The hearer or reader is to assume that narrative events are part of the theme line unless they are marked to the contrary.

Thus, Inga uses an unmarked form of the verb to present theme-line events, but a marked form for backgrounded events (e.g. *samú* versus *samu-rka* 'came'). English uses the simple past to present theme-line events, but more complex forms for backgrounded events (e.g. *used to wait*). Written French uses the *passé simple* to present theme-line events, Greek uses the aorist, and many African languages use a simple 'neutral' or 'narrative' form of the verb. In other words, the default way in many languages of presenting the events of a narrative is with some sort of unmarked or minimally marked verb form.[4]

Review question

If a language presents the events of a narrative with more than one verb form, which form is most likely to be used for the theme-line events: the simplest or the more complex?[5]

Application to the language you are analysing

Examine the verb column of your charted narratives to determine how many ways the events are presented. Which would you judge to be the default verb form for presenting theme-line events?

Note: When answering the above question, you must ignore the verbs that occur in reported speeches. Such verbs do NOT constitute part of the narrative superstructure, but belong to embedded conversations (see 3.2). Thus, in the opening sentences of the Bekwarra text (from table 4, repeated from 1.5.2), the verbs that are part of the narrative superstructure are *e-ngwìà* 'they entered' (1) and *e-dè* 'they said' (2). *È-káá* 'they should fry' and *ja* 'eat' (2) belong to an embedded conversation and must be ignored.

Table 4. Chart of part of the Bekwarra text

Ref.	Pre-S	S	V	(O)	Adjunct
1	únyang kìn time one	ùbuhó àhe dog 3s n'-anyamchù with-hare	e-ngwìà p-entered	iyìm agreement	
2		abe 3p ---- ----	e-dè p-said è-káá p-fry ja eat	èbwa íbere children their ----	

---

[4] In some languages, though, the default way of presenting theme-line events in a narrative is NOT with a minimally marked verb form. For example, Hebrew uses the *wayyiqtol* form of the verb. Also, some languages include a particle in the verb phrase when the event concerned represents a significant development in the story (see ch. 6).

[5] **Suggested answer:**
If a language presents the events of a narrative with more than one verb form, the form that is most likely to be used for the theme-line events is the simplest one.

5.2 Sentences that present background information in narrative

Because narratives are made up of events, a sentence that describes an event is generally assumed to constitute foreground (theme-line) information unless it is marked in some way. Background information consists of the **nonevents** of the narrative, together with those **events** that are **marked** as being of secondary importance (nonthematic). These two types are considered in turn (5.2.1–5.2.2). Sections 5.2.3–5.2.4 respectively discuss devices that background whole sentences and those that background some of the information in a sentence in relation to other information in the same sentence.

5.2.1 Nonevents

Because of the nature of narratives, nonevents are **automatically** viewed as background information when appearing in a narrative. This does not mean that the information they convey is unimportant for the narrative; indeed, they may be highlighted (5.4). Rather, their background status is simply a consequence of the fact that the sentence describes a nonevent.[6]

Grimes (1975, ch. 4) distinguishes a number of types of nonevent information. They include setting, explanatory, evaluative, collateral and performative information.

Settings describe the time, place and circumstance of the events of a narrative and may include the introduction of some participants. The following sentence sets the scene for a folktale in the Kambaata [ktb] (Cushitic, Ethiopia) language:

Once, in a certain country, there were two friends who loved each other very much.

Explanatory information clarifies and explains the events of a narrative. It includes comments about the participants. The bolded sentence in the example below explains why only *three of the four children came running*:

Three of the four children came running. ***Jimmy, aged 10, was visiting friends.***

Evaluative information conveys the author's feelings about the narrative, its events and participants. The following bolded sentence from a folktale in Gude conveys an evaluation of Cock:

He said to Cock, 'Let's go to my in-laws!' ***Now Cock, he was really clever.***

Collateral information tells what did not happen, **as a basis for what did happen**. It includes some negative statements and rhetorical questions.

She considered staying in the car*, but the garage door opened …* [implying: *so she didn't stay there*].

A negative sentence may present an event; it is NOT automatically classified as collateral information. For example, when Herod questioned Jesus, *Jesus answered him nothing* (Luke 23:9). This clause does NOT present collateral information because Jesus didn't do something else instead. Rather, it simply presents a negative event.

Performative information concerns the devices used by the author to relate him or herself to the audience. It includes material directed by the author (first person) to the audience (second person), such as the moral the audience should draw from a story.[7] In addition, the events, participants, etc. of the story may be related to the audience's situation. In the following sentence from a folktale in Gumawana (Olson 2014:233), for instance, the bolded sentence is performative information, because the author is addressing the audience:

The giant thought he was by himself. ***You, though, know that the hero was with him.***

---

[6] Heimerdinger (1999:261) rejects this classification of nonevents as background, as they may be "foregrounded" (highlighted, in the present work). "Foregrounding" for Heimerdinger means the same as "foreground".

[7] Clif Olson points out that, in Gumawana, performative information such as the moral of the story uses the first person inclusive. For example, the conclusion of one folktale reads, 'So, although we see that Gilibo is split when we go to it, a long time ago it was not split' (2014:236).

Nonevent information can often be recognised from such things as the connective used (e.g. *Now*), the way it is introduced (e.g. *you know, she considered*), the verb type employed (see 5.3.1 – e.g. *was*), the presence of a negative, etc.

5.2.2 Secondary events

Whereas nonevent information in narrative is automatically viewed as background, events are viewed as foreground (theme line) **unless** they are backgrounded. Rather than marking the theme-line events as foreground, languages tend to mark those that are NOT theme-line events.

Three types of event information are commonly marked as being of secondary importance in relation to the theme-line events:

1. **preliminary** events that occur **prior** to the theme-line events (often marked as **past** or **perfect** – e.g. sents. 1–4 of the Inga folktale presented in 5.1)
2. **resulting** events that occur **after** the theme-line events (often marked as **perfect** – e.g. in the Bonggi [bdg] (Malayo-Polynesian, Sabah) language (see Boutin 1988) or as **future**)
3. **reported speeches** that **lead to** theme-line events (see ch. 7)

Review questions

1. What two types of background information are commonly found in narratives?
2. What condition must a negative sentence meet if it is to be viewed as conveying background information?[8]

5.2.3 Devices used to background sentences

Sentences are commonly backgrounded either by distinct verb forms or with a spacer. These devices are now considered in turn.

1. Specific verb forms

Two verb forms lend themselves to being associated with backgrounding:
- a **past** tense which implies 'prior to the point of reference' (e.g. the English pluperfect), because the event concerned takes place prior to the time of the theme-line events. A **completive** aspect has a similar effect, because the event concerned is completed prior to the time of the theme-line events. A particle translated '**already**' may also function in the same way (e.g. in Thai [tha] (Kra-Dai, Thailand)).
- a **perfect** tense or aspect, since the event concerned often results in a **state** which holds at the time of the theme-line events, and states are usually background information in narrative (5.3.1).[9]

---

[8] **Suggested answers:**
1. Two types of background information commonly found in narratives are nonevent information and events that are marked as being of secondary importance.
2. If a negative sentence is to be viewed as conveying background information, it must describe what did not happen, as a basis for what did happen.

[9] When a verb has **perfect** tense or aspect, it typically portrays the event concerned as past or completed at the point of reference, with results or effects that are still relevant at the point of reference. Bhat (1999:168–175) claims that, in tense-prominent languages such as English, the perfect is viewed temporally, whereas in aspect-prominent languages (which would include many African languages), the perfect is viewed aspectually.

"Perfect" has a different meaning for **Hebrew** grammarians. *(W)qtl* forms that **begin** clauses may be used to background events because they are preliminary to following theme-line events. This is illustrated in 1 Kings 21:12–13; the events of verse 12 (presented with *(w)qtl* forms) are readily interpreted as preliminary to and backgrounded with respect to the theme-line events of 13 (presented with *wyyqtl* forms).

12	qarʾû	ṣôm	wəhošîbû	ʾet-nabôt	bəroʾš	haʿam
	they called	fast	& they seated	(et) Naboth	at the head	of the people

Both of the above verb forms are used for backgrounding in the following extract from a folktale in the Guayuyacu dialect [inj] of Inga (alt. Jungle Inga). In this particular dialect, the past tense (marked by *-rka*) is reserved for nonevents (sents. 1–3). A verb form similar to the perfect (*marked by -ska*) is used in connection with events that build up to each set of theme-line events (see also 5.3.3). The theme-line events themselves are in the morphologically unmarked form (Ø, *-n* preceding certain suffixes).

1. *After God made this world, it was (-**rka**) not like now: proper days.*
2. *The sun used not to appear (-**rka**).*
3. *At that time there was (-**rka**) a very wise medicine man.*
4. *He said (-**ska**), 'We are not enjoying proper days, as there is a great tree which is darkening the whole world. If we could cut down that tree, there'd be good days, since there is a thing to give us light called "sun."'*
5. *Then everyone, meeting together, asked each other (Ø) what could be done to cut down that tree.*
6. *Then he answered (-**ska**), 'It is not yet known how to cut it down.'*
7. *After that, all the medicine men, meeting together, drank (-**ska**) [a hallucinatory drug].*
8. *Then they said (-**n**), 'That tree can be cut down just by drinking the drug and chanting.'*
9. *Then they asked (-**ska**) which medicine man could chant like that until the tree fell.*
10. *And he answered (-**n**), 'The great owl will be able to.'*
11. *Having said that, having asked him, they took (-**ska**) him [to it].*
12. *Then, standing beside it, he began (-**n**) to chant ...*
13. *While he was chanting, the tree actually began (Ø) to bend.*
14. *It became (Ø) as though about to fall.*
15. *And then breath failed (Ø) the chanter.*
16. *With that, the tree again became upright (Ø).*

In the Inga dialect illustrated above, the verb forms containing *-rka* and *-ska* are always associated with backgrounding when they are used in narrative. In some languages, however, the same verb form is used for both backgrounding and highlighting, to "**detach**" the events concerned from their context because of their differing importance. For example, the perfect in Bonggi is used to present both preliminary events and concluding ones of a climactic nature (Boutin 1988).

Waugh and Monville-Burston (1986) analysed French newspaper reports of incidents. They found that, in some, the introductory and concluding paragraphs used the *passé simple*, whereas the body of the article used the *passé composé*. In others, the pattern was reversed:

Introduction:	*passé simple*
Body of article:	*passé composé*
Conclusion:	*passé simple*

Introduction:	*passé composé*
Body of article:	*passé simple*
Conclusion:	*passé composé*

---

13 wayyabo'û   šənê   ha'anašîm   bənê-bəliyya'al ...
    & they came two   the men   sons-of worthlessness

'They proclaimed (*qtl*) a fast and seated (*wqtl*) Naboth in a prominent place among the people. Then the two scoundrels came (*wyyqtl*) ...'

In other words, it was the switch from one verb form, that marked the transition from the background information to the theme-line information, rather than the actual form used. A similar phenomenon appears to occur in the Oroko [bdu] (Bantu A, Cameroon) language.

Jarvis (1991:219) describes another verb form that is used to background events: the "focus perfective". She finds that theme-line events in the Podoko [pbi] (alt. Parkwa; Chadic, Cameroon) language are presented with default topic-comment perfective verb forms. In contrast, "[b]ackground material uses the focus perfective for events that took place prior to that point on the event line. The focus imperfective is used for repeated events, for events and states that are concurrent with the main events, and for explanations of a general nature" (p. 213).[10]

Application to the language you are analysing

Examine your narrative texts to see whether a past tense, completive aspect or perfect tense-aspect is ever used **instead of** the default tense-aspect to present events. If so, ask yourself whether it is being employed to background the event concerned.

2. A spacer

Many languages use a spacer WITHIN sentences to separate information of unequal importance (see 5.2.4). Sometimes the same particle occurs at the beginning of a sentence to indicate that the information preceding it has been backgrounded with respect to what follows. Such is the case in the Teribe [tfr] (Chibchan, Panama) language.

> "When *ga* occurs at the beginning of a sentence, it indicates that the whole of the preceding unit (which can on occasion be a sentence, though in general it is a paragraph) is complementary information and that the nuclear clause of the next sentence is a key event of the theme line." (Koontz and Anderson 1978:73 [my translation of the Spanish])

The following is one of the examples cited in Koontz and Anderson's article (1978:74):

a BACKGROUND: *After telling her, 'Do not come down!', he continued to hold it [the animal] by the hair until it became tired.*
b THEME LINE: ***Ga** he told her ...*

The same phenomenon has been observed in Gumawana and Herde [hed] (Chadic, Chad).

Review questions

1. What two devices are commonly used to background sentences?
2. Which two verb forms lend themselves to being associated with backgrounding?[11]

5.2.4 Backgrounding *within* a sentence

Three devices are commonly used to background some of the information within a sentence in relation to the rest of the information: subordination, a spacer, and the same verb forms that are used to background whole sentences (see 5.2.3). These devices are now considered in turn.

---

[10] See 5.4 regarding an apparent exception to this pattern.

[11] **Suggested answers**:
1. Two devices that are commonly used to background sentences are distinct verb forms and a spacer.
2. Two verb forms that lend themselves to being associated with backgrounding are a past tense or completive aspect and a perfect tense or aspect.

1. Subordination

Cross-linguistically, the information conveyed in **prenuclear** subordinate clauses is backgrounded in relation to that conveyed in the main clause.[12]

The following is a Koine Greek example from Luke 2:42–43. The theme-line event (bolded) is presented in the main clause. It is preceded by four subordinate clauses presenting nonevent information or preliminary events:

> 42 *And, when he was twelve years old, having gone up according to custom (43) and the feast having ended, as they were returning,* **the boy Jesus stayed behind in Jerusalem** ...

2. A spacer

In some languages, a spacer is used to separate information of **unequal importance**. In the following extract from a folktale in Gumawana (Olson 2014:231), the spacer *go* separates the preliminary events of the sentence from the theme-line events (this is reflected in the free translation in English by subordination of the initial clauses):

E	*Gumasai*	*ina*	*bwae*	*i-kabi-di,*	*i-na,*	*i-tega-tega*	***go***
then	Gumasai	his	jug	3s-get-3p	3s-went	3s-fill-fill	SPACER

si-sowoya,	*ina*	*oga*	*si-kailave,*	*si-lokoine,*	*si-me*	*Kitava.*
3p-embark	his	canoe	3p-depart.with.TR	3p-run.with.TR	3p-bring.TR	Kitava

'Then, while Gumasai got his jugs and went and was filling them, they embarked and left with his canoe, sailed it and brought it to Kitava.'

In the following extract from the Bekwarra folktale (18–22), the spacer *áná* separates the preliminary events of each sentence from the following theme-line events. In contrast with Gumawana, this spacer is only found in the sentences that build up to the climax of the story (see 5.4).

a
é-kuo	*anyamchù*	*bé*	*chi*	***áná***	*é-kuo*	*ùbuhó*	*bé*	*chi*	***áná***
p-called	hare	came	sat	SPACER	p-called	dog	came	sat	SPACER

é-bii	*ùbuhó*	*dèè*	*abe*	*n'-anyamchù*	*e-ngwìà*	*iyìm*	*èbwan*
p-asked	dog	say	3p	with-hare	p-entered	agreement	children

àjini	*bu*	*à*
eating	indeed	QUESTION

'Hare was called (and) came (and) sat ***áná*** Dog was called (and) came (and) sat ***áná*** Dog was asked whether he and Hare had indeed made an agreement to eat their children.'

b
ùbuhó	*á-chi*	*ngá*	*nè*	*he*	*chùù*	*k'-àchì*	*ékáànì*	***áná***	*á-kung*	*bàng*
dog	s-sat	there	looked at	3sO	carefully	in-face	of elders	SPACER	s-took	agreed

'Dog sat there looking at him carefully before the elders ***áná*** agreed.'

---

[12] **Postnuclear** subordinate clauses often contain theme-line information (Hwang 1990:69). An example from the story of 'The Three Little Pigs' is *He was picking apples* **when the wolf arrived**. The effect of using such a structure is to highlight the event expressed in the postnuclear subordinate clause (see 5.4.2).

In some OV languages, linguists distinguish between two types of prenuclear subordinate clause: adverbial clauses that present background information and gerundive or participial clauses that may present theme-line information. See Longacre 1990:11ff. and Levinsohn 2003 for discussion of this point. See also Fast 2008.

It is not unusual for the same spacer to be used in all four of the following circumstances:

topic	**spacer**	comment (especially in equative clauses that lack a verb)
point of departure	**spacer**	rest of the sentence
less important information	**spacer**	more important information
focus/more important	**spacer**	presupposition/less important information.

For example, in the next sentence of the Gumawana folktale illustrated above (Olson 2014:231), the spacer *go* separates the point of departure from the rest of the sentence:

Kina	*go*	*i-sowodo,*	*i-doiwo,*	*oga*	*geya.*
3s.PN	SPACER	3s-go.out	3s-look.seaward	canoe	not

'He for his part went out and looked seaward [but saw] no canoe.'

3. Distinct verb forms

In other languages, the same verb forms that are used to background whole sentences (5.2.3) may background individual clauses within a sentence. In other words, a single sentence contains verb forms with marked tense-aspect (usually sentence-initial) and the default tense-aspect.

In the following word-by-word translation of an extract from a folktale in the Cerma [cme] (Gur, Burkina Faso) language, the first clause is in completive aspect (COMP),[13] whereas the verbs of the other two clauses have 'narrative' verb forms (NARR). The effect is to background the arrival in relation to the events of the other two clauses (this is again reflected in the free translation by subordination of the initial clause):

3P *come*.COMP *arrive, partridge pull.out*.NARR *his feathers, fish enter*.NARR *water-in*

'When they came and arrived, Partridge took back his feathers and Fish re-entered the water.'

Review questions

1. What is the preferred device in English for backgrounding some of the information in a sentence in relation to other information in the same sentence?
2. What other two devices for backgrounding within a sentence are cross-linguistically common?[14]

Application to the language you are analysing

1. Identify the devices that are used in your texts to background whole sentences. If more than one device is used, distinguish their functions.
2. Identify the devices that are used in your texts to background some of the information in a sentence in relation to the rest of the information. If more than one device is used, distinguish their functions.

5.3 Natural prominence: verb semantics and verb aspect

We have been looking at languages that have one or more markers for backgrounding whole sentences.[15] In many languages, though, such markers are rare or nonexistent. This is because there is a significant

---

[13] The completive marker is attached to the first verb of the clause.

[14] **Suggested answers**:
1. The preferred device in English for backgrounding some of the information in a sentence in relation to other information in the same sentence is the **subordination** of prenuclear clauses.
2. Two other devices for backgrounding within a sentence that are cross-linguistically common are the use of a **spacer** and the use of a **marked verb form** in the backgrounded clauses. Where a language prefers one of these latter two devices, this constitutes a major **mismatch** with English and other European languages.

[15] Section 5.3 is based on sec. 10.2 of Levinsohn 2000, though some of the footnotes have been omitted.

correlation between the verb form used and foreground versus background information. In particular, Foley and Van Valin (1984) note two areas of correlation. One is with the "semantic verb type" (Longacre 1990:63) or "lexical meaning" (Fanning 1990:127) of the verb used in the clause; this is briefly considered in 5.3.1. The other correlation is with the aspect of the verb; this is discussed in 5.3.2. Section 5.3.3 concerns marked uses of verbal aspects.[16]

5.3.1 Verb types and natural prominence

If we encounter a main verb such as *was* in a narrative, we expect the sentence concerned to be conveying background information.[17] Foley and Van Valin go further; they discern a natural correlation between four basic verb types and background versus foreground information. They use syntactic and semantic criteria proposed by Vendler (1967) to distinguish the following types:[18]

- achievement (e.g. *recognise, find, die*)
- accomplishment (e.g. *make something, paint a picture*)
- activity (e.g. *run, drive a car*)
- state (e.g. *know, have*).

Foley and Van Valin point out (1984:371) that clauses "with achievement and accomplishment verbs will strongly tend to occur in the temporal structure". In other words, such clauses **tend** to present foreground information in narrative. In contrast, clauses "with activity and state verbs [will strongly tend to occur] in the durative/descriptive structure". That is to say, such clauses **tend** to present background information in narrative.

The selection of a particular semantic verb type therefore tends naturally to determine whether the clauses in which it appears will convey information of more or less importance for the genre concerned. What is significant for translators is that different languages tend to allocate individual verbs to the **same** semantic type. Consequently, the verb that is most likely to be selected as the translation of an achievement verb in the source language is likely also to be an achievement verb, etc. In other words, translators will probably preserve the natural prominence conveyed by a particular verb in the source language even if they have not classified the verbs of the receptor language into semantic types.

5.3.2 Verbal aspect and background versus foreground

Before looking at the correlation between certain verbal aspects and background versus foreground, let me remind you what linguists mean by aspect![19] Verbal aspect is a way of **portraying** an event. It is "the speaker's subjective view of a process or event" (Reed and Reese 1996:183). It "reflects the subjective conception or portrayal by the speaker" (Fanning 1990:31).

When the **imperfective** aspect describes an event, the event is portrayed as **not completed**. The Greek imperfect has imperfective aspect. Thus, *suneporeuto autois* 'he was journeying with them' (Luke 24:15b) indicates that the journeying is portrayed as an action that has not been completed at the point the story has reached. Fanning (1990:84–85) calls the imperfect the "internal" aspect, which views the action "from a reference-point *within* the action, without reference to the beginning or endpoint of the action".

When the **perfective** aspect describes an event, the event is portrayed **as a whole**. The aorist in Greek has perfective aspect. Thus, *ēlthon* 'they came' indicates that the act of coming is viewed as a single journey, including its beginning and end. Though the use of the aorist presupposes that the journey was completed, it does not focus on the end of the journey; it simply views the journey as a whole.

---

[16] In addition, Hopper and Thompson (1980:252) found that "high transitivity" correlates with foreground, whereas "low transitivity" correlates with background (using the term "transitivity" in a broader sense than that of having a direct object); see Dooley and Levinsohn 2001:79–80.

[17] Longacre's "storyline scheme" uses both the "semantic type" and the tense-aspect-mood of the verb to rank the sentences of a narrative into seven or eight bands. I follow Gutt in separating the different parameters involved (see Longacre 1990:63).

[18] Although linguists have since proposed additional verb types, the correlation being discussed here is best seen between these four types.

[19] See Aaron 1999:36 on 'perfectivity'.

5.3 Natural prominence: verb semantics and verb aspect

Fanning (1990:84) calls the aorist the "external" aspect, which views the action "from a vantage-point *outside* the action ... without reference to its internal structure".

Foley and Van Valin point out that there is an inherent **correlation** between perfective versus imperfective aspect and foreground versus background (see also Hopper 1979:215–216):

> [T]he perfective aspect is the primary aspectual category found in the temporal structure of narrative discourse ... and imperfective aspect is primary in durational/descriptive structure. (1984:373)
>
> This finding [the statement on p. 373] is not surprising, since perfective aspect codes completed actions and events and imperfective incomplete events and actions and the former fit more naturally into the temporal structure of narrative, the latter into durational/descriptive structure. (1984:397)

Thus, it is natural in a narrative in Koine Greek for a clause with the verb in the imperfect (having imperfective aspect) to be conveying information of less importance than one with the verb in the aorist (having perfective aspect); this is due to the nature of the respective aspects.

For example, the imperfect is used in Greek to encode **habitual** actions, since habits are not viewed as completed. In turn, such actions are typically viewed as events of secondary importance in narrative. This is seen in Luke 2:41–42. The fact that Jesus' parents habitually went to Jerusalem for the festival of the Passover is of secondary importance to the events that took place after they went there when he was twelve years old.

41   *Now his parents **used to travel** (IMPERFECTIVE) each year to Jerusalem for the feast of the Passover.*

42   *And, when he was twelve years old, having gone up according to custom and the feast having ended, (43) as they were returning, the boy Jesus **stayed behind** (PERFECTIVE) in Jerusalem ...*

Thus, in narrative, the imperfective (imperfect) tends to correlate with background information and the perfective (aorist) with foreground events, because of their inherent nature.

Nevertheless, the presence of the imperfect in a narrative in Greek is NOT a signal that the information concerned is of a background nature. This is seen in Luke 2:36–38. Verses 36–38 are all in the imperfect; 36 gives nonevent information with the verb *ēn* 'was', the relative clause of 37b describes a habitual action, and the foreground events of 38 are also portrayed as incomplete (*NRSV* translates, "began to praise God ...").

36   *There was (IMPERFECTIVE) also a prophetess, Anna the daughter of Phanuel, of the tribe of Asher. She was of a great age, having lived with her husband seven years after her marriage, (37a) and as a widow to the age of 84,*

37b   *who **used not to depart** (IMPERFECTIVE) from the temple ...*

38   *At that very hour, coming up, she **was praising** (IMPERFECTIVE) God and **was speaking** (IMPERFECTIVE) of him to all who were looking for the redemption of Jerusalem.*

The above passage shows that the primary function of the imperfect in Greek is not to mark background but to portray events as incomplete. Habitual actions and other events of secondary importance in a narrative are often viewed as incomplete. It is this tendency that explains the correlation between the imperfect and background information.[20]

Before continuing, I must emphasise that any correlation between the imperfective aspect and background information, on the one hand, and between perfective aspect and foreground information, on the other, is specific to **narrative**.

5.3.3 Marked uses of aspects

The last section argued that the primary function of the imperfect in Greek is not to mark background but to portray events as incomplete. However, there appear to be occasions when the imperfect is used but it is NOT obvious that the event described can be viewed as being incomplete. John's use of *elegen*

---

[20] See also Reed and Reese (1996:190): "the use of verbal aspect ... to indicate prominence is a secondary role."

(the imperfect of 'say') in 8:31 is a case in point. It does not seem likely that the imperfect is used here because Jesus habitually made this statement. Nor is there any suggestion that the speech is portrayed as incomplete because Jesus was interrupted.

30   *As he was saying these things, many believed* (PERFECTIVE) *in him.*

31   *Jesus said* (**elegen** – IMPERFECTIVE) *to the Jews who had believed in him, 'If you continue in my word, you are truly my disciples;* (32) *and you will know the truth, and the truth will make you free'.*

33   *They answered* (PERFECTIVE) *him, 'We are descendants of Abraham and have never been slaves to anyone. What do you mean by saying, "You will be made free"?'*

If an event cannot readily be viewed as incomplete yet the imperfect is used, we may consider such an imperfect to have been used in a **marked** way. The message to the reader in this case is that, because the writer did not select the default way of portraying a completed event (with, say, an aorist), there must be "added implicatures" (Sperber and Wilson 1995:220).

Elegen in John 8:31 (above) could be such a marked usage of the imperfect. Possible confirmation for this interpretation is that the speech follows a paragraph break in some versions and can readily be interpreted as the speech which incites or provokes the conversational exchange of the rest of the chapter.[21]

The imperfective is not the only aspect that can be used in a marked way. The same is true of the **perfect**. In its default usage in Tsuvadi, for instance, the perfect portrays an event as "completed ... with continuing (imperfective) relevance" (Bhat 1999:170). Consider the following pair of sentences from a Tsuvadi folktale:

a   *The tree came down-***PERFECT** [with continuing relevance: *and remained down*].

b   *They climbed-*PERFECTIVE *it ...*

In sentence a of the above extract, *came down* is portrayed as a completed event which produces an ongoing resultant state, namely that the tree remained down while the event of sentence b took place. In other words, *they climbed it* while it remained down.

The following passage from another Tsuvadi folktale illustrates what I judge to be extended uses of the perfect. In this folktale, the aunt keeps sending the orphan to Hoka to get water, where she will be abducted. Each time she goes, though, the tamarind tree directs her to Zurundum. Finally, the aunt sends her own daughter with the orphan, to ensure that she goes to Hoka. They get to the tree. The story continues (Lovelace 1992:11ff.):

a   *She (the orphan) called out-*PERFECTIVE, *'Tamarind, Tamarind, shall I go to Zurundum or to Hoka?'*

b   *Tamarind replied-***PERFECT**, *'Go to Zurundum, not Hoka'.*

c   *She returned-***PERFECT** *again to Zurundum, fetched water and went home.*

d   *The aunt said-***PERFECT**, *'I told you to go to Hoka, didn't I?'*

e   *She (daughter) said-*PERFECTIVE, *'No, Mom, there's a Tamarind there; it stopped us going to Hoka'.*

In sentences b–d of the above passage, the completed events do not produce an ongoing resultant state. Rather, they point forward to the speech of sentence e, when the daughter tells her mother about the talking tamarind tree (which in turn leads to the mother cutting the tree down). The pragmatic effect of such occurrences of the perfect is to highlight the resulting event (see 5.4).[22]

---

[21] Longacre (1994:72) notes that imperfective *wqtl* forms in Hebrew are used to present "the denouement of a story". See 1 Kings 20:21c, for example: *'The king of Israel went out* [wyyqtl], *attacked* [wyyqtl] *the horses and chariots, and defeated* [wqtl] *the Arameans with a great slaughter'* (NRSV). The imperfective may indicate that the episode it terminates forms part of a larger story, with the event so marked setting the scene for a further episode.

[22] The use of *-ska* in the Guayuyacu dialect of Jungle Inga (5.2.3) has a similar pragmatic effect. See Levinsohn 2000:200ff. on the use of the historical present in Koine Greek to point forward to and highlight what follows.

Review questions

1. What are two correlations that Foley and Van Valin have observed in narrative between verb forms and foreground versus background?
2. When the imperfective aspect is used to describe an event, how is the event portrayed?
3. When the perfective aspect is used to describe an event, is the event portrayed as completed?
4. Under what circumstances is it valid to consider an imperfective to have been used in a marked way? And the perfect?[23]

Application to the language you are analysing

Examine your narrative texts to see whether the imperfective or perfect is ever used in a marked way.[24] If so, what appears to be its function?

5.4 Highlighting of sentences

We noted in 4.6.2 that thematic prominence may be given to a point of departure or connective when it introduces a significant event of the theme line. The effect of marking either as prominent is to highlight the following material.[25]

Sentences are typically highlighted when they relate to a **climax** (as defined in 5.1) or when a **significant development** (e.g. an 'inciting incident' or a 'complication') or a **change of direction** occurs. Typically, some of the same rhetorical devices are used for both, but climaxes are more extensively marked.

An **inciting incident** is "that which is unexpected and routine-breaking" (Longacre 1996:141). It often introduces a problem or creates an imbalance that needs to be resolved. A **complication** increases the problem and moves it further from a resolution. In the Bekwarra folktale, Dog's refusal to fry his pup (sent. 9) introduces a problem and creates an imbalance that is only resolved after Hare appeals to the elders (see further in 5.4.2).

5.4.1 Climaxes

Both the overall story and subgroupings MAY build up to a climax (but do not have to). Such events may be highlighted by:
- introducing **nonevent** (background) information immediately before it (see Acts 19:14 below) or
- **backgrounding** the event(s) that immediately precede it (see below for an example from Podoko).

---

[23] **Suggested answers:**
1. The two correlations that Foley and Van Valin have observed in narrative between verb forms and foreground versus background are:
   - the semantic type of the verb: achievement and accomplishment verbs tend to correlate with foreground, whereas activity and state verbs tend to correlate with background;
   - verbal aspect: the perfective (external) aspect tends to correlate with foreground, whereas the imperfective (internal) aspect tends to correlate with background.
2. When the imperfective aspect is used to describe an event, the event is portrayed as **not completed**.
3. No, when the perfective aspect is used to describe an event, the event is portrayed **as a whole**. In the context of narrative, the event concerned is usually completed, but it does not have to be. See Luke 15:20 (*So setting off, he came to his father. But while he was still far off, his father saw him and was filled with compassion, and ran and put his arms around him and kissed him*). The verb *came* (Greek *ēlthen*) is perfective, but the father runs to meet his son **before** he finishes coming.
4. It is valid to consider an imperfective to have been used in a marked way if the event concerned cannot readily be viewed as incomplete. Similarly, it is valid to consider a perfect to have been used in a marked way if the event concerned does not produce an ongoing resultant state.

[24] The **inchoative** ('began to') may also be used in a marked way; see 6.5.4.

[25] Highlighting may be thought of as thematic prominence at the level of a sentence or group of sentences.

Introducing nonevent information immediately before the climax

The following extract from Acts 19:13–14 illustrates the introduction of nonevent information immediately before a climax. Once the event of 13 has been presented, the reader expects to be told the result. Instead, a nonevent is introduced, thus slowing the story down and creating the expectation that a particularly significant event is about to be described:

13		*Then some itinerant Jewish exorcists tried to use the name of the Lord Jesus over those who had evil spirits, saying, 'I adjure you by the Jesus whom Paul proclaims'.*
14		*Now there were seven sons of a Jewish high priest named Sceva who were doing this.*
15	CLIMAX:	*But the evil spirit said to them in reply, 'Jesus I know, and Paul I know, but who are you?' (16) Then the man with the evil spirit leaped on them, mastered them all, and so overpowered them that they fled out of the house naked and wounded.*

Backgrounding the event(s) that immediately precede the climax

The Inga folktale presented in 5.1 included an example (sent. 7) of the **backgrounding** of the event that immediately precedes the climactic event. The same phenomenon is found in Podoko. I cited in 5.2.3 Jarvis' claim, "Background material uses the focus perfective for events that took place prior to that point on the event line". Sentences b and c of the following extract from a folktale (see Jarvis 1991:235 for the Podoko text) use the "focus perfective" to background the events that take place immediately before the climactic event of sentence d:

a		*Now they caught Squirrel.*
b		*When Squirrel said, 'Let me escape to the termite hill', they quickly* FOCUS-*grabbed his feet.*
c		*They* FOCUS-*knocked him over on the ground and hit him.*
d	CLIMAX:	*They untied the baby on his back and all the jewellery.*

In the following passage from Hebrew (1 Samuel 17:35), imperfective *wqtl* forms present a series of events that were done repeatedly in the past. However, the act performed by the wild animal that leads to the climactic event performed by *ego* uses a perfective *wyyqtl* form (the English translation captures the intended effect with a subordinate clause: "When it turned on me"):

35	**wəyaṣa'tî**	'aḥarayw	wəhikkitîw	wəhiṣṣaltî	mippîw
	& I went out	after him	& I struck him	& I delivered	from his mouth
	wayyaqom	'alay	wəheḥezaqtî	bizqanô	wəhikkitîw	wahamîtîw
	& he rose	against me	& I seized	by his beard	& I struck him	& I killed him

'I would go (*wqtl*) after it, strike (*wqtl*) it and rescue (*wqtl*) the sheep from its mouth. When it turned (*wyyqtl*) on me, I would seize (*wqtl*) it by its hair, strike (*wqtl*) it and kill (*wqtl*) it.'

Other slowing-down devices

In addition to the rhetorical devices described above, other devices **slow down** the narrative immediately before a climax or significant development (some of them occur at the beginning of the climactic sentence itself). They include:
- a conjunction or referential connective, in languages that use these sparsely
- tail-head linkage instead of the default means of conjoining (see 3.2.3)
- heavy participant encoding (see ch. 8)
- a review of past events that led up to the climax.
  For example, Revelation 5:3 (*But no one in heaven or on earth or under the earth could open the scroll or look inside it*) is reviewed in 4 (*I wept and wept because no one was found who was worthy to open the scroll or look inside*), prior to the climactic events of 5ff. (see discussion in 3.2.3).

5.4 Highlighting of sentences 83

Further highlighting devices

Other highlighting devices include:
- a prominence marker attached to a point of departure or connective (see 4.6.2). For example, the use of an *it*-cleft structure in English (4.9) to give prominence to a point of departure by renewal and thereby highlight what follows, as in *It was there that disaster struck*.
- a change of tense, aspect or agent orientation (e.g. from *go* to *come* – see ch. 9)
- a change in sentence length
- a change in the way speech is reported (e.g. from indirect to direct – see ch. 7)
- increased frequency of ideophones and other dramatic features.

The following free translation of the end of a folktale in the Karai Karai [kai] (alt. Karekare; Chadic, Nigeria) language illustrates the use of a change of **aspect** as a highlighting device. The default form for theme-line events has no aspectual marker (indicated by Ø in sents. a–c). The events leading up to the climax have imperfective aspect (IMPF – sents. d–e), but the climactic event itself (sent. f) is in the perfect (PER):

a		and so	he [Cat]	bent-Ø his head towards Cock [to feel the coxcomb].
b		Where Cat touched-PER, then	he	felt-Ø them like liver.
c		Then	Cat	said-Ø, 'So that's your thing, is it? It's nice to touch …'
d	PRECLIMAX:		Cat	was talking (IMPF)
e	PRECLIMAX:		Saliva	was leaking (IMPF) from his mouth.
f	CLIMAX:	Before Cock could do anything,	Cat	**finished**-PER **swallowed**-PER Cock's coxcomb,
g	END OF STORY:	[and]		was licking (IMPF) his lips.

Another highlighting device that is more often found in behavioural texts (including reported speeches) is the **repetition** of important, focal information (see Speece 1989 and Levinsohn 2015, 5.4).

The point about the above list of devices associated with highlighting is that they are noteworthy because they are **different from the norm**. For instance, the presence of a conjunction is significant because it is NOT normally used; the presence of ideophones is significant because they are NOT normally so frequent, etc.

It is therefore very important that you identify what are the norms or default forms, so that you can recognise when a marked form has been used. For instance, before claiming that a change in sentence length is significant, you need to know what sentence length is typical. This in turn implies that you have worked on many texts and have seen the device used on a number of occasions.

5.4.2 Highlighting significant developments and changes of direction

Key events that change the direction of a narrative or are otherwise of particular significance to the outworking or purpose of the story are generally highlighted in some way. Some of the same devices used to highlight climactic events may be used, such as tail head linkage (e.g. *Now, while he was going, who do you think came round the corner but …*). In the Bekwarra text (see appendix C in chapter 2), the **problem** presented in sentence 9 is highlighted both by the use of the imperfective and by the exceptional length of the sentence.

Backgrounding the event that immediately precedes the significant development. One way of giving prominence to a significant development is to background the event that immediately precedes it. Typically, the backgrounded event is expected (e.g. if one squanders one's property, one will eventually have spent everything). A pragmatic effect of backgrounding such an event is to highlight what follows.

In Kangri [xnr] (Indo-Aryan, India), for example, relative clauses of time or cause are used to background the event that precedes a significant development. Prior to the sentence given below, an old woman has persuaded the miller to grind some grain for her, and gives him her sack.

The event expressed in the relative clause (opening the sack and looking inside) is one that would be expected:

> *[The] time that he opened and looked, he saw it was sand!*

One device used in Koine Greek to background the event that immediately precedes a significant development is by means of a participial clause called the **genitive absolute** (GA – in which both the subject and the participle are in the genitive case). GAs in Koine Greek have a different subject from the clause to which they are subordinated. Sentence-initial GAs with the **same subject** as that of the **previous** main clause are used to highlight the **following** main clause, which will describe a significant event involving a different subject. In Luke 15:14, for instance, the GA has the same subject as the previous sentence. By using the GA, the famine is highlighted.[26]

13b and there he squandered his property in dissolute living.

14   **When he had spent everything** [lit. *having.spent of.him everything*], *a severe famine took place throughout that country.*

Another way of highlighting significant developments is by means of a **special marker or construction**. In Koine Greek and Biblical Hebrew, a word traditionally translated as 'it came to pass' (followed by an adverbial phrase or clause of time) marks the transition from less to more important events.

In Hebrew, the word concerned is **wayyəhî**, which occurs twice in the following extract from Genesis 4:1–8. *Wayyəhî* in 3a marks the transition from background information to the "inciting event" (Van der Merwe 1999:114) of the story. In 8b, it introduces a climactic event.[27]

1–2 *Adam lay with his wife Eve, and she became pregnant and gave birth to Cain. She said, 'I have brought forth a man with the help of the LORD'. Later she gave birth to his brother Abel. Now Abel was a shepherd, and Cain was a tiller of the ground.*

3–8a **Wayyəhî** <u>in the course of time</u> *Cain brought some of the fruits of the soil as an offering to the LORD and Abel brought fat portions from some of the firstborn of his flock. The LORD looked with favour on Abel and his offering, but on Cain and his offering he did not look with favour. So Cain was very angry, and his face was downcast. Then the LORD said to Cain, 'Why are you angry? Why is your face downcast? If you do what is right, will you not be accepted? But if you do not do what is right, sin is crouching at your door; it desires to have you, but you must master it.' Now Cain spoke to his brother Abel.*

8b   **Wayyəhî** <u>while they were in the field,</u> *Cain attacked his brother Abel and killed him.*

The equivalent word in Greek is **egeneto**. In Acts 9:37, *egeneto* (plus a temporal point of departure) marks the transition from background information to the first significant event of the story:[28]

36   *Now in Joppa there was a disciple whose name was Tabitha, which in Greek is Dorcas. She was devoted to good works and acts of charity.*

37   **Egeneto** <u>at that time</u> *she became ill and died.*

The equivalent of *it came to pass* in many Indian languages is the expression *what happened*; e.g. *After that, one day what happened (was that) the village people heard (about the tiger)* (Ho [hoc]; Munda, India).

---

[26] In English, one appropriate way to highlight an event is to express it in a **postnuclear** subordinate clause (see fn. 12 in 5.2.4). For example, "He had spent it all **when a severe famine fell upon that country**" (Luke 15:14 NEB).

[27] Van der Merwe's article includes a valuable summary of previous observations about *wayyəhî* plus a temporal expression. For example, he notes Schneider's (1982:251–252) claim that such expressions 'provide the bridge between the introduction and the main section of narrative' (p. 89) and 'highlight the main event(s) of a narrative' (p. 90).

[28] See Levinsohn 2015, 5.4, for discussion of highlighting devices used in non-narrative passages (including reported speeches) in Koine Greek and Hebrew. See ch. 12 of Levinsohn 2000 for other devices used for highlighting in Greek.

A word traditionally translated '**lo, behold**' is used in Hebrew and Greek to highlight the information that immediately follows. This is illustrated in Exodus 4:6, where Hebrew **wəhinneh** highlights the state of his [Moses'] hand:[29]

6   *Again, the* LORD *said to him, 'Put your hand inside your cloak'. He put his hand into his cloak and he took it out,* **wəhinneh** *his hand [was] leprous like the snow.*

In Matthew 2:9b, Greek ***idou*** highlights the reappearance of the star:

9a   *When they had heard the king, they set out;*

9b   *and* **idou** *the star that they had seen at its rising went ahead of them until it stopped over the place where the child was.*

One way of highlighting key **speeches** is by means of a cataphoric expression (e.g. *He said* **as follows**) or by spreading the introduction of the speech over two clauses (e.g. *He asked them a question. The question was …*).

Review question

What are five devices that are used to slow down a narrative immediately before a climax or significant development?[30]

Application to the language you are analysing

Look for highlighting devices in your texts. Which devices are used to highlight both climaxes and significant developments? Which devices highlight only climaxes or only significant developments?

Suggested reading

Chapters 12 "Foreground and Background Information" and 15 "Conventionalized Aspects of Text Organization" of Dooley and Levinsohn 2001 relate to the topics covered in this chapter.

---

[29] "*Hinnēh* draws attention to a proposition indicating that it is important or salient in the given context" (Follingstad 1995:22). Sim (2010) considers *hinnēh* to be an 'interpretive-use' marker (see 7.10 of this course) which, in this instance, indicates that the event is presented from the point of view of the experiencer.

[30] **Suggested answer:**
The following five devices slow down a narrative immediately before a climax or significant development:
- the introduction of nonevent (background) information immediately before the event to be highlighted
- a conjunction or referential connective, in languages that use these sparsely
- tail-head linkage instead of the default means of conjoining
- heavy participant encoding
- a review of past events that led up to the climax.

example from Arop-Lokep [apr] (Austronesian, Papua New Guinea), which uses the conjunction *a*:
So then the two of them followed that river **and** (*a*) *went inland.*
In other words, the two of them went inland following that river.
- **Distinctive**: the events described by the conjoined propositions are distinct. In the following example from the same Arop-Lokep story, the conjunction used is *inbe*:
They went inland **and** (*inbe*) *their eyes went up to the edge of the riverbed.*

Questions about the charted Bekwarra text (chapter 2, appendix C: Bekwarra text)

1. What is the default way of conjoining sentences in the text? (Look at the prenuclear column.)
2. When is a sentence-initial intersentential conjunction used in the text? [2]

Application to the language you are analysing

What is the default way of conjoining sentences in your narrative texts: juxtaposition or a connective? If the latter, which connective is the default one?

6.2 Pragmatic connectives

This section considers Reboul and Moeschler's (1998) definition of a connective. Sections 6.3–6.5 will discuss three specific types of pragmatic connective: those that require an additive interpretation, those that require a countering interpretation, and those that require a developmental interpretation.

What do connectives do? They guide and **limit** the way the material they introduce is processed in the light of the context. The following is my translation, with modifications, of Reboul and Moeschler's (1998:77) definition of a connective:

> A **connective**[3] is a linguistic marker, drawn from a number of grammatical categories (coordinating conjunctions [e.g. *but*], subordinating conjunctions [*since*], adverbs [*thus*], adverbial expressions [*after all*]), which
> a) links a linguistic or discourse unit of any **size** to its context;
> b) gives instructions as to **how** to relate this unit to its context; and
> c) requires conclusions to be drawn on the basis of this discourse connection **that might not have been drawn had it been absent.**

Now for some observations on the above definition.
a) One cannot tell the **size** of the unit being linked from the connective itself. The Greek connective *gar* 'for' indicates that what follows strengthens the material that immediately precedes it. However, one cannot tell from the presence of *gar* how far the strengthening material will extends.

Thus, in the extract below (1 Timothy 4:7b–8), *gar* indicates that what follows strengthens the command of verse 7b, but does not indicate how far this strengthening material extends. In fact, the strengthening material extends over two clauses (8a–b), but this is not indicated by *gar* (see 6.4 and 6.5.3 on the function of the connective *de*).

7b *Teach yourself to be godly.*

8a *The* **gar** *physical training is of some value.*

8b *The* **de** *godliness has value for all things.*

---

[2] **Suggested answers**: about the charted Bekwarra text:
1. The default way of conjoining sentences in the text is by juxtaposition.
2. The only time a sentence-initial intersentential conjunction is used in the text is to introduce sentence 10, at a point of discontinuity. (The function of the verb phrase particle *kà* will be discussed in 6.5.5.)
[3] Reboul and Moeschler's definition includes the adjective 'pragmatic'. I have omitted the word as I am not trying here to distinguish 'pragmatic' connectives from other sorts of connectives.

b) The presence of *gar* in the above extract guides or **constrains** the reader to interpret what follows (8a–b) as strengthening the immediately preceding material (7b). Each connective places a **different** constraint on the way the material it introduces is to be related to its context.[4]

c) The presence of the connective requires conclusions to be drawn **that might not have been drawn had it been absent**. This is illustrated in the following extract from the *NIV* translation of Romans 8:17–18. Although the translation does not show it, *gar* introduces 18. Failure to translate *gar* (e.g. by "After all"), together with the presence of a title, means that the reader is unlikely to draw the conclusion that 18 is strengthening 17, even though the presence of *gar* indicates that it is!

17 *Now if we are children, then we are heirs – heirs of God and co-heirs with Christ, provided we share in his sufferings in order that we may also share in his glory.*

Future Glory

18 *I consider that our present sufferings are not worth comparing with the glory that will be revealed in us.*

Blass (1990:126) says that connectives "facilitate the interpretation process by, on the one hand, economising on processing effort, and, on the other hand, decreasing the risk of misunderstanding". She continues:

> Imagine we had to interpret two utterances of a discourse. Without any further information, we would be faced with the problem of discovering not only how each one is relevant, but also whether/how each of them is related to the other. (1990:127)

To illustrate this point, consider the following extract from Koine Greek (Mark 13:21–22), but with the connective for 22 omitted (I chose this example because some manuscripts have *gar* and others, *de*):

21 *If anyone says to you at that time, 'Look! Here is the Messiah!' or 'Look! There he is!' – do not believe it.*
22 *False messiahs and false prophets will appear and will produce signs and omens, to lead astray, if possible, the elect.*

In the absence of a connective to introduce 22, the reader is unsure how to relate it to 21. Is it intended to strengthen 21 (the relation constrained by *gar*) or is it a new point in the argument (the relation constrained by *de*)?

Review question

According to Reboul and Moeschler, what are three tasks of a connective?[5]

The next sections concern connectives that constrain three specific pragmatic relationships: addition, countering and development.

6.3 Connectives that constrain an additive interpretation

This section discusses connectives such as *also, too, as well, furthermore* and *moreover* which guide or constrain the hearer or reader to add what follows to corresponding material in the context.[6] One

---
[4] Blakemore (2002:184) refers to "clusters of discourse connectives with similar (but not identical) meanings".
[5] **Suggested answer**:
According to Reboul and Moeschler, the following are three tasks of a connective:
a) to link a linguistic or discourse unit of any **size** to its context
b) to give instructions as to **how** to relate this unit to its context
c) to constrain conclusions to be drawn on the basis of this discourse connection **that might not have been drawn had it been absent**.
[6] On additives or "inclusives" as "focus particles", in contrast with "exclusive (restrictive) particles" such as *only*, see König 1991:33. In some languages, the same expression is used both as an additive and as a coordinating

reason for looking in some detail at additives is because they are used in significantly different ways in different languages.

The section begins with ways in which additives involving **parallelism** between propositions have been found to differ in the same language (6.3.1). It then considers the varied pragmatic effects that one and the same additive may convey in different contexts, including occasions when the material that is added **confirms** a previous statement or assumption (6.3.2). Finally, it discusses default versus marked **positions** for additives (6.3.3).

6.3.1 Ways in which additives involving parallelism between propositions have been found to differ in the same language

Additives like *also* are used "to encourage a search for parallelisms" (Blass 1990:145). Consider the following excerpt from Dorothy Sayers' novel, *The Documents in the Case*:[7]

> I looked into the cupboard. In it there was a large cottage-loaf, uncut. On the table was another ... [There follows a long sentence about the two loaves.] The cupboard also contained about a pound of shin of beef ... (Sayers 1989:124–125)

"In the above extract, *also* instructs the reader to find a parallel with some previous proposition or assumption. In this instance, the reader finds a parallel in earlier statements, 'I looked into the cupboard. In it there was a large cottage-loaf, uncut.'" (Levinsohn 2001b:4).

The following distinctions involving parallelism between propositions have been found in some languages between DIFFERENT *also*-type additives (marked with **ADD**).

- One additive is used when the added proposition has a different **subject** but the same or similar predicate as before: *Bill has a computer. Susan* ADD *has one*. A different additive is used when the added proposition has a different **predicate** but the same subject as before: *Bill is good at sports. He is* ADD *a good linguist.*

    In Gude, for example, *boo* is used when the added proposition has a different subject but the same or similar predicate. In contrast, *ésé* is used when the added proposition has a different predicate but the same subject (Levinsohn 2002:176–177 cites examples from Perrin n.d.).

- The default additive is used when the added proposition is **similar** to what has already been presented. A different additive is used when the added proposition is the **same** in certain respects.

    Such is the case in the Bwamu [box] (Gur, Burkina Faso) language. One folktale describes Hyena out walking and, on a later occasion, Monkey out walking. Because the events take place on different occasions, the additive *bén* is used to indicate the parallelism between them. Had they been out walking on the same occasion, the additive *mún* would have been used.

    The two additives may be used together. In another Bwamu folktale, Dog is courting a girl. The storyteller then informs his audience, 'That same girl, Hyena *bén mún* was courting her'. The additive *bén* is used to append a parallel proposition with the same predicate but a different subject. The additive *mún* adds the idea of sameness: both actions took place on the same occasion.

- One additive is used when what is added is a distinct **constituent** with part of the proposition unchanged. A different additive is used when a distinct **proposition** is added.

    The following examples contrast two additives in Koine Greek. Nonconjunctive *kai* adds a distinct constituent to a corresponding constituent in the context, whereas *te* adds a distinct proposition.[8] In Acts 21:16a, *kai* adds the **constituent** *some of the disciples from Caesarea* to *we* (15); all the referents travelled to Jerusalem together (see 6.5.3 for the function of *de* in 16a):

---

conjunction (1991:65–66 – see Levinsohn 2000:125 on Greek *kai* and 2000:102ff. for evidence that the constituent modified by the additive *kai* is not necessarily focal). See Levinsohn 2002 for a preliminary typology of additives.

[7] The paragraphs concerning the three extracts from Sayers' novel are taken from Levinsohn 2002:172, 179.

[8] *Kai* is also used to add propositions that **confirm** a previous proposition (see 6.3.2). Propositions added by *te* "are characterized by *sameness*, in the sense that they refer to different aspects of the same event, the same occasion, or the same pragmatic unit" (Levinsohn 2000:106–107).

6.3 Connectives that constrain an additive interpretation

15   *After these days we got ready and started to go up to Jerusalem.*

16a   *Travelled* **de kai** *some of the disciples from Caesarea with us.*

In Acts 21:18b, *te* adds the proposition *all the elders were present* to the proposition of 18a; the elders are not added to *Paul with us* as people who went to [visit] James. Rather, they were there with James on the same occasion that we visited him:

18a   *The next day Paul went with us to [visit] James;*

18b   *all* **te** *the elders were present.*

- The default additive is used when the relative **status** of the adjoined propositions is **unspecified**. A different additive is used when what is added is **more important** than or **at least as important** as the item to which it is being added.

   Too is the default additive in English, whereas *also* indicates that the added material is at least as important as that to which it is added. This is illustrated in the following extract from a court scene. *Also* adds a second symptom of poisoning by muscarine that is just as relevant to the question as the first.

   > *What would be the symptoms of poisoning by muscarine?*
   > *– They vary in different cases. Generally speaking, a sensation of acute sickness would be experienced almost immediately after the meal, followed by violent vomiting and diarrhoea. There might also be a feeling of suffocation and dizziness, sometimes accompanied by blindness.* (Sayers 1989:141–142)

   When *too* is used to append information, in contrast, there is no guarantee that the information concerned is of equal relevance; it may be of more or of less importance than the material to which it is appended. In the following extract, for instance, the reference to women is **incidental** to the rest of the sentence:

   > *Like most men, and women, too, when left to themselves, I [masc.] found solitary meals uninspiring.* (Sayers 1989:113)

   Similarly, an additive may be used rather than the default **conjunction** to suggest that the units so linked are of **unequal relevance**. In the Greek of John 6:18, the pragmatic effect of using the additive *te* instead of the conjunction *kai* is to suggest that the added proposition is of particular significance (English might use 'Furthermore'):

16   *When evening came, his disciples went down to the sea*

17a   **kai** *having got into a boat, started across the sea to Capernaum*

17b   **kai** *it had become dark*

17c   **kai** *Jesus had not yet come to them*

18   *the* **te** *sea was becoming roused because a strong wind was blowing.*

Review question

What are four ways in which additives involving parallelism between propositions have been found to differ?[9]

---

[9] **Suggested answer:**
Additives involving parallelism between propositions have been found to differ in the following four ways:
- One additive is used when the added proposition has a different **subject** but the same or similar predicate as before. A different additive is used when the added proposition has a different **predicate** but the same subject.
- The default additive is used when the added proposition is **similar** to what has already been presented. A different additive is used when the added proposition is the **same** in certain respects.
- One additive is used when what is added is a **distinct constituent** with part of the proposition unchanged. A different additive is used when a **distinct proposition** is added.

Application to the language you are analysing

If more than one additive occurs, check whether any of the above distinctions helps to distinguish them.

6.3.2 The varied pragmatic effects that the same additive may convey in different contexts

The SAME additive may convey different pragmatic effects in different contexts. The following paragraphs describe the most common ones.

- **Confirmation**. A number of languages use the same additive not only when some parallelism is to be discerned, but also to confirm a previous statement or assumption. The following example involves the additive *má* in Sissala [sid] (Gur, Burkina Faso) (Blass 1990:135). *Má* is here translated 'Indeed' because English does not use *also* for confirmation.

    Speaker A: *Zimpeale is a Dagaati.*
    Speaker B: ADD *he is; I know him* … (i.e. **Indeed** *he is, I know him.*)

    It is common in some languages for an additive to be used for confirmation in **stimulus-response** situations when the "response proposition … is anticipated by the stimulus, fulfills the conditions of the stimulus, or is closely associated with the stimulus" (Follingstad 1994:168). The following example is from the folktale in the Tyap [kcg] (Plateau, Nigeria) language that is cited in 6.5.1.

    He said that she could pass. The woman ADD *passed.*
    'He told her she could pass. So she did so.'[10]

- Confirmation by adding **the least likely possibility** (see Blass 1990:152–153). This is illustrated in the following example from Greek. The additive *kai* appends the least likely member of the set of all things that one might be able to examine, in order to confirm that the Spirit truly examines **all** things. In contrast, English uses the "scalar additive" *even* (König 1991:68):

    the for Spirit all.things examines ADD *the depths of.the God*
    'For the Spirit examines all things, **even** the depths of God.' (1 Corinthians 2:10b)

    A related instance of confirmation involves what Blass (pp. 1990:151–152) calls **pseudo-relatives**. In Inga, for instance, the effect of appending the additive *-pas* to an indefinite pronoun such as *ima* 'thing' is to include (or exclude) even the least likely thing (see also König pp. 1991:66–68). English would translate the combination *ima-pas* 'anything whatever' or, following a negative, 'nothing whatever'.

- **Concession**. A number of languages use additives to append a proposition that counters a previous proposition (English would use *However* or *although*). The following example involves the additive *kîî* in Bafut (see Mfonyam 1994:199):

    Jacob is banging at Joshua's door. ADD *Joshua slept.*
    'Jacob was banging at Joshua's door. However, Joshua slept on.'

The third of Reboul and Moeschler's tasks for a connective was to constrain conclusions to be drawn on the basis of this discourse connection that might not have been drawn had it been absent (6.2). This task provides a **motivation** for choosing an additive; namely, to **add** a proposition when it would otherwise be interpreted as a new development (discussed in 6.5) or as in contrast with respect to the previous one.

For instance, the propositions of Genesis 4:3–4a would be interpreted as being in contrast (see 6.4), were it not for the presence of the Hebrew additive *gam*: In other words, the presence of *gam* "cancel[s] the contrastive connotations" (Blakemore 1987:99).

- The default additive is used when the relative status of the adjoined propositions is **unspecified**. A different additive is used when what is added is **more important** than or **at least as important** as the item to which it is being added.

[10] See 7.5.3 on the tendency for languages to associate together proposals and their execution.

3   *In the course of time Cain brought some of the fruits of the soil as an offering to YHWH.*

4a *Abel, brought* **ADD**-*he fat portions from some of the firstborn of his flock.*

Review questions

1. In some languages, the same particle can be translated into English 'also', 'so', 'indeed' and 'even', depending on the context. What does this suggest?
2. In some languages, a particle which is clearly additive in some contexts seems to mean 'but' in others. What does this suggest?[11]

6.3.3 Default and marked positions for additives

It is important to establish the default position of each additive, so that deviations from the norm (marked positions) can be recognised. Here are some examples from English.

- The default position of *too* is at the end of the clause. As we saw in previous chapters, when placed in a marked position **earlier** in the sentence, *too* acts as a spacer, setting off a point of departure (3.1) or dominant focal element (DFE – 4.2.4).
- In contrast, the default position of *also* is immediately preceding the main verb (Taglicht 1984:82 – e.g. *John [has] also phoned Mary*). When placed in a marked position **later** in the sentence, it also sets off DFEs (as in *He invited also his wife's cousin Jane* – p. 83).

In many languages, additives occur **next** to the constituent that is being added to a corresponding constituent of the context.

- In a **VO** language, the additive is most likely to **precede** the constituent that is being added:

    (Greek)   **kai** *the depths of.the God*   '**even** the depths of God' (1 Corinthians 2:10b)

    (Hebrew)   *Abel, brought* **gam**-*he fat portions from some of the firstborn of his flock.* (Genesis 4:4a)

- In an **OV** language, the additive is most likely to **follow** the constituent that is being added:

    (Inga)   *ima-***pas**   [thing-ADD]   'anything whatever'.

When adding a whole **proposition**, additives typically occur **early** in the proposition:

(English)   ***Also**, he seemed quite delighted about the whole thing …* (Sayers 1989:38)

(Greek)   *the* **te** *sea was becoming roused because a strong wind was blowing.* (John 6:18)

(Hebrew)   ***Gam** you must allow us to have sacrifices and burnt offerings to present to the* LORD *our God.* (Exodus 10:25b)

Application to the language you are analysing

1. If more than one additive is found, distinguish their functions. Which of the above pragmatic effects does each additive convey?
2. What is the default position of each additive? What is its function when in other positions?

---

[11] **Suggested answers:**
1. If the same particle can be translated into English as 'also', 'so', 'indeed' and 'even', depending on the context, this suggests that it is an additive which is used not only for parallelism between propositions, but also to confirm a previous statement or assumption, for example by adding the least likely possibility.
2. If a particle which is clearly additive in some contexts seems to mean 'but' in others, this suggests that it is being used to group sentences together and cancel contrastive connotations. (See also 6.5.2.)

6.4 Connectives that constrain a countering interpretation

If a particular connective constrains a countering interpretation, then it will **always** introduce material that counters some event or expectation.[12] If it appears that the connective sometimes introduces countering material and sometimes does not, then the following are possibilities:
- the analyst is overlooking some expectation that the material is countering; OR
- the connective does not in fact constrain a countering interpretation. It is more likely to be an additive (grouping material together – see 6.3.2) or a development marker (see 6.5).

In Koine Greek, for example, *de* is NOT a countering connective, even though it is often translated 'but', because it is not always used for countering (see Levinsohn 2000:112–117 on this point).[13] In contrast, *alla* is a countering connective, even though it is not always translated 'but'. For example, in Philippians 1:18 (*And because of this I will rejoice.* **Alla** *I will continue to rejoice*), *alla* indicates that *I will continue to rejoice* is contrary to what one would have expected in the circumstances, yet it cannot be translated 'but'. Rather, a rendering such as 'Yes and' (*NRSV*) is needed.

The countering connective in the Lobala [loq] (Bantoid; Democratic Republic of Congo) language is *ka* (Morgan 1994). In many sentences, it can be translated 'but', as the following exchange illustrates; speaker B asks a question that counters the statement made by speaker A:[14]

> Speaker A: *I've no plans to go to X.*
>
> Speaker B: **ka** *you and I, aren't we going there next week?*

Now consider the following pair of sentences, in which *ka* cannot be translated 'but':

> Reported Speaker: *'Scrape your hands with this knife!'*
>
> **ka** *with the hunger he felt, Monkey was not able to refuse.*

Since *ka* is a countering connective, it constrains the hearer to recognise an expectation that is being countered by the following action. In this particular instance, the demand that Monkey scrape his hands with a knife before eating is so unreasonable that one would have expected him to refuse.

The following subsections consider mismatches between languages in encoding countering relations and factors that may determine when a countering relation is marked or left implicit.

6.4.1 Encoding countering relations in specific contexts

A common error in translation is to insert a countering connective (at times, borrowed from the *lingua franca* of the area) when the natural way to encode the relation in the receptor language is different. The following paragraphs note alternative ways of encoding countering relations in specific contexts.

Double-difference contrast. This occurs when two propositions have a point of similarity and two points of contrast (Longacre 1996:55; Mann and Thompson 1987:8). Consider the following propositions:

> *You'll be in the water,* **but** *I'll be in the bush.*

The above propositions are in double-difference contrast because they have a point of similarity (*Someone will be in some place*) and two points of contrast (*you* versus *I* and *water* versus *bush*).

In some languages, it is not natural to use any countering connective in cases of double-difference contrast. In the Mono [mnh] (Ubangi, Democratic Republic of Congo) language, for instance, the same effect is achieved by **left dislocation** of the contrasting subject:

---

[12] The 'newly presented proposition … may lead to the abandoning of an existing assumption' (Blakemore 1987:53).

[13] *De* constrains a developmental interpretation – 6.5.3.

[14] Most of the examples of this section are taken from non-narrative material. I have included them in this chapter because of the need to contrast countering markers with those that constrain an additive or developmental interpretation.

6.4 Connectives that constrain a countering interpretation

> *When the day comes,   you'll   be in the water.*
> ***Me**, I'll   be in the bush.*

Replacing focus (see 4.4). In some languages, it is not natural to use any countering connective when the second proposition involves the replacement of an earlier constituent by another. Rather, **juxtaposition** is the norm. So, instead of *He didn't go to X, but to Y*, one might find:

> *He didn't go to X. Ø he went to Y.*

In the Dogosé/Khissé language, replacing focus is achieved by juxtaposition and **preposing** the constituent concerned:[15]

> *He didn't go to X. **To Y** he went.*

Contrasting predicates. When predicates are in contrast, as in the sentence *I wanted him to visit you, **but** he stayed*, natural ways of encoding the second proposition in African languages include:

(Mambila, Bantoid)	(*I wanted him to visit you.*)	*He stayed **turned** + **VERB FOCUS**.*
(Kako [kkj], Bantu A)	"	*He **returned** stayed.*
(Mbuko [mqb], Chadic)	"	*He stayed, **however**.*
(Kera [ker], Chadic)	"	***Doloy*** (onomatopoetic word for surprise) *he stayed.*

For example, the following extract is from a hortatory text in Dogosé/Khissé:

> (*You are still in your sins.*)   *Jesus **returns** calls you because he loves you.*
>   (i.e. ***But*** *Jesus calls you because he loves you.*)

In addition, some languages use juxtaposition plus negation of the first proposition before presenting the contrast:

> (*I wanted him to visit you.*)   ***He didn't** (visit you). He stayed.*

Contrasting actions. When actions are in contrast, as in *I'm not washing clothes, **but** eating*, natural ways of encoding the second proposition include:

(Mambila)	(*I'm not washing clothes.*)	*I eat* + **VERB FOCUS**
(Kako)	"	*I'm eating **eating*** (**nominalised verb**)
(Chadic)	*I'm eating; I'm not washing clothes.*	(**POSITIVE-negative with juxtaposition**)
(Kenyang [ken])	*Don't clear-clear the grass; cut it …*	(**negative counterpoint + main point**)

Contrasting adjuncts. In a narrative example from Gude, the speaker wished to communicate, *Father said, 'Throw the grass on the river bank'. **But** the child threw it behind him*. To do so, the noncontrastive part of the second proposition was **left-dislocated** (*ma* = marker of nominal points of departure):

> *Father says, 'Go throw grass onto river bank'.*
> [***Ma** INFINITIVE child throw*], *he throws behind him.*

Concessive. When a concessive relation exists between two propositions, as in *It's market day, **but** there aren't many people here*, many languages use an **additive** (see 6.3.2). For example, natural ways of encoding the second proposition include:

(Bafut)	(*It's market day.*)	***Also*** *there aren't many people here.*
(Mambila)	"	***Even with this*** *there aren't many people here.*

---

[15] I am grateful to Lassina Ouatara and Graeme Lawson (p.c.) for the examples from Dogosé/Khissé.

6.4.2 Factors that may determine when a countering relation is marked or left implicit

Particularly in languages that rarely use a countering connective, the following are some factors that may determine **when** a countering relation is marked or is left implicit.

- The **default** way of expressing the relation may be to leave it implicit, so that the countering relation is conveyed only by the content of the propositions concerned. The relation is marked only when it would otherwise be **unclear** or to **draw attention** to it.

    Under such circumstances, care must be taken not to make a relation explicit when to do so would produce the wrong effect. An early draft of Luke 2:19 in one African language began with a countering connective (**But** *Mary treasured up all these things and pondered them in her heart* – NIV). The effect was to draw an explicit contrast with the events described in the previous verse (*all who heard it were amazed at what the shepherds said to them*). This implied that Mary was NOT amazed at what the shepherds said! The translation has been changed!

- In some languages, certain relations are only made explicit when the proposition being introduced is **more important** than the preceding one. In Dogosé/Khissé, the auxiliary verb *return* (see above) is used only when the proposition concerned is more important than the one being countered. Otherwise, no countering connective occurs. In the following extract, for instance, *They are not all bad children* is not the main point, so no connective is used, even though the proposition counters what the mother says. Rather, the THESIS occurs later (*but some are normal*).

    (If a child is born at a certain time, the mother) *will say, 'I've given birth to a bad child'.*

    Ø *They are not all bad children. Some are; some* ***return*** *are normal.*

- When one proposition of a contrastive pair is POSITIVE and the other one is negative, the **order** of the propositions may well affect the connective used. Roberts (1997:29) found the following correlation between the order of the verb (V) and the object (O), on the one hand, and the order of the POSITIVE and negative propositions, on the other:

    Table 8. Constituent order and propositional order correlations

Constituent order	Preferred propositional order
VO	POSITIVE–negative
OV	negative–POSITIVE

    Although the above correlations reflect the preferred order of propositions, most languages also allow them to be put in the opposite order. Often, however, the preferred or default order uses the default means of conjoining, whereas the marked order needs a marked connective:

    Table 9. Propositional order and means of conjoining correlations

Propositional order	Means of conjoining
default/preferred	default
marked	marked connective

    This is illustrated with the POSITIVE-negative correlation in Koine Greek and English (VO). When the propositions occur in their preferred order, the default connective (*kai* 'and') is used. When they occur in the opposite order, a marked connective (*alla* 'but') is required:

    default order: *Allow the children to come to me*   **kai/***and do not prevent them!* (Luke 18:16)
    marked order: *Lead us not into temptation*   **alla/***but deliver us from evil!* (Matthew 6:13)

    The converse is found in Konso [kxc] (Cushitic, Ethiopia) – OV. When the default negative-POSITIVE order occurs, the default connective ***ka*** is used. When the marked POSITIVE-negative order occurs, the marked connective ***umma*** is used. (However, POSITIVE-connective-negative is the preferred order in a number of Ethiopian OV languages, including Amharic [amh] (Semitic, Ethiopia).)

6.4.3 Application to Koine Greek

A number of connectives are used to link propositions in a countering relationship. The following factors enable the most common ones (*alla*, *kai*, and *de*) to be distinguished.

- When the first proposition of the pair is **negative** and the second **positive**, then the DEFAULT way of conjoining them is with *alla*, as in 1 Thess. 5:6:
  So then, let us not be like others, who are asleep, **alla** *let us be alert and self-controlled.*
- Otherwise, when the propositions in a countering relationship are more or less of **equal importance**, the default conjunction *kai* occurs, as in Luke 1:52:
  He has brought down rulers from their thrones **kai** *has lifted up the humble.*
- This includes occasions when the first proposition is POSITIVE and the second negative, as in Luke 18:16: *Allow the children to come to me* **kai** *do not prevent them!*
- To MARK the second proposition in a countering relationship as **more important** than the first, the development marker *de* is used (see 6.5.3), as in 1 Timothy 4:8:
  For physical training is of some value, the **de** *godliness has value for all things.*

Review questions

1. If it appears that a connective sometimes introduces countering material and sometimes does not, what are two possible explanations?
2. If a countering connective is rarely used in natural texts, what three factors may determine when a countering relation is marked or is left implicit?[16]

Application to the language you are analysing

1. Look for instances of countering relations in your texts, including examples where the relation is left implicit.
2. If more than one countering connective occurs, then distinguish their functions.
3. Under what circumstances is the countering relation normally left implicit?

6.5 Particles that constrain a developmental interpretation

Some particles that introduce distinctive information (6.1) may be used to "constrain the reader to *move on to the next point* … they indicate that the material so marked represents a new development in the story or argument, as far as the author's purpose is concerned" (Dooley and Levinsohn 2001:93).[17]

---

[16] **Suggested answers:**
1. If it appears that a connective sometimes introduces countering material and sometimes does not, the following are possible explanations:
   - the analyst is overlooking some expectation that the material is countering; OR
   - the connective does not in fact constrain a countering interpretation. It is more likely to be an additive or development marker.
2. The following factors may determine when a countering relation is marked or left implicit:
   - The default way of expressing the relation is to leave it implicit. The relation is marked only when it would otherwise be unclear or to draw attention to it.
   - The relation is only made explicit when the proposition being introduced is more important than what precedes.
   - When a countering relation exists between a POSITIVE and a negative proposition, the relation may be marked only when their relative order is not the default or preferred one.

[17] In Gojri ([gju] (alt. Gujari; Indo-Aryan, India), for example, the connective *te* coordinates "constituents that belong to the same grammatical class, provided the coordinated constituents are distinct. … Noun phrases, verb phrases, certain subordinated clauses, independent clauses, and sentences are all coordinated with their own class by *te*. … When *te* accompanies some indicator of 'discontinuity' (Givón 1984:245), it marks the beginning of a new package of events … [or] 'development unit'" (Fast 2008:68, 79).

New developments typically involve change: "a change of spatiotemporal setting or circumstances, a change in the underlying subject, or a change to or from a background comment." However, for a development marker (DM) to be used, the information must not only contain an element of change; "it must also represent a **new step or development in the author's story or argument**" (Levinsohn 2000:72).

Because new developments always contain an element of change, DMs are sometimes confused with markers of contrast (see 6.4).

DMs are typically NOT used in a narrative **until the scene has been set** for the theme-line events (see discussion in next section).

6.5.1 Extract 1: Tyap

The extract displayed in chart form below is from a folktale in Tyap.[18] Prior to the extract, introductory sentences have told about the healer, his wife Bashila and their having a child. They have also indicated that she did not know that he was a cannibal, that he looked after the child while she was away grinding, and that he kept the child quiet by singing to it while entertaining it with a necklace made from his victims' fingernails. **No DM is used during these scene-setting sentences.**

The DM in Tyap is the particle *kàn*. The particles *kìn* and *ma* are additives. All three occur between the subject and the verb (a further particle, *si*, has been omitted from the chart – see appendix E in chapter 8). The sentences are numbered, with individual clauses being given letters.

Now study the chart, which is followed by comments about it.

Table 10. Chart of a Tyap folktale

Ref.	Prenuclear clauses	Subject	Particles	Predicate
1a–b	*Bashila was coming from grinding,*	she	**kàn**	heard the healer singing to their child [that he used to go to eat people],
1c		she		stood behind the room,
1d		she		heard the song that he was singing.
2a		Bashila	**kìn**	passed,
2b		she		entered,
2c–d		she		returned, kept quiet.
3a		He		took the child,
3b		he		gave it to Bashila.
4	*It became morning,*	he		got up.
5	*After he got up,*	he		left, again went to eat people.
6a	*After he went to eat people,*	Bashila	**ma kàn**	got up,
6b		she	**kìn**	gathered her things,
6c		she		fetched ashes,
6d		she		added an egg,
6e		she		put the things on her head,
6f		she		caught the road.
7a–e	*She caught the road, went, went,*	she	**kàn**	looked,
7f		she		saw the healer.

---

[18] See Follingstad 1994:155, 165–166.

6.5 Particles that constrain a developmental interpretation

Table 10, continued

Ref.	Prenuclear clauses	Subject	Particles	Predicate
8		Healer	**ma kàn**	saw her.
9		Healer		said, 'What kind of woman looks like this?'
10a–e	He walked, walked, the woman was drawing close,	she	**kàn**	rubbed the ashes on her face,
10f		she	**kàn**	put the egg in her mouth.
11a–b	She reached him,	she	**kàn**	bit down on the egg,
11c		she		bit down on it in her mouth,
11d		the egg	**kàn**	burst [all over her face].
12	There	he		said the woman was not his wife, that she could pass.
13		The woman	**kìn**	passed.

I have already pointed out that the DM *kàn* is not used during the sentences that set the scene for the above extract. The first time it is used is in connection with the event that changes Bashila's attitude to her husband: while returning from grinding, she overhears what he is singing, and thereby discovers that he is a cannibal (sent. 1). The next developments in the story, again marked by *kàn*, are found in 6, 7, and 8–9. Then, as the climax of the extract is reached, each individual act by which the woman disguises herself is marked by *kàn* as a new development (10–11).

The presence of *kàn* in 6a rather than 6b is a further illustration of the fact that the size of the unit being introduced is not conveyed by the connective itself. *Kàn* indicates that what follows is a new development. The story will develop through Bashila's actions, not those of her husband, but the significant event is not her getting up (6a – something she does every day), but the events of the rest of the sentence. These events are appended to 6a by the additive *kìn*. Thus, the unit introduced by *kàn* is larger than a single clause.

Two functions of the **additive** *kìn* are illustrated in this passage:[19]

- **confirmation** (6.3.2). The healer says the woman can pass (12) ADD (*kìn*) she does so (13).
- adding information of **unequal importance** (see 6.3.1). The material added by *kìn* can be less or more important than the material to which it is added.

In sentences 1–2, the information added by *kìn* is **less** important. Bashila *kàn* overhears a song which reveals that her husband goes and eats people, she *kìn* performs actions which are not a consequence of her overhearing the song but, rather, are the commonplace actions that she would have done anyhow on returning from grinding.

In sentence 6, the information added by *kìn* is of **great** importance. Bashila *kàn* gets up as she does every morn; she *kìn* performs actions which she does not normally do on getting up, but which rather represent crucial preparations for when she catches up with her husband.

Kàn and *kìn* thus constrain the hearers to interpret in a particular way the events with which they are associated. If we think of the material introduced by *kàn* as a **development unit** (DU), then *kàn* marks the beginning of new DUs. *Kìn* adds one or more propositions to other(s) of the same DU, for confirmation or when they are of unequal importance. Both particles contrast with the **absence** of any constraining particle (juxtaposition – the default means of conjoining in Tyap).

The following diagram seeks to capture the developmental structure of sentences 4–7 of the extract in Tyap. Each box represents a DU. Within the DU, propositions are normally juxtaposed. *Kìn* adds 6b–f to 6a within the same DU. *Kàn* marks the shift from one DU to the next.

---

[19] In sentences 6 and 8, the additive particle *ma* indicates parallelism between similar actions performed by different participants (see 6.3.1).

4	It became morning,	he got up.
5	After he got up,	he left, again went to eat people.

↓*kàn*

| 6a | After he went to eat people, | Bashila also got up, |

+ *kìn*

6b		she gathered her things,
6c		she fetched ashes,
6d		she added an egg,
6e		she put the things on her head,
6f		she caught the road.

↓*kàn*

| 7a–e | She caught the road, went, went, | she looked, |
| 7f | | she saw the healer |

6.5.2 Extract 2: Koorete

The following extract gives an overview in English of part of a Koorete fable.[20] The interaction between a DM, an additive and the presence of neither is similar to that of Tyap. New developments are marked by the prominence marker *-kko* attached to a sentence-initial constituent (e.g. *hinne-kko* 'It was then that'). The additive marker *-ni* is attached to sentence-initial constituents when what follows is closely associated with the previous proposition, rather than representing a new development. This is seen in sentences 8d and 8e, which describe events anticipated in 8c (the numbers in the extract represent different DUs, not different sentences).

1a   *A certain man had three children.*

1b   Ø *Two of them were rich.*

1c   Ø *The third and youngest was poor.*

1d   Ø *The youngest was called Buxho.*

1e   Ø *He had just one fat ox.*

2   **Hinne-kko** *instead of killing one of their many cattle, Buxho's brothers slaughtered his fat ox.*

3a   **Hinne-kko** *Buxho asked his brothers for the skin and they gave him it.*

3b   Ø *He took it, dried it, and climbed a tree under which traders rest.*

4   **Hinne-kko** *many traders came and unloaded their animals, Buxho beat the hide, and they fled, leaving their goods and animals.*

5   **Hinne-kko** *Buxho climbed down, loaded their goods on the animals, and left.*

6   **Ye e geede-kko** ('After that') *his brothers asked him where he got all this.*

7   **Hinne-kko** *Buxho said, 'I traded them for the skin of my fat ox'.*

8a   *His brothers-**kko** killed their oxen, dried the skins, and took them to a far country.*

8b   Ø *Buxho was afraid for himself.*

8c   Ø *Thinking they would come and burn his house, he dug an escape hole.*

8d   *His brothers-**ni** returned and burnt his house.*

8e   *Buxho-**ni** escaped through the hole.*

---

[20] These observations are based on an analysis of three Koorete texts which SIL linguist Lydia Hoeft (p.c.) obtained, glossed and charted for a 'Discourse for Translation' workshop in Addis Ababa in 2001.

6.5 Particles that constrain a developmental interpretation

The developmental structure of 7–8 may be represented as follows:

↓ **-kko**

7	Then Buxho said, 'I traded them for the skin of my fat ox'.

↓ **-kko**

8a	His brothers killed their oxen, dried the skins, and took them to a far country.
8b	Buxho was afraid for himself.
8c	Thinking they would come and burn his house, he dug an escape hole.

+ **-ni**

8d	His brothers returned and burnt his house.

+ **-ni**

8e	Buxho escaped through the hole.

6.5.3 Extract 3: Koine Greek

De is a DM in Greek. This is seen in the following extract (Luke 2:1–7). Verses 1–3 set the scene. The first development is when Joseph and Mary act for the first time in the episode (4–5). The second development is the birth of Jesus (6–7 – see further in Levinsohn 2000:75–76).[21]

1. *In those days a decree went out from Emperor Augustus that all the world should be taxed.*
2. Ø *This was the first registration, while Quirinius was governor of Syria,*
3. **kai** *everyone went to their own towns to be registered.*
4. *Joseph* **de** *also went from the town of Nazareth in Galilee … (5) to register with Mary …*
6. *It happened* **de** *that, while they were there, the time came for her to deliver her child,*
7a. **kai** *she gave birth to her firstborn son,*
7b. **kai** *wrapped him in bands of cloth,*
7c. **kai** *laid him in a manger, because there was no place for them in the inn.*

Review questions

1. What does a development marker (DM) constrain the hearer or reader to do?
2. It is common for a DM not to occur in the first few sentences of a story. Why is this?
3. Represent the developmental structure of Luke 2:1–7 in a boxed diagram similar to those given above for Tyap and Koorete.[22]

---

[21] The DM *de* also occurs in 2:1, to show that the episode as a whole represents a further development of the theme line.

[22] **Suggested answers:**

1. A DM constrains the hearer or reader to move on to the next point. The material so marked represents a new development in the story or argument, as far as the author's purpose is concerned.
2. It is common for a DM not to occur in the first few sentences of a story because the scene usually has to be set before the first development is described.
3. The following boxed diagram represents the developmental structure of Luke 2:1–7:

1	In those days a decree went out from Emperor Augustus that all the world should be taxed.
2	Ø This was the first registration, while Quirinius was governor of Syria,
3	**kai** everyone went to their own towns to be registered.

↓ *de*

4	Joseph also went from the town of Nazareth in Galilee … (5) to register with Mary …

↓ *de*

6	It happened that, while they were there, the time came for her to deliver her child,
7a	**kai** she gave birth to her firstborn son, (7b) **kai** wrapped him in bands of cloth,
7c	**kai** laid him in a manger, because there was no place for them in the inn.

6.5.4 Marking new developments

Some languages mark new developments, whereas others indicate when the material concerned does NOT represent a new development.

- Languages that **mark** new developments may use a specific DM (e.g. *kàn* – Tyap, *de* – Koine Greek) and/or markers that both have semantic content and signal a new development (e.g. *-kko* – Koorete, *then* – English). Alternatively, they may employ a connective that introduces distinctive information (6.1), but is not in itself a development marker (e.g. *tɛ* in Gojri – see Fast 2008).
- Some languages mark development on **two** axes: "the linkage axis and/or the agent axis" (Levinsohn 2006:31); others tend to mark it on only one. Development on the **linkage** axis is typically marked by means of connectives, either early in the sentence (e.g. in Greek) or in the verb phrase (Tyap).[23] Development on the **agent** axis is marked on references to participants, by a DM (extract 4 below), by a thematic determiner (9.2.1) or simply by the seemingly redundant naming of the participants (e.g. in Hebrew – see 8.3).

    There appears to be a correlation between the marking of development primarily on the agent axis and the use of juxtaposition as the default means of conjoining sentences or groups of sentences (6.1). Marking of development on both axes is most common in OV languages, though it is also found also in some Bantu (SV/VO) languages in which the default means of conjoining sentences or groups of sentences is with a connective (Levinsohn 2012).
- Alternatively, new developments may be indicated by **constituent order** (see text 5 below).
- Some languages do not have a development marker. Instead, they signal when, for example, a theme-line event is **not** a new development in a narrative, often by means of an associative or additive connective.[24]

    Such is the case in Yoruba; the language uses an additive to indicate that the event concerned does not represent a new development, but rather is part of the same DU as the previous event (e.g. *Cramp took him and he* ADDITIVE *died in that place*).
- In many **OV** languages, the chaining of events into a single sentence with participial clauses and/or switch reference markers produces the equivalent of a DU. Associative markers, including tail-head linkage, may then be used to indicate that a particular sentence does not represent a new development, but rather belongs to the same DU as the previous sentence.

Extract 4: Inga

In Inga, which is a typical OV language, the enclitic *-ka* may be attached to two types of expressions to signal story development:[25]

- expressions that indicate **temporal succession** or some other relation of the sentence to its context (the linkage axis)
- expressions that refer to the **agents** who perform the actions of the story (the agent axis).[26]

The absence of *-ka*, in turn, "represents lack of movement with respect to the relevant ... axis" (Levinsohn 1976:122).

To illustrate the function of *-ka*, consider the translation into English of an extract from a traditional folktale in Inga narrated by Lázaro Mojomboy Pujimoy (see Longacre and Levinsohn 1978:112).

---

[23] In a number of languages, an inchoative auxiliary (typically translated *come*) is used to mark new developments (e.g. in the Obolo language of Nigeria and in Moroccan Arabic).

[24] However, languages that have a development marker may permit an additive to co-occur with it. See, for example, sentence 6a of the extract from a Tyap text (6.5.1).

[25] The discussion of extract 4 is taken from Levinsohn 2006.

[26] Occasionally, references to **patients** are marked in the same way in Inga (Levinsohn 2006), so it might be preferable to call the 'agent axis' the 'participant axis'.

6.5 Particles that constrain a developmental interpretation

Table 11. Illustration of the affix -*ka* in storyline development in Inga

Ref.	Linkage axis	Agent axis	Action
1	*At.that.time*	*mother-in-law*-**ka**	*went ahead, weeping, to where she had buried the piece of fruit.*
2	*Arriving*-**ka**	Ø	*said, 'Here is where the child is buried'.*
3	*Thus having.said*-**ka**	Ø	*fled to hang herself.*
4	*At.that.time*-Ø	*father*-**ka**	*dug up the grave.*
5	*Removing the earth*-Ø	Ø	*found just a piece of fruit.*
6		Ø	*said, 'Oh no! Now it's clear to me.'*
7	*Thus having.said*-**ka**	Ø	*followed her trail.*

In the above extract, -*ka* marks the **agents** through whom the story develops: first, the mother-in-law (1–3), then the father (4–7). The presence of -*ka* on the **linkage** axis divides the mother-in-law's actions into three distinct "bursts of closely related actions" (Heimerdinger 1999:124): her journey to the place of burial (1), her speech (2) and her fate (3). The absence of -*ka* in 4 and 5 "constrains the finding of the piece of fruit not to be viewed as a new development (perhaps because the hearers already know what will be found), but as part of the same" DU (Dooley and Levinsohn 2001:94). A new DU begins in 7, with the father's decision to follow the mother-in-law's trail.

Text 5: Gude

The following chart presents a folktale in Gude.[27] Labelled columns indicate whether the order of constituents in the clause(s) concerned is SV or VS. 'V$_{prior}$' refers to verbs which indicate that the event took place prior to the time of the main events (see 5.2.2). *Ma* introduces points of departure. Double lines across the page mark the divisions of the folktale into Episode 1 (1–12), Episode 2 (13–22) and Conclusion (23–24). Single lines across the page precede each sentence with SV order (a signal of new developments – see further below).

Table 12. Illustration of constituent order in Gude storyline

Ref.	Prenuclear	SV	VS	V$_{prior}$S	Postnuclear
1	**ma** *long ago*			*Squirrel got up.*	
2			*He went, found Goat*		*so that they go to his in-laws.*
3			*They got up, left.*		
4	**ma** *they arrived,*	*people brought them foufou.*			
5		*Squirrel tasted,*			
			he said to Goat, 'No salt! Go home for salt!'		
6			*Goat got up, left.*		
7	**ma** *he left to find salt,*	*Squirrel took, ate all the foufou.*			
8	**ma** *Goat returned with salt,*			*Squirrel had eaten the foufou.*	
9			*He said to him, 'What about the foufou?'*		
10			*He said to him, '[EXPLANATION]'*		
11			*They got up, left for home.*		
12			*Goat was angry*		*as he came to house.*
13	**ma** *another day*		*he went to Cock.*		
14			*He said to Cock, 'Let's go to my in-laws!'*		

---

[27] I am grateful to Mona Perrin (p.c.) for providing this text.

Table 12, continued

Ref.	Prenuclear	SV	VS	V$_{prior}$S	Postnuclear
15	Now, **ma** Cock,				he was truly clever.
16			He took salt, put it under wing.		
17			They left, arrived,		
				people brought them foufou, as they did before.	
18			He tasted,		
				he said to Cock, 'No salt!'	
19			Cock brought out salt, they put it in, they ate.		
20				Squirrel was upset.	
21			They got up, left for home.		
22			Cock walked along mocking him.		
23	Thus,			he had failed	to fool Cock
24	but			he had fooled Goat.	

Gude does not have a DM marker as such, but the above chart shows how SV ordering is used to introduce each new development. Further events of each DU are presented with VS ordering.

Both episodes begin with one or more events with VS order (1, 13–14). These events set the scene for the first development of the episode.

In the first episode, no further developments occur after sentence 7. This is because Squirrel has already fooled Goat (the purpose of the trick – see the conclusion in sents. 23–24).

6.5.5 Stories which build up to a moral or other teaching point

The above examples have illustrated how DMs work in narrative when the story is an end in itself. Each new development along the theme line tends to be marked with a DM. When the reason for telling a story is to draw a moral, however, DMs typically mark the events or groups of events that contribute to bringing out the point of the moral. Quite often, as a consequence, the DMs are relatively infrequent in such stories.

This is illustrated in the Bekwarra folktale that we have already considered. The moral of the story is that, once you have entered into an agreement, you must see it through. The DM *kà* marks the developments in the story that lead to this moral. The developmental structure is shown in the following diagram (see comments below).

1–6	Dog & Hare made an agreement to eat their children.
	Because Dog's pup was ill, they ate Hare's pup.

↓*kà*

7–9	When Dog's pup became well, he hid it and fled.

↓*kà*

10–27	Hare tried to get him to keep to the agreement
	first, by appealing to him directly (10–15)
	then, by taking the case to the elders, who ruled in Hare's favour (16–27)

↓*kà*

28	Dog finally kept his part of the agreement.

↓*kà*

29	MORAL: *Once you've entered into an agreement, you must see it through.*

The above diagram shows that the first six sentences of the Bekwarra text set the scene for the rest of the story. Dog and Hare enter an agreement and put it into practice. The first development of the story occurs when Dog refuses to go along with his part of the agreement (7–9). The second development concerns Hare's efforts to get Dog to keep to the agreement (10–27). Dog's acquiescence (28) is the final development of the narrative proper. This leads to the presentation of the moral. *Kà* thus marks each development in the folktale that leads to this moral.

In the Gospels, it is normal for an episode to be recounted, not as an end in itself, but because of the results it produces. This is reflected in the way the Greek DM *de* is used in such episodes.

In Matthew 9:1–8, for instance, no DM is used until Jesus pronounces the words that lead to the healing of the paralytic (6b – see Levinsohn 2000:97 on the DM *tote* 'then'). *De* is used only to introduce the response of the crowds to the manifestation of Jesus' authority. This suggests that the author has a larger purpose than the simple narration of the episode; his primary interest is rather in the response of those with whom Jesus is interacting.

1a	**Kai** *having embarked in a boat, he crossed over*
1b	**kai** *came into his own city.*
2a	**Kai** *behold they brought to him a paralytic lying on a stretcher*
2b	**kai** *having seen their faith, Jesus said to the paralytic, 'Cheer up, child, your sins are forgiven'.*
3	**Kai** *behold some of the scribes said among themselves, 'This one is blaspheming'.*
4	**Kai** *having seen their thoughts, Jesus said, 'Why are you thinking evil in your hearts?'*

↓*tote*

6b	*he says to the paralytic, 'Rise up, take your stretcher and go to your house'.*
7	**kai** *rising up, he went away to his house.*

↓***de***[28]

8a	*having seen [this,] the crowds were afraid*
8b	**kai** *glorified God, who had given such authority to men.*

Review question

Why do DMs occur frequently in some narratives and infrequently in others by the same author?[29]

Application to the language you are analysing

Describe the (positive or negative) means used to indicate new developments in a narrative. If more than one means is used, then distinguish their functions.

6.6 Packaging information in development units

This section seeks to place the marking of new developments into a larger picture by representing basic developmental relationships in diagrams. The following are basic developmental relationships between units (propositions, sentences or groups of sentences):

---

[28] See Levinsohn 2000:71ff. for a more detailed discussion of *de* as a DM.
[29] **Suggested answer:**
DMs occur most frequently in narratives that are an end in themselves. In narratives that build up to a moral or other teaching point, DMs tend to be less frequent, as they typically mark only the events or groups of events that contribute to bringing out the teaching point.

a) Unit 2 develops from Unit 1:

```
    ┌─────┐
    │  1  │
    └─────┘
       ↓
    ┌─────┐
    │  2  │
    └─────┘
```

In the extract from Tyap (6.5.1), for example, *kàn* marks the development from 6 to 7. In the extract from Luke 2:1–7 (6.5.3), Greek *de* marks the development from 4–5 to 6–7.

b) Proposition 2 is associated with Proposition 1:

```
    ┌─────┐
    │  1  │
    │  2  │
    └─────┘
```

In the extract from Tyap, for example, 1c–3b are associated with 1b by the additive *kìn* or by juxtaposition. In the extract from Luke, 2:2–3 are associated with 1 by juxtaposition or by *kai*.

Possible relationships between Propositions 1 and 2 include the following:
- Proposition 1 may be the primary assertion (the new development), and Proposition 2 supplementary material (e.g. an Event 2 that is associated with Event 1 – see sentences 8a–8e of the Koorete extract presented in 6.5.2).
- Proposition 2 may be the primary assertion, and Proposition 1 preliminary material (e.g. Setting 1 for Event 2).
  In Acts 5:7, for example, the significant event is presented in the second sentence of the DU (7b):

  7a An interval **de** *of about three hours passed*

  7b **kai** *his wife came in, not knowing what had happened.*
- The combination of Propositions 1 and 2 may represent the new development.
  In the Koorete extract, for instance, the third development consists both in Buxho obtaining the skin (3a) AND in what he did with it (3b):

  3a **Hinne-kko** *Buxho asked his brothers for the skin and they gave him it.*

  3b Ø *He took it, dried it, and climbed a tree under which traders rest.*

c) No developmental relationship exists between Units 1 and 2:

```
    ┌─────┐
    │  1  │
    └─────┘

    ┌─────┐
    │  2  │
    └─────┘
```

In the extract from Tyap, for instance, the events of 4ff. begin an episode, and no developmental relation with the events of the previous evening is marked.

d) Unit 1 presents theme-line information; unit 2 supplies background information:

This is illustrated for Koine Greek in John 11:4–6. Verse 4 presents a theme-line event, whereas 5 (introduced with *de*) supplies background information (see the diagram following point e):

   4 *When Jesus heard that Lazarus was ill, he said, 'This illness is not unto death.'*

   5 *Jesus* **de** *loved* (IMPERFECTIVE) *Martha and her sister and Lazarus.*

   6 *When* **oun** *he heard that he was ill, he stayed two days longer in the place where he was.*

e) Unit 1 supplies background information; unit 2 presents theme-line information, which may or may not be **resumptive**, representing a new development with respect to an earlier proposition:

```
         (↓)              ┌─────┐
                          │  1  │
      ┌─────┐             └─────┘
      │  2  │
      └─────┘
```

6.6 Packaging information in development units

This is illustrated in John 11:5–6 (see above). Verse 5 supplies background information, whereas 6 (introduced with *oun*) resumes the event line:

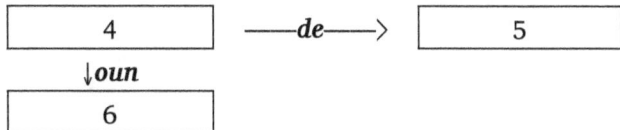

Alternatively, unit 1 may supply information on another topic. This is illustrated in the following extract from a folktale in the Makaa [mcp] (Bantu A, Cameroon) language. Following several sentences concerning Ant, sentence 3 (introduced with *ka* 'then') resumes the theme line as it concerns Dog.

1. *So Dog arrived outside quickly (and) went behind the house, embarrassed because he had abandoned the food.*
2. *As for Ant, the woman then sent him water ...* [several sentences]
3. *Dog* **ka** *went (and) arrived behind the house with this embarrassment, and went went ...*

Resumptives

The following two devices are commonly used to mark the resumption of a theme line:
- tail-head linkage (3.2.3) or some other way of **reiterating** an earlier point in the story or argument, following assertions concerning a different topic; and/or
- a **development** marker or similar connective, following supportive material (e.g. *de* or *oun* in Koine Greek [point d above], *ka* in Makaa [point e above]).[30]

Application to the language you are analysing

Describe the means used to indicate the resumption of an earlier theme line.

---

[30] In the Greek and Makaa examples, both devices were used, but that is by no means always the case.

7

The Reporting of Conversation in Narrative

Reported conversations tend not to be presented like ordinary theme-line events in a narrative.
- In many languages, no verb is used to introduce the speech (instead, a complementiser like *that* may be the norm), or the introductory verb is not conjugated, or it is in imperfective aspect or some other form that is not normally associated with theme-line events.
- The default encoding of references to a reported speaker who was the previous addressee may not be the same as for other changes of subject. For example, the default encoding of references to a speaker who was the previous addressee in Koine Greek is often an articular pronoun rather than a full noun phrase, even though the latter is the norm for many other changes of subject (see ch. 8).

This chapter first discusses factors that influence an author's decision to report speeches directly, indirectly or semidirectly (7.1). The position of the 'orienter' (the clause that identifies the speaker and addressee of a reported speech) in relation to the speech itself is addressed in 7.2. 'Closed' conversations are defined in 7.3 as those that involve only two participants. The relation between the individual speeches of a reported conversation is considered in 7.4. Section 7.5 distinguishes between reported speeches that are treated as theme-line events and those that only lead up to the next theme-line event. Means of indicating changes of direction in reported conversations are recorded in 7.6. Section 7.7 takes a preliminary look at how the speaker and addressee are referred to in orienters (a topic that is further developed in ch. 8). Section 7.8 asks why speech orienters are sometimes repeated. Section 7.9 notes how the relative status and authority of the participants may affect the way their speeches are reported. Finally, 7.10 makes some observations about 'interpretive-use' markers, since they often appear in orienters.

7.1 Forms of reporting speeches

Speeches are typically reported in one of three basic ways: directly, indirectly or semidirectly. The following are third-person examples of these basic ways (see below on the meaning of LOG):[1]

- DIRECT: *John said (that) I can see you.* (speaker: 1st person, addressee: 2nd person)
- INDIRECT: *John said (that) he/LOG can see him.* (speaker: 3rd/LOG, addressee: 3rd person)
- SEMIDIRECT: *John said (that) he/LOG can see you.* (speaker: 3rd/LOG, addressee: 2nd person)

In **indirect** speech in English, the tense of the reported speech changes, e.g. from *can* to *could*. In many languages, there is no change of tense when speech is reported indirectly. Similarly, the

---
[1] For further ways of reporting speech, see Aaron 1992.

presence in English of *that* implies that what follows is indirect speech; such is not the case in many other languages.

In **semidirect** speech (also called 'combined' speech), references to the reported speaker are indirect, but some or all of the remaining content is same as for speech (see Perrin 1974; Hedinger 1984).

The abbreviation LOG means **logophoric** pronoun. Such pronouns are used in indirect and semidirect reporting to indicate that the referent is the reported speaker.

A logophoric pronoun, *àhe*, occurs in sentence 14 of the Bekwarra folktale. The referent of *àhe* is the reported speaker (Dog). In contrast, the referent of the third-person singular pronoun *ámín* is someone other than the reported speaker (in this case, Hare).[2]

a-dè	àhe	n'-ámín	e-ngwìà	iyìm	ùngwan	ạjini	rẹ
s-said	LOG	with-3s	p-entered	agreement	child	eating	not

'He said, "I did not make a child-eating agreement with you."'

In some languages, **direct** reporting predominates or is default (e.g. in English, Bantu A, Greek and Hebrew). In other languages, **indirect** reporting predominates (e.g. in Bekwarra). In yet other languages, **semidirect** reporting is the default (e.g. in some Grassfields languages of Cameroon).[3]

7.1.1 Factors that may determine the form of reporting

If a language reports speech both directly and indirectly, the form of reporting selected is determined by a number of factors. I discuss these factors under three categories: a) verbatim reporting, b) language-related constraints and c) text-related factors.

a) **Verbatim reporting**. The use of direct versus indirect speech may be related to whether the author wishes to suggest that the message is being reported verbatim or not (Li 1986:38–40).
- By using **direct** speech in English, "the reporter-speaker intends for the hearer to believe that the form, the content and the nonverbal messages such as gestures and facial expressions of the reported speech originate from the reported speaker".
- In **indirect** speech, in contrast, "the reporter-speaker may communicate his own feelings through the form (e.g. intonation) and nonverbal messages of the reported speech as a comment on the content of the reported speech".

Li's point is illustrated with Acts 12:14b (*She [the maid] announced that Peter was standing at the gate. 'You are out of your mind!' they told her*). Because the maid's speech is reported indirectly, the hearer does not know what she actually said; only the gist of the message is communicated. In contrast, the hearer is led to believe that the addressees actually said, *You are out of your mind!*[4]

b) **Language-specific constraints**. The use of direct versus indirect speech may be affected by language-specific constraints such as the following.
- Certain sentence types (e.g. questions – 7.1.2) have to be given in direct speech in some languages. Others (e.g. speeches reported in subordinate clauses) may have to be given in indirect or semidirect speech.
- If the speaker or addressee is referred to in the reported speech, the speech must be reported indirectly or semidirectly in some languages: *He told me I/you have to go*. In such languages, one cannot use *you* to refer to *ego*.

c) **Text-related factors**. The use of direct versus indirect speech may be affected by a number of text-related factors.

---

[2] In addition to LOG (logophoric), the following abbreviations are used: p: plural; s: singular; 3: 3rd person.
[3] This chapter does not discuss "referred-to speech" (Chafe 1994:247) such as *I spoke to him*. Such sentences are interpreted as ordinary narrative events.
[4] See the following discussion to understand **why** an author chooses to report one speech directly and another indirectly. See Chafe 1994 for extensive discussion of reporting speech directly, indirectly and in other ways. Chafe makes further subdivisions – pp. 247–248 gives a useful summary.

7.1 Forms of reporting speeches

- In some languages, the basic distinction is a **two-way** one with indirect or semidirect speech as the default, particularly if the language has logophoric pronouns. In such languages, direct reporting is only for highlighting. In the Bekwarra folktale, for example, only the moral (*The elders told him, 'What you have eaten, you must pay in full'* – sent. 29) is given in direct speech; the remaining speeches are reported indirectly (see sent. 14 above).

In other languages with a two-way distinction, direct speech is the default; indirect reporting backgrounds the speeches concerned.

- In some languages, the basic division is a **three-way** one, with semidirect reporting as the default, direct reporting for highlighting, and indirect reporting for backgrounding speeches. Such is the case in Bafut (see Mfonyam 1994:195).
- In some languages, direct reporting is default in **folktales**, especially those involving animals, whereas semidirect or indirect speech is the norm in reports of **real events**!
- The relative **status** of the participants may be reflected in the type of reporting; the speeches of those occupying an authority role (see 7.9) are given directly, whereas those of other participants are reported indirectly or semidirectly.
- In all languages where there is a text-related choice, indirect reporting is the **least prominent** (see Lowe and Hurlimann 2002:75).

7.1.2 Extract 1: Goemai

The following extract from a folktale in Goemai [ank] (Chadic, Nigeria) illustrates a two-way distinction between indirect and direct reporting. Indirect reporting is default (sents. 1, 3–5). Direct reporting is obligatory in questions (sents. 2, 4b), and is used to highlight declarative speeches (sent. 6).

1   When she went and met the herbalist, she said, *What disturbs her is this; she came .... so that he help her.*
2   The herbalist said, '*What is it that disturbs you?*'
3   She said, *she wants her husband to love her more than her cowives.*
4   The man said, *he will be able to do it, but he has work he will give her to do first. Then he will find medicine for her, so that she will return and give it to her husband so that he will love her more than her cowives. Are you able to do that work?*
5   The woman answered, *she is able.*
6   Ø '*OK, what you are to do is this. .... I warn you: don't be afraid!*'

Review questions

1. What characterises semidirect speech?
2. When a logophoric pronoun occurs in reported speech, what does it indicate?
3. What are three categories of factors that may affect the form of reporting speech?
4. If there is a text-related choice in the form of reporting speech, which is the least prominent form?[5]

---

[5] **Suggested answers:**
1. In semidirect speech, references to the reported speaker are indirect, but some or all of the remaining content is same as for direct speech.
2. When a logophoric pronoun occurs in reported speech, it indicates that the referent is the reported speaker.
3. Three categories of factors that may affect the form of reporting speech are verbatim reporting, language-related constraints and text-related factors.
4. If there is a text-related choice in the form of reporting speech, the least prominent form is indirect reporting.

Application to the language you are analysing

1. Determine the default way of reporting speech (direct, indirect or semidirect).
2. Determine the functions of any other ways of reporting speeches.
3. Are there any restrictions if the narrator or his/her addressee is referred to in the reported speech (e.g. *He told me **you** have to go*, where *you* in English could refer either to the narrator or to his/her addressee, depending on the intonation or punctuation)?
4. Are there any restrictions on the embedding of a reported speech inside a reported speech?
5. Are the restrictions more severe if the reported speaker or addressee is referred to in the embedded speech (e.g. the second reference to *the* LORD in Exodus 8:1: *Then the* LORD *said to Moses, 'Go to Pharaoh and say to him, "This is what the* LORD *says:"'*)?

7.2 The speech orienter

The term *speech orienter* refers to the clause that identifies the reported speaker and/or addressee.[6] It most often occurs either before or after the reported speech (see below for other patterns).

In the following extract from a folktale in Gumawana (Olson 2014:233–234), the orienter sometimes occurs before the reported speech, and sometimes after it.[7] We shall see in 7.5.3 that such variations in its position are significant (DET: determiner; DM: development marker – 6.5).

Extract 2: Gumawana

Table 13. Chart of a Gumawana folktale

Ref.	Prespeech orienter		Reported speech				Postspeech orienter	
1	*Dokanikani-ya-na*	*ka-na,*	*'Akeke,*	*kom*	*moe,*	*ava*	*tau?'*	
	giant-DET-3s	talk-3s	OK	you	there	which	one	
2			*'O*	*tubu-gu*	*yau'*		*Gumasai*	*ka-e-na.*
			oh	elder-my	me		Gumasai	talk-?-3s
3			*'Yoi-m*		*manakoyoi-na?'*		*dokanikani*	*ka-e-na.*
			name-your		what-3s		giant	talk-?-3s
4			*'Yau,*	*tubu-gu,*	*yoi-gu*	*Gumasai'*	*Gumasai*	*ka-e-na.*
			I	elder-my	name-my	Gumasai	Gumasai	talk-?-3s
5	*E dokanikani*	*i-digo ka-na,*	*'O*	*dedei-na,*	*ku-kaika ....'*			
	DM giant	3s-say talk-3s	oh	good-3s	you-eat			

1. The giant said, 'Alright, you there, who are you?'   2. 'Oh sir, it's me', said Gumasai.
3. 'What is your name?' said the giant.   4. 'My name, sir, is Gumasai', said Gumasai.
5. So the giant said, 'Oh, fine, eat. [Don't be worrying; I'm a good man.]'

In **Koine Greek**, orienters almost always occur before the speech (see extract 3 – 7.3). The orienter occurs within the speech in Matthew 14:8 (*Give me, **she says**, here on a platter the head of John the Baptist!*). It follows the speech in Revelation 1:8 (*I am the Alpha and the Omega, **says the Lord God***). It is omitted completely in John 1:21c (*Are you the prophet?*). More often, though, it is the verb of the orienter that is omitted, as in Acts 9:11 (**And the Lord to him**). (See below on Luke 7:40b.)

---

[6] Longacre (1996:89) uses the term "quotation formula".
[7] In fact, most Gumawana speakers rarely place the orienter after the reported speech (Clif Olson p.c.).

Orienters also precede the speech in **Biblical Hebrew**. However, divine pronouncements often have an orienter both before and after the speech (e.g. '*Thus says YHWH*. ... *Utterance of YHWH*' – Jeremiah 30:18–21), presumably to highlight its origin.

In written **English**, the most common position for an orienter, if it occurs at all, is following or within the speech (Thompson 1994:78–79):

> '*What, kissing her hand, and he a clergyman!*' **said Miss Dunstable**. '*I did not think they ever did such things, Mr. Robarts*'.
> '*Still waters run deepest*', **said Mrs. Harold Smith**. (Anthony Trollope, 1860, *Framley Parsonage*.)

In verb-final languages such as Korean [kor] (Koreanic, Korea), the orienter is often split, with the reference to the speaker before the speech and the speech verb after it. Luke 7:40b in Greek (**And he**, *Teacher, say on,* **says**) would sound very natural in such languages.

A shift to **drama** (speech orienters omitted) may be associated with a climax, especially in oral texts (see sent. 6 of the Goemai folktale cited in 7.1.2). In written English, in contrast, it is the norm to omit orienters for noninitial speeches of a reported 'closed' conversation (see 7.3).

Application to the language you are analysing

1. Determine the normal position of the orienter relative to the speech being reported (prior to the speech, following the speech, both, split).
2. Is the orienter found in other positions? (If so, you will be asked about the factors that determine its position after 7.5.4.)
3. When is the orienter omitted completely: in oral material? in written material?

7.3 Closed conversations

I use the term **closed conversation** to refer to reported **dialogues**; i.e., conversations with only two speakers or groups of speakers. Each new speaker was the previous addressee, and vice versa.

Acts 10:3–4 exemplifies a closed conversation in Greek; the angel and Cornelius address each other in turn (the DM is *de*; *ho* is an articular pronoun glossed 'he').

Extract 3: Acts 10:3–4

3   *He clearly saw an angel of God coming in and saying to him, 'Cornelius'.*

4a *ho* DM *said, 'What is it, Lord?'*

4b *said* DM *to him, 'Your prayers and your alms have ascended as a memorial before God ....'*

Luke 15:21–22 is an example of a conversation that is NOT closed, since the addressees of the speech of 22 (the slaves) were not the previous speaker (the son).

Extract 4: Luke 15:21–22

21 *And the son said to him, 'Father, I have sinned against heaven and before you; I am no longer worthy to be called your son ....'*

22f *said* DM *the father to his slaves, 'Quickly bring out a robe – the best one – and put it on him.'*

Question

Is the reported conversation in Gumawana (extract 2 – 7.2) closed or not?[8]

---

[8] **Suggested answer:**
The reported conversation in Gumawana is closed; only two speakers are involved (the giant and Gumasai). Throughout the conversation, each new speaker was the previous addressee, and vice versa.

7.4 The relationship between successive speeches in a reported conversation

Though the speeches of a reported conversation follow each other in time, they are not always treated as a series of theme-line events in natural chronological sequence, linked by the default connective for narrative. Instead, the relation between them may be marked as **logical**: one of stimulus-response, using a connective such as 'so'.

In Bwamu, for instance, a stimulus-response conjunction links noninitial speeches of a reported conversation, instead of the default conjunction. Such is the case also in Inga.

In the Iten [etx] (Benue-Congo, Nigeria) language, in contrast, the default conjunction is absent with the noninitial speeches of a reported conversation. This sometimes happens also in Koine Greek (see Levinsohn 2000:235ff. on why this happens in Matthew's Gospel).

Application to the language you are analysing

Is the default way of coordinating sentences (6.1) typically used also to link noninitial speeches of a reported conversation? If not, what means of coordination is typically used?

7.5 The status of reported speeches in the overall story

Typically, in the narrative texts that I am shown in a workshop, the majority of reported speeches are **not an end in themselves**. Rather, they lead up to and point forward to later speeches or nonspeech events that form the theme line of the narrative. They "are simply *intermediate steps* en route to the goal of the conversation" (Levinsohn 2000:218). Furthermore, if a reported conversation consists of several speeches, they are often not treated as the equivalent of that number of individual theme-line events.

The status of reported speeches is usually reflected in their orienter. Sections 7.5.1–7.5.3 describe three ways of indicating that a reported speech is not an end in itself, but is an intermediate step pointing forward to a later speech or nonspeech event. Section 7.5.4 considers instances in which a reported speech IS treated as a theme-line event.

7.5.1 Many reported speeches are backgrounded

The most overt way of recognising when reported speeches are intermediate steps en route to later speeches or nonspeech events is when perfective aspect is used to present the theme-line events, whereas the aspect of the verb of the speech orienters is **imperfective**. Such is the case for the vast majority of reported speeches in narratives in the Hixkaryána [hix] (Carib, Brazil) language (see Derbyshire 1986:283–303) and in the Longuda [lnu] (Adamawa, Nigeria) language.[9]

Alternatively, some other indicator is present in the speech orienter that elsewhere correlates with a backgrounded event of a preliminary nature (5.2.2). For instance, it is common for **no verb** to introduce the speech (instead, a complementiser like *that* may be the norm), or for the speech verb not to be conjugated. In Gumawana, for instance, orienters for intermediate steps lack the speech verb *-digo* 'say' and instead use only a nominalised form (*ka-na* or *ka-e-na* 'his talk'). This is illustrated in extract 2 (table 13, repeated from 7.2).

---

[9] The historical present [HP] in Greek, which occurs frequently in speech orienters, is also an imperfective (Levinsohn 2000:203, fn. 6. "[T]he use of a HP in a speech orienter most often points forward to and highlights a later speech or event" [p. 248]).

7.5 The status of reported speeches in the overall story 115

Extract 2: Gumawana

Table 13. Chart of a Gumawana folktale

Ref.	Prespeech orienter		Reported speech				Postspeech orienter	
1	**Dokanikani-ya-na ka-na,**		'Akeke, kom moe, aya tau?'					
	giant-DET-3s	talk-3s	OK	you	there	which one		
2			'O tubu-gu yau'				*Gumasai*	*ka-e-na.*
			oh elder-my me				Gumasai	talk-?-3s
3			'Yoi-m manakoyoi-na?'				*dokanikani*	*ka-e-na.*
			name-your what-3s				giant	talk-?-3s
4			'Yau, tubu-gu, yoi-gu Gumasai'				*Gumasai*	*ka-e-na.*
			I elder-my name-my Gumasai				Gumasai	talk-?-3s
5	**E dokanikani i-digo ka-na,**		'O dedei-na, ku-kaika ....'					
	DM giant	3s-say talk-3s	oh good-3s you-eat					

1. The giant said, 'Alright, you there, who are you?'   2. 'Oh sir, it's me', said Gumasai.
3. 'What is your name?' said the giant.   4. 'My name, sir, is Gumasai,' said Gumasai.
5. So the giant said, 'Oh, fine, eat. [Don't be worrying; I'm a good man.]'

7.5.2 Many reported speeches are not treated as new developments

A second way to recognise when reported speeches are intermediate steps en route to later speeches or nonspeech events is when they are not treated as new developments in the story. In other words, the orienters concerned lack development markers.

This is evident in the extract from Gumawana cited above; only the final speech (5) is introduced with the DM *e*. See also the Gude text that was presented in 6.5.4; VS order was used in all the speech orienters, whereas SV order marks the beginning of new development units.

7.5.3 Many reported speeches are grouped into couplets

Further evidence that reported speeches are often not treated as the equivalent of that number of individual theme-line events is the tendency for them to be grouped into couplets (Coulthard 1977:70), especially in oral material. Typical couplets, in which reported speeches are paired together, are:
- Question + Answer
- Remark + Evaluation or Reply.

For instance, reported speeches may be grouped into couplets which open with a prespeech orienter and terminate with a postspeech orienter (see sents. 1–2 of extract 2 above):

PRESPEECH ORIENTER	Question	
He said to him,	*'Who are you?'*	(no POSTSPEECH ORIENTER)
	Answer	POSTSPEECH ORIENTER
(no PRESPEECH ORIENTER)	*'I'm Gumasai'*	*he replied.*

In addition to the above couplets which involve the pairing of reported speeches, it is common for a reported **proposal** to be paired with its nonspeech **execution**. For example, an additive may be used to pair the execution of a proposal with the proposal itself – see 6.3.2 and sentences 12–13 of the Tyap folktale cited in 6.5.[10]

---
[10] For evidence of couplets in the Greek of John's Gospel, see Levinsohn 2000:248–249.

Languages may use more than one of the above methods of indicating when reported speeches are not an end in themselves, but are intermediate steps that point forward to later speeches or nonspeech events.

7.5.4 Speeches as theme-line events

I said earlier that, in most of the narrative texts that I see in a workshop, the majority of reported speeches are not an end in themselves. In the Greek New Testament, in contrast, several reported conversations are presented as a series of theme-line events; e.g. the debate of John 8:12ff., the conversation between Mary and the angel (Luke 1:30–38), and the conversation between the rich man and Abraham (Luke 16:24–31). In such exchanges, each speech is introduced just like any nonspeech theme-line event in Greek (with the DM *de* or *oun* and the *say* verb initial in the orienter).

The language you are analysing will also have ways of presenting reported speeches as theme-line events. To achieve this in Hixkaryána, for instance, the aspect of the verb of the speech orienters will be perfective (contrast 7.5.1). In Gude, the order of constituents in the orienter will be SV (contrast 7.5.2). In Gumawana, the orienter will precede the speech and contain a DM. That is why I recommended that your text corpus of narratives (1.3) should include the report of a debate.

I must add, though, that, as in other languages, the individual speeches of many reported exchanges in the Greek New Testament are NOT treated as the equivalent of nonspeech theme-line events, but as intermediate steps en route to them. A number of devices are used to indicate this. For example, the combination of an articular pronoun plus DM is used in Luke-Acts and John to introduce noninitial speeches that lead to the next theme-line development (Levinsohn 2000:218–220). See Acts 10:4a (extract 3, 7.3) for an example.

Review question

What are three ways that languages employ to indicate when reported speeches are not an end in themselves, but are intermediate steps en route to later speeches or nonspeech events?[11]

Application to the language you are analysing

1. What is the default form of the orienter for noninitial speeches of a reported conversation (e.g. with the verb in the imperfective, without any speech verb)?
2. Describe the function of each other form of the orienter (e.g. with the speech verb in the perfective, with a speech verb).
3. If the position of the orienter varies, indicate the factors that determine when it does not occur in its default position.

7.6 Changes of direction in reported conversations

A reported conversation is **tight knit** if it is a closed one (7.3) in which each successive speaker takes up the same topic as that of the previous speech and develops the conversation from the point at which the last speaker left off.

Extract 3 (7.3) is a tight-knit conversation, since Cornelius responds appropriately to the angel's greeting, and the angel in turn answers Cornelius' question.

---

[11] **Suggested answer:**
The following are three ways that languages employ to indicate when reported speeches are not an end in themselves, but are intermediate steps en route to later speeches or nonspeech events:
- Use in the speech orienter of a device associated with backgrounding, such as imperfective aspect or the lack of a conjugated speech verb.
- Failure to treat the reported speech as a new development.
- Pairing the reported speeches into couplets, instead of treating them as individual theme-line events.

Extract 5 is NOT a tight-knit conversation. It starts off the same way as extract 3, with Ananias responding appropriately to the Lord's greeting and the Lord giving his instruction. However, Ananias then breaks the tight-knit nature of the exchange by voicing an objection (13–14).

Extract 5: Acts 9:10b–14

10b *The Lord said to him in a vision, 'Ananias'.*

10c *ho DM said, 'Here I am, Lord'.*

11–12 *the DM Lord to him, 'Rising, go to the street called Straight, and at the house of Judas look for a man of Tarsus named Saul'.*

13–14 *answered DM Ananias, 'Lord, I have heard from many about this man, how much evil he has done to your saints in Jerusalem.'*

Reported speeches that break the tight-knit nature of a conversation and take it in a new direction generally are **marked** in some way. If the language groups its speeches into couplets, for instance, such speeches will **open a new couplet**, instead of terminating the one opened by the previous question or other initiative:

PRESPEECH ORIENTER	Question
PRESPEECH ORIENTER	Counter-Question

Other devices that mark changes of direction in a reported conversation include the use of:
- a **noun** rather than a pronoun to refer to the speaker (true for all languages – see Acts 9:13 above)
- a **development marker** (true of all languages that use a DM)
- a **specific orienter verb or expression**, such as *answer* (Koine Greek), *respond* (Bantu A), *answered and said* (Biblical Hebrew), *return* (Iten), *open his mouth* (Karai Karai) or a *come* auxiliary (Mambila).

Review question

What is meant by a **tight-knit** conversation?[12]

Application to the language you are analysing

Describe the means of indicating a change of direction within a reported conversation (e.g. a verb such as *answer*).

7.7 References to the speaker and addressee in speech orienters

Chapter 8 will discuss how participants in a narrative are activated (introduced) and the significance of different ways of referring to active participants. Consequently, the purpose of this brief section is to make two observations about participant reference that are specific to reported conversations.

First of all, an observation about references to the speaker and addressee of a **noninitial** speech of a reported conversation.[13] The form of reference may depend on whether the speech is the first or the

---

[12] **Suggested answer:**
A tight-knit conversation is a closed one in which each successive speaker takes up the same topic as that of the previous speech and develops the conversation from the point at which the last speaker left off. (Reported speeches that break the tight-knit nature of a conversation generally are marked in some way.)

[13] The noninitial speeches of a conversation are the second and subsequent ones. In extract 5, for instance, 10b is the initial speech, whereas those of 10c, 11–12 and 13–14 are noninitial.

second part of a **couplet** (7.5.3). If that is so, then references to both the speaker and the addressee in the orienter for the **second** part of a couplet will typically be **minimal**.[14]

The form of reference in a noninitial **round** may also be minimal. When an episode contains more than one conversation between the participants, each conversation may be thought of as a round. For example, the temptation of Jesus by the devil (Matthew 4:3–11) contains three conversational rounds between the devil and Jesus. In noninitial rounds, references to both the speaker and the addressee in the orienter are often minimal.

Second, I have already indicated that, if a reported speech changes direction, then the reference to the speaker in the orienter is typically a **full noun phrase** (7.6). The same is true if the speech is **highlighted** (this point is discussed further at the end of 8.2.2).

This is exemplified in the Hebrew of Genesis 22:8a. References to the speaker in 7c–d are minimal, whereas the speaker is identified by name in 8a. The effect is to highlight the reported speech because its assertion *God will provide* is "the turning point of the story," explaining the name of the place *the LORD will see* (Wenham 1994:109, 100).

7a–b	& spoke	Isaac to Abraham his father and said,	'*My father.*'
7c	& said	Ø,	'*Here I am, my son.*'
7d	& said	Ø,	'*See, the fire and wood! but where [is] the lamb for a burnt offering?*'
8a	& said	**Abraham**,	'*God will provide the lamb for a burnt offering ….*'

Application to the language you are analysing

What is the default way of referring to the speaker and addressee in the orienters of noninitial speeches? If relevant, distinguish between references in the first and the second part of a speech couplet.

7.8 Repetition of speech orienters

If an orienter is repeated in the middle of a speech, you should assume that its presence is motivated. Typically, orienters are repeated:
- to mark the introduction of a new point within the same reported speech
- to slow down the discourse immediately preceding a key assertion (see 5.4.1).

In the Hebrew in Numbers 5:21, for instance, the orienter of 19 is repeated in expanded form in the middle of a sentence. It follows the protasis of the sentence (the conditional point of departure *if you have gone astray while married to your husband …*). The effect is to slow down the discourse and thus highlight the apodosis (*may the* LORD *cause your people to curse and denounce you …*).

19f	& the priest shall cause the woman to swear & shall say to the woman, '*If no other man has slept with you and you have not gone astray and become impure while married to your husband, may this bitter water that brings a curse not harm you. (20) But if you have gone astray while married to your husband and you have defiled yourself by sleeping with a man other than your husband*' –
21	**& the priest shall cause the woman to swear with an oath of cursing & the priest shall say to the woman** – '*may the* LORD *cause your people to curse and denounce you when he causes your thigh to waste away and your abdomen to swell ….*'

Application to the language you are analysing

Explain any repetitions of the same speech orienter in your texts.

---

[14] References to addressees tend to be explicit in the Greek New Testament. In Acts 10:4 (extract 3) and Acts 9:10 (extract 5), however, they are omitted in the second part of the couplet (the response of the human participant to the divine voice).

7.9 The relative status and authority of the participants

The author has the option of indicating that one participant in a reported conversation has an authority role over the other or otherwise is in control of the situation.

In the Mofu-Gudur [mif] (Chadic, Cameroon) language, for instance, a "nonsalient" marker is used to refer to speakers in a nonauthority role (see ch. 9 and Pohlig and Levinsohn 1994:66–68).

Johnstone (1987) finds that, if the Historical Present (HP) is used in speech orienters in certain varieties of American English, one of the reported speakers occupies an authority role. If the HP is not used, neither speaker is credited with an authority role.

Finally, Koontz (1978:48) finds that, when the speeches of one of the participants in a closed conversation in Teribe are backgrounded, this indicates that the other participant is in control. For example (see 5.2.3 on the use of *ga* as a spacer in Teribe):

Table 14. Chart of a Teribe conversation

Ref.	Prenuclear clause	Spacer	Nuclear clause
1	*'Let's eat!' he added,*	*ga*	*'No!' said his little wife.*
2			*The sun was now setting.*
3	*'Let's lie down; let's eat!' he said,*	*ga*	*'No!' she said, 'I will not eat'.*

7.10 Interpretive-use marker

When a speech is reported directly, it usually purports to **describe** a state of affairs – what was said on a particular occasion (a "descriptive use" – Sperber and Wilson 1995:224–231). However, some reported speeches do not inform the reader of what was said so much as **represent** an utterance or thought that resembles it.

Some languages have "an explicit linguistic indicator of interpretive use" (Blass 1990:104) whose function is to indicate that the speech concerned is not describing what was said on a particular occasion, but rather represents an utterance or thought. Such markers are often found in speech orienters.

A variety of circumstances motivate the presence of interpretive-use markers. Four are exemplified below. To start with, the speaker may wish to indicate that the reported speech:

a) was not said on a particular occasion, or

b) is to be related back to a previous utterance.

Both of these motivations are exemplified in Southern Toussian [wib] (Gur, Burkina Faso).[15] The interpretive-use marker in Toussian is distinct from the complementiser that introduces reported speech and other clausal complements: *nɛ* is the complementiser; *nké* is the interpretive-use marker (Wiesmann n.d.).

a) Following (a), in examples 1–4, *nké* occurs before speeches that were **not** said on a **particular** occasion.

By using *nké* in example 1, the speaker is putting in his own mouth words that he hopes never to say on any occasion:

1 *That is not to say that, if you don't listen, I will rise up and say* **nɛ nké** *You are my enemy.*

By using *nké* in example 2, the speaker avoids suggesting that anyone will actually say on a particular occasion, 'We will come on the Day of the Festival...':

2 *But, if you all stay at home, (saying)* **nɛ nké** *We will come on the Day of the Festival.*

The reason that *nké* is used in example 3 is that the speaker is not reporting what the Word of God said on a particular occasion, but what it always says:

3 *We have seen in the Word of God itself* **nɛ nké** *...*

---

[15] Blass (1990:93–123) describes "an explicit linguistic indicator of interpretive use" in Sissala.

Proverbs in Toussian are also introduced with *nké*, since they "are not the particular thought of anybody, but of people in general" (Blass 1990:106). In the following example, the complementiser *nɛ* is omitted:

4 **nké** *the teeth and the tongue stay together.*

b) Following (b) above, Toussian also uses *nké* to indicate that the speech concerned is to be **related back to a previous utterance**. Contrast the following pair of utterances from the same discourse. In (5), the speaker is making a new assertion, and *nké* is not used. In (6), however, he relates what he is about to say to something he has already said, and *nké* is used:

5 *Because of that* [conflict] *I say to you* **nɛ** *I want to speak to you, so you should listen carefully.*
6 *Because of that, when I told you* **nɛ nké** *you should pardon ....*

Koine Greek also has an interpretive-use marker (see Levinsohn 2009a), though the term "*hoti recitativum*" has traditionally been applied to some of its uses.[16] The factors that motivate it include those that apply to Toussian.

a) Again, following (a), the speech was **not** said on a **particular** occasion. In John 4:20, there is no suggestion that the speech which *hoti* introduces was uttered on a particular occasion; rather, it represents a précis of what *you* (Jews) say:

20 *The woman said to him [Jesus], '... Our ancestors worshiped on this mountain, and you (pl.) say* **hoti** *Jerusalem is the place where one should worship.'*

b) Again, following (b) from above, the speech is to be **related back to a previous utterance**. In John 4:17b, Jesus repeats the utterance of the woman with whom he is conversing (17a), but changes the order of constituents in order to give prominence to the focal constituent (because it is a foil for a later constituent – 4.8). By using *hoti*, he relates his words back to what the woman has said, while modifying them:

17a *The woman answered him, 'I have no husband'* [lit. not I.have husband].
17b *Jesus said to her, 'You rightly say* **hoti** *I have no husband* [lit. husband not I have]; *(18) for you have had five husbands, and the one you have now is not your husband.'*

The interpretive function of *hoti* is also seen by contrasting two utterances from John 10:1–7 that begin with 'Very truly I tell you'. The assertion of 1, which lacks *hoti*, introduces a **new** theme: that of the false and true shepherds, together with the image of the gate of the sheepfold. This speech is followed by the observation (6), 'Jesus used this figure with them, but they did not understand what he was saying to them'. Consequently, the assertion of 7 interprets the figure for Jesus' audience. The presence of *hoti* indicates that 7 is to be related back to a previous utterance (see also Levinsohn 2000:266):

1 *'Very truly, I tell you Ø anyone who does not enter the sheepfold by the gate but climbs in by another way is a thief and a bandit.'*
6 *Jesus used this figure with them, but they did not understand what he was saying to them.*
7 *So again Jesus said to them, 'Very truly, I tell you* **hoti** *I am the gate of the sheep.'*

c) A third motivation for employing the interpretive-use marker *hoti* is to introduce some types of **indirect** speech. This employment of *hoti* is appropriate because indirect speech does not purport to describe the original form of the speech, but only **represents** it in an indirect way. In John 4:51, for instance, *hoti* introduces the indirect speech 'his child lives'. Whether the speech was originally 'Your child lives' or something more extensive, 'his child lives' only represents the original:

51 *As he was going down, his slaves met him, saying* **hoti** *his child lives.*

---

[16] Concerning *kî* in Biblical Hebrew, Follingstad (2002:152) states, "Throughout its uses, *kî* has this 'mention' [interpretive use] function". However, he goes on to describe its use in general in terms of Mental Space Theory.

d) A fourth motivation for using an interpretive-use marker is to **avoid endorsing** the contents of the speech by underlining the fact that it was someone else who said it. In Matthew's account of the temptation of Jesus by the devil, for instance, the devil uses *hoti* when he cites Scripture to support a temptation (Matthew 4:6), whereas Jesus' citation of Scripture in reply does not (Matthew 4:7):[17]

6   *... and says to him, 'If you are the Son of God, throw yourself down, for it is written* **hoti** *"He will command his angels concerning you" and "On their hands they will bear you up, so that you will not dash your foot against a stone."*

7   *Jesus said to him, 'Again it is written* Ø *"Do not put the Lord your God to the test."*

Review questions

1. What do interpretive markers indicate?
2. What are four circumstances under which an interpretive-use marker might introduce a reported speech?[18]

Application to the language you are analysing

1. Check whether any particle associated with speech orienters is functioning as a marker of interpretive use.
2. Describe any other variation in the speech orienters in your texts (e.g. the function of each verb or particle used).

Suggested reading

Chapter 14 of Dooley and Levinsohn 2001 relates to the topics covered in this chapter.

---

[17] Hearsay evidentials, which indicate that the current speaker is not the source of the utterance, are "markers of echoic interpretive-use" (Blass 1990:102). See Dooley and Levinsohn 2001:74 for examples in Mbyá Guaraní [gun] (Guarani, Brazil).

[18] **Suggested answers**:
1. Interpretive markers indicate that the speech concerned is NOT describing what was said on a **particular** occasion, but rather **represents** an utterance or thought.
2. Four circumstances under which an interpretive use marker might introduce a reported speech are to indicate
   - the speech was not said on a particular occasion,
   - the speech is related back to a previous utterance,
   - the speech is only reported indirectly (the original form of the speech is only represented indirectly), or
   - the speaker wishes to avoid endorsing the contents of the speech.

8

Participant Reference

We now look at two aspects of participant reference:

1. how the basic system works (which is fairly similar from language to language – this chapter), and
2. language-specific details, especially as they relate to the use of articles or demonstratives and the organisation of paragraphs around individual participants (ch. 9).

Languages typically have a fairly extensive range of forms of reference to participants in a story. They extend from complete ellipsis to an implicit reference conveyed only by the inflection of the verb, to two or more sets of independent pronouns (personal and demonstrative, among others), to a full noun phrase (with or without a determiner). This chapter looks at factors that determine when each is to be used. An understanding of these factors sheds light on the author's intentions as to the status of the participants in the story, on whether or not certain events or speeches are highlighted, and on the degree to which successive incidents are associated together.

Section 8.1 considers various factors that may affect the way participants are **introduced** to a narrative. Section 8.2 discusses further reference to **activated** participants – participants who have already been introduced to a narrative. Section 8.3 is devoted to the system of references to active participants in **Hebrew** and how this contributes to story development.

8.1 Introduction of new participants

This section considers five factors that may affect the way a participant is introduced to a narrative. Is the participant a major or a minor one 8.1.1)? Is the participant being introduced into an existing mental representation or into a new one (8.1.2)? Is a morpheme for *one* or *certain* used in connection with the introduction (8.1.3)? Is the introduction in connection with a point of departure (8.1.4)? And is the introduction being highlighted (8.1.5)?

8.1.1 Major versus minor participants

The way participants are introduced differs according to whether they are major or minor ones. "Notionally, major participants are those which are active for a large part of the narrative and play leading roles; minor participants are activated briefly and lapse into deactivation" (Dooley and Levinsohn 2001:119).

Question

The following participants in the Bekwarra text are listed in order of appearance. Which are major participants, and which are minor ones: Dog, Hare, Dog's pup, Hare's pup(s), the elders?[1]

As the examples of the next section show, most (but not all) **major** participants are introduced in a nontopic, noninteractive role, BEFORE they become the topic of a topic-comment sentence.[2] In contrast, **minor** participants typically just appear and disappear; they may be introduced as topic in an interactive role (e.g. *Then* **someone** (Greek *tis*) *arrived and announced* – Acts 5:25). Minor participants are often identified in full each time they are involved in the story.

One of the major participants may be the centre of attention throughout the narrative or a major section of it. The term *global VIP* (Dooley and Levinsohn 2001:119) will be used to refer to such a participant. In some languages, the global VIP is introduced before other major participants.

8.1.2 Introduction to a new versus an existing mental representation

The author may choose to introduce a participant to a new or to an existing mental representation of the discourse context.

Introductions in connection with the establishment of a **new** mental representation are most often in the **title** (e.g. *Hansel and Gretel*) or in a **nonevent** clause (1). In some languages, the introductory reference is **left-dislocated** (2):

1 ***A certain man*** *had two sons.* (Luke 15:11)

2 ***A certain man****, he had two wives.* (Toussian)

Utterances with **presentational articulation** may be used in connection with the establishment of a new mental representation (3) or to introduce a participant to an **existing** mental representation (4):

3 *There was* ***an old woman*** *[who lived in a shoe].*

4 *Now there was in Damascus* ***a certain disciple called Ananias****.* (Acts 9:10)

Other introductions to an existing mental representation may be:

- with a verb of arrival or appearance:

5 ***A Samaritan woman*** *came to draw water.* (John 4:7)

- as the object of a perception verb or in some other nonsubject role:

6 *and he saw* ***a tax collector named Levi*** (Luke 5:27)

- by association with a schema. For example, reference to a synagogue in Luke 13:10 presupposes the existence a synagogue leader:

7 *But* ***the leader of the synagogue****, indignant because Jesus had cured on the Sabbath, said …*
   (Luke 13:14)

- by association with another participant:

8 *After a while,* ***his master's wife*** *took notice of Joseph.* (Genesis 39:7)

---

[1] **Suggested answer:**

Dog and Hare are major participants, since they are active for a large part of the narrative and play leading roles. Dog's pup and Hare's pup are minor participants, since they are activated briefly and lapse into deactivation. The elders are probably major participants, as they play a leading role in the latter part of the narrative.

[2] Lambrecht (1994:185) finds that, in **oral** French, the following principle generally holds: "Do not introduce a referent and talk about it in the same clause." It is useful to determine the extent to which Lambrecht's principle holds in **written** material in the language under investigation.

The opening sentence of the Bekwarra text (*Once Dog and Hare made an agreement*) is an exception to Lambrecht's principle. Perhaps, the story began with a title such as *Dog and Hare*. Alternatively, it may have been elicited by a specific request such as, *Tell me the story of Dog and Hare*.

The existence of **local authorities, leaders** and **supernatural** participants is often assumed, in which case they may not be introduced before acting:

9   **King Herod** heard of it ... (Mark 6:14)

10 Jesus left the synagogue and went to the home of **Simon** (Luke 4:38)

11 But at night **an angel of the Lord** opened the prison doors. (Acts 5:19)

8.1.3 One, a certain

In many languages, the presence or absence of the morpheme for *one* or *a certain*, in connection with the introduction of a participant, depends on whether or not it is thematically **salient**. In other words, use of *one* or *a certain* with a head noun depends on whether or not the participant continues to feature in a meaningful way in the following material.

Hopper and Thompson (1984:719) cite the following Modern Hebrew [heb] (oral) example. *Exad* 'one' is used in 12a because 'book' continues to be salient. In contrast, *exad* is not used in 12b because 'book' does not feature in the following material.[3]

12a *I sat there and read a book (**sefer-exad**), and it was an excellent book.*

12b *I read a book (**sefer**), and a couple of newspapers, and then went home.*

Participants introduced with *one* or *a certain* in written material in Biblical Hebrew and Koine Greek are often but not always thematically salient. The presence of the morpheme allows the writer both to introduce a participant (who may not even be named or otherwise identified) and to make a comment about him or her as topic in a single sentence (see (1) above and 2.1.3).

8.1.4 Points of departure and the introduction of a participant

The use of a point of departure in connection with the introduction of a participant signals a discontinuity of some type with respect to the existing mental representation. For instance, presentational sentence 13b begins with a point of departure by renewal *in the synagogue*. The point of departure indicates that, although 13b occurs in the same setting as 13a, it begins a **different** episode.

13a *Then Jesus went down to Capernaum, a town in Galilee, and began to teach the people on the Sabbath. They were amazed at his teaching, because his message had authority.*

13b *And <u>in the synagogue</u> there was a man possessed by an evil spirit.* (Luke 4:31–33)

In contrast, presentational sentence 14b provides detail about the **same** episode as that which has begun to be described in 14a.

14a *Then Levi held a great banquet for Jesus at his house.*

14b *And (there) was a large crowd of tax collectors and others who were eating with them.* (Luke 5:29)

When a participant is introduced in a **referential** point of departure in Koine Greek, then this participant temporarily displaces the global VIP of the section and becomes thematically salient (see ch. 9 for ways of signalling this fact in other languages).[4] In Acts 10:1, for example, Cornelius is introduced into a section in which Peter is the global VIP.

15 *Now <u>a certain man in Caesarea called Cornelius</u> ... saw ... an angel of God.*

---

[3] In the Hebrew of Ruth 1:1, 'one' is not used when Ahimelech is introduced, as he is not thematically salient. Unfortunately, translations into Swahili have used 'one' when introducing him. Unaware of this mistake, Tanzanian rural pastors understood Ahimelech to be a salient participant and offered me a number of explanations as to how he could be so viewed.

[4] For further examples in Greek, see Acts 8:9 (Simon is introduced in a point of departure and Philip is the VIP) and Acts 16:14 (Lydia is introduced in a point of departure and Paul is the VIP).

8.1.5 Highlighting the introduction of a participant

Many languages have devices to highlight the introduction of a participant. They include:
- the use of tail-head linkage immediately prior to the introduction ([16] – 3.2.3):

16 *While they were still speaking to the people, the priests ... approached them* (Acts 4:1)

- a thematic demonstrative such as *this* (17) in oral English (see ch. 9):

17 *Then **this** man arrived.*

Alternatively, a nondefault construction may be used. In one story in a Mixtec language of Mexico, the temporal setting for the introduction of the new participant was expressed in the main clause instead of a subordinate clause. The participant himself was introduced in a postnuclear subordinate clause:[5]

18 *They were still eating when **his godfather** arrived.*

In Koine Greek, *idou* 'behold' precedes the reference to a new participant "to focus special attention ... as he/she/it is introduced onto the event line of an episode" (Van Otterloo 1988:34):

19 *Now when Jesus was born in Bethlehem of Judea in the days of Herod the king,* **idou** *wise men from the East came to Jerusalem...* (Matthew 2:1)

In Matthew 1:20, *idou* highlights the introduction to an existing scene of a supernatural participant (contrast Acts 5:19 – 8.1.2):

20 *While he was considering this,* **idou** *angel of Lord appeared to him in dream.*

Review questions

1. How are major and minor participants typically distinguished?
2. In what sort of role are most major participants introduced?
3. On what does the presence or absence of the morpheme for *one* or *a certain*, in connection with the introduction of a participant, typically depend?[6]

Application to the language you are analysing

1. Describe the different ways that **major** participants are activated (introduced) in your texts. Distinguish introductions into a NEW mental representation from introductions into an EXISTING mental representation.
2. Describe how **minor** participants are activated in the texts.
3. Describe how the introduction of participants is **highlighted**.

8.2 Further reference to activated participants

Once participants have been introduced to a story, the way they are referred to depends on a number of factors, such as the number of participants currently on stage, their relative status, whether or not

---

[5] I am grateful to Inga McKendry (p.c.) for providing this example. The same device can be used in English; e.g. *They were still speaking to the people when the priests ... approached them* (Acts 4:1 – example 16 above).

[6] **Suggested answers**:
1. Major participants are typically active for a large part of the narrative and play leading roles; minor participants are activated briefly and lapse into deactivation.
2. Most major participants are introduced in a nontopic, noninteractive role.
3. The presence or absence of the morpheme for *one* or *a certain*, in connection with the introduction of a participant, typically depends on whether or not it is thematically **salient**.

their role changes, and the position of the sentence in the text.[7] Reflecting these factors, three tasks for a scheme of reference have been identified (Dooley and Levinsohn 2001:112):

semantic: identify the referents unambiguously, distinguishing them from other possible ones
pragmatic: signal the activation status and prominence of the referents or of the actions they perform
processing: overcome disruptions in the flow of information

Note 1. The term "activation status" refers to whether the referent is being introduced (activated) or reintroduced (reactivated), is currently on stage (active), or otherwise is accessible (see 9.2.4).

Note 2. In well-known folktales, the characteristics of the participants may be sufficient to identify each referent unambiguously. One must not, therefore, determine the scheme of reference for the language under consideration solely on the basis of folktales. It is important also to analyse narratives that concern incidents which are NOT generally known to the audience.

This section first states Givón's Iconicity Principle for referring to participants, and points out some limitations (8.2.1). It then describes an alternative method for determining how activated participants will be referred to, in terms of default and marked encoding values (8.2.2–8.2.3). It ends with some cross-linguistic observations about default encoding values (8.2.4).

NO step-by-step methodology for determining default and marked encoding values is presented here. Such a methodology is provided in chapter 18 of Dooley and Levinsohn 2001 ("A Methodology for Analyzing Reference Patterns").

8.2.1 Givón's Iconicity Principle

Givón's (1983:18) Iconicity Principle reflects the above three tasks of a scheme of reference, and is an attempt to predict how participants in a narrative will be referred to. It states:

> "The more disruptive, surprising, discontinuous or hard to process a topic is, the more *coding material* must be assigned to it."

For Koine Greek, the coding material for **third**-person referents, with the least coding material at the top of the scale and the most at the bottom, is as follows:
- implicit reference reflected in the verb inflection
- articular pronouns (e.g. *ho* 'he')
- "independent" (demonstrative or intensive) pronouns
- full noun phrases (NPs – including proper nouns), with or without the article

I find that Givón's Iconicity Principle works up to a point. For example, it correctly predicts that, when there is a **discontinuity** because a participant is being reactivated after an absence, it is normal for reference to be with a full NP. Similarly, it is normal to use a full NP when a sentence is **highlighted** because the event described is "disruptive, surprising" (1983:18).

However, sentences may be highlighted and a full NP employed when the information concerned is important but NOT disruptive nor surprising (e.g. a key speech). Also, it is not clear whether the principle covers the use of full NPs at the beginning of new "narrative units" (Fox 1987:168) when the participants remain the same and occupy the same roles in successive paragraphs.

The following are three factors that Givón's principle does NOT seem to cover:
- the **status** of the participant, in particular whether two major participants are interacting or whether the interacting participants are one major and one minor (see 8.2.2).
- the **salience** of the participant: a participant who is central to a whole book (the "global VIP") is referred to in different ways than other major participants. In addition, references by name to a locally important participant ("local VIP") are often marked in a special way.
- whether or not the reference to a participant follows the **reporting of a speech**.[8]

---
[7] Most of this section is taken from sec. 8.2 of Levinsohn 2000, though citations from Greek have been omitted.
    For an alternative approach to participant reference, see the "Givenness Hierarchy Model" of Gundel, Hedberg and Zacharski (1993).
[8] Givón (1983) used statistical studies to validate his Iconicity Principle. Unfortunately, such studies only reveal

An alternative to Givón's Iconicity Principle is to analyse the system of reference to activated participants in terms of default and marked encoding values.

- **Default** encoding values are identified for various situations in which, in Givón's terms, there is no great discontinuity or surprise.
- **Marked** encoding values are those that are other than the default encoding for a specific situation.

8.2.2 Default encoding values for activated subjects

First, default encoding values for activated subjects in certain specific contexts are determined:

S1   when the subject is the same as in the previous clause or sentence

S2   when the subject was the addressee of a speech reported in the previous sentence*

S3   when the subject was involved in the previous sentence* in a nonsubject role other than S2

S4   other changes of subject than those covered by S2 and S3 (including instances where the new subject is a subgroup of the previous subject).[9]

(*or earlier in the same sentence)

These encoding rules are then modified, as appropriate, to reflect more accurately the actual system being used in the language under investigation.

For example, default encoding rules for third-person subjects in Koine Greek include the following:

1. (S1) If the subject is the **same** as in the previous clause, no overt reference other than verb inflection is made to the subject, unless the construction requires an overt subject (rule 5 below).
2. (S2) If the subject was the **addressee** of an immediately preceding speech, an articular pronoun or no overt reference is used (depending on factors discussed in part V of Levinsohn 2000).
3. If a nonsubject in one clause becomes the subject of the next and a major participant is interacting with a **minor** participant or is **alone**, no reference is made to the subject. (This rule is based on S3, but applies in more restricted circumstances.)
4. In all other occasions that involve a **change** of subject, a full NP is used to refer to the subject. (These include occasions in which a participant is reactivated [S4] and those in which two major participants are interacting [S3].)
5. If the subject of a **genitive absolute** is the same as the subject of the previous clause, an independent pronoun is used (in genitives absolute, the subject generally is obligatory). Similarly, if a **point of departure involving renewal** has the same subject as that of the previous sentence, an independent pronoun is used (see below).

I now illustrate these rules from the parable of the Prodigal Son (Luke 15:11–32), before adding some provisos to rule 1.

---

tendencies. For example, Derbyshire (1986:252) gives the following statistics for the relation between the "average referential distance" in clauses since a participant had last featured in a Hixkaryána story and the form of reference used.

Category	Number of occurrences	Average referential distance
Ø	9	1.33
verb affix	298	1.31
pronoun	12	1.58
NP	121	5.65

Although these statistics show that Hixkaryána is likely to use an NP to refer to a participant who has not recently featured in the story, they do not indicate the circumstances under which the other forms of encoding would be used. The same is true of the other statistics cited by Derbyshire (1986:252).

[9] Similarly, determine default encoding values for activated **nonsubjects** in certain specific contexts (see 8.3.2).

8.2 Further reference to activated participants

Default rule 1 is illustrated in Luke 15:13b. The subject of 13b is the same as in 13a and no overt reference occurs (other than 3rd person singular verb inflection).

13a   *Not long after that, having got everything together the younger son set off for a far country*

13b   *and there Ø squandered his wealth in wild living.*

Default rule 2 is illustrated in Luke 15:12b. The subject of 12b was the addressee of the speech of 12a and is referred to by an articular pronoun (*ho*) or no overt reference, depending on the variant.

11b   *A certain man had two sons*

12a   *and the younger of them said to the father, 'Father, give me my share of the estate.'*

12b   *and **he/Ø** divided his property between them.*

Default rule 3 is illustrated in Luke 15:15–16a, which describe the interaction of a major participant (the younger son) and a minor participant (a citizen of the country). In 15b and 16, the subject was a nonsubject in the previous clause and no overt reference is made to him.

15a   *and, going, Ø became associated with one of the citizens of that country,*

15b   *and Ø sent him to his fields to feed pigs.*

16a   *and Ø was longing to be fed from the pods that the pigs were eating,*

Default rule 4 is illustrated in Luke 15:12a. There is a change of subject from 11b (a certain man) to the younger son and a full NP is used.

11b   *A certain man had two sons*

12a   *and **the younger of them** said to the father, 'Father, give me my share of the estate.'*

Default rule 5 is illustrated in Luke 15:14a. The subject of the genitive absolute of 14a is the same as the subject of 13b, so an independent pronoun (*autou* 'of him') is used.

13b   *and there Ø squandered his wealth in wild living.*

14a   *After **he** had spent everything ...*

Luke 2:36–37 illustrates rule 5 when a point of departure involving renewal has the same subject as the previous sentence. In both 36b and 37, the point of departure is an independent pronoun.

36a   *There was also a prophetess, Anna, the daughter of Phanuel, of the tribe of Asher.*

36b   ***This** (was) very old, having lived with a husband seven years after her marriage,*

37a   *and **she** (was) a widow for eighty four years.*

In regard to **rule 1** above, it should be noted that, if the subject is the same as in the last **independent** clause that describes a theme-line event, no overt reference is necessarily made to it even if an intervening background comment has a different subject. This is illustrated in Acts 5:2c; the subjects of 2a and 2c are the same (Ananias), and no overt reference is made to him in 2c even though the intervening genitive absolute has a different subject:[10]

2a   *and Ø kept back part of the money,*

2b   *his wife also having knowledge (of this),*

2c   *and, having brought the rest, Ø put it at the apostles' feet.*

---

[10] Changes of subject from a body part to its possessor (e.g. 'His feet and ankles became strong and he jumped up') are often treated as S1, as well. "[B]ody parts are not in general discourse-salient entities. ... They are undifferentiated from their possessors, and don't participate in discourse apart from their owner" (Hopper and Thompson 1984:726).

I now consider instances in which the subject and other participants in the action of the previous clause are included in a **plural** subject in the next clause. This is treated as the same subject (rule 1 above) for the purposes of participant reference encoding (the symbol **S1+** denotes this context).

Luke 15:24b (below) provides an example; the subject of the speech of 22–24a was the father and he, together with the addressees, is included in the plural subject of 24b. No overt reference is therefore made to the subject (*3p-* refers to the 3rd person plural inflection on the verb):

22   But the father said to his servants, … (23) 'and bring the fattened calf and kill it. Let's have a feast and celebrate.'

24b   and Ø *3p-began to celebrate.*

Note: In many languages, 3rd person plural forms are also used to refer to generic subjects. In sentence 8 of the Bekwarra text (p. 35), for instance, the subject of *e-dè* 'they said' must be 'someone' or 'some people', as Dog certainly was not among those who said, 'Let's fry Dog's (pup) and eat it'!

8.2.3 Marked encoding values for activated subjects

Deviations from default encoding values may involve the use of **more** or of **less** encoding material than predicted.

When **more** coding material is used than the default rules predict, this typically occurs for one of two reasons:

a) to mark the beginning of a narrative unit, following a discontinuity[11]
b) to highlight the action or speech concerned.

a) More coding material is used to mark the beginning of a narrative unit.

This is illustrated in the following extract from a Mofu-Gudur text (Dooley and Levinsohn 2001:134). The default value for context S1 in Mofu-Gudur is no overt reference (other than verb inflection). The initial adverbial phrase *one day* indicates that sentence b occurs immediately following a discontinuity, hence the motivation for the increased coding material (*the chief*).

a   *After that,* **Ø** *(chief) put it in its place.*
b   *One day,* **the chief** *left for his field.*

b) More coding material is used to highlight the action or speech concerned.

This is illustrated in sentence 9 of the Tyap text cited in 6.5.1 (see also appendix E in this chapter). The default encoding for context S1 in Tyap is a third-person pronoun. The increased coding material (*healer*) highlights his decision to discover who the woman is.

8   *Then healer also saw her.*
9   **Healer** *said, 'What kind of woman looks like this?'*

Similarly, in the Greek of Luke 15:22, the default encoding of reference to the father would be an articular pronoun, as he was the addressee of the previous speech (context S2). The marked encoding (*the father*) contributes to the highlighting of what he says.

21   *The son said to him, 'Father, I have sinned against heaven and against you. I am no longer worthy to be called your son.'*

22   *But* **the father** *said to his servants …*

---

[11] Sentence 2 of the Bekwarra text amplifies (is a restatement of) sentence 1. It begins with the pronoun *abe* 'they' to mark this discontinuity of action (2.4.4).

c) Less coding material is used for some references to a VIP.

When less coding material is used than the default rules predict, the referent is usually a VIP.[12] Section 9.1.3 further discusses this point. For references to VIPs in Koine Greek, see Levinsohn 2000:142ff.

8.2.4 Cross-linguistic default encoding values

The default coding values for references to activated third-person participants vary with the language. There appears to be a tendency for African languages to follow one of two patterns of default encoding:

- S1 (same subject) references use minimal coding material, whereas
  S2–S4 (all changes of subject) references use a full NP (e.g. in Tyap, in Chadic languages)
- S1–S3 references (to active participants) use minimal coding material, whereas
  S4 (reactivating) references use a full NP (e.g. in Bekwarra, in Bantu A languages).[13]

In other languages around the world (including Koine Greek – 8.2.2), the default encodings for S2 and S3 are different. For example, S1 and S2 references may use minimal coding material, whereas S3 and S4 references are a full NP (e.g. in Balochi of Sistan [bgn] (Iranian, Iran) – see Barjasteh Delforooz 2010:279).

Nevertheless, whichever pattern is followed in a particular language, the default encoding for context S1 (the subject is the same as in the previous clause or sentence) is always minimal.

Review question

Typically, for what two reasons is more coding material used than the default rules predict?[14]

Application to the language you are analysing

(The page references are to Dooley and Levinsohn 2001.)

1. Give the encoding scale for further reference to activated participants (see pp. 127–128).
2. Prepare a chart of participant encoding in one of your third-person texts (see pp. 128–130).
3. Track the participants in the text (p. 130).
4. Identify the context in which each reference to a participant occurs in the text (pp. 130–132).
5. Propose default encoding values for the following contexts involving activated **subjects** in the text (p. 132):
   - S1: the subject is the same as in the previous sentence;
   - S2: the subject was the addressee of the previous reported speech;
   - S3: the subject had some other nonsubject role in the previous clause/sentence;
   - S4: the subject was not involved in the previous clause/sentence.

   [As time permits, also propose default encoding values for the following contexts involving activated **nonsubjects** in the text:
   - N1: the referent occupies a nonsubject argument role in the current clause and in the previous clause or sentence;
   - N2: the referent was the speaker of the previous reported speech;
   - N3: the referent was involved in the previous sentence in a role other than N1 or N2;
   - N4: other nonsubject references than those covered by N1–N3.]
6. Inspect all your texts for other than default encoding (pp. 132–134).

---

[12] For less coding material in noninitial rounds of a reported conversation, 7.7.

[13] As noted earlier, it is important to check that this system of encoding holds in other than well-known folktales.

[14] **Suggested answer:**
Typically, more coding material is used than the default rules predict:
- to mark the beginning of a narrative unit, or
- to highlight the action or speech concerned.

7. Incorporate any modifications to the proposals of point 5 (p. 134).
8. Generalise the pragmatic motivations for deviations from default encoding in the texts you are analysing (see pp. 134–135 and 8.2.3).

8.3 NP references to active participants and story development in Biblical Hebrew

In Biblical Hebrew,[15] the default encoding of reference to active participants in contexts S1 and S2 is minimal.[16] This is illustrated in the following extract from Genesis 22:1–14 (see also appendix D); the subject of 1c is the same as that of 1b (S1), whereas the subject of 1d was the addressee of 1c (S2). In both instances, there is no overt reference to the subject (other than verb inflection).

1b   & *the God tested Abraham*

1c   & *Ø (S1) said to him, 'Abraham'.*

1d   & *Ø (S2) said, 'Here I am'.*[17]

8.3.1 Marked encoding of references to subjects in contexts S1 and S2

As in other languages, increased encoding is used in Biblical Hebrew in contexts S1 and S2 to mark the beginning of a narrative unit and to highlight the action or speech concerned. In 22:4a, for example, the initial adverbial phrase *on third day* signals a discontinuity of time, hence the motivation for the increased encoding material (*Abraham*) in context S1.

3f   & *Ø went to the place which the God had said to him.*

4a   *On third day* & **Abraham** *(S1) lifted up his eyes*

Similarly, increased encoding (*Abraham*) is used in context S2 in 22:8a to highlight the reported speech (see discussion in 7.7).

7a   & *Isaac spoke to Abraham his father*

7b   & *Ø (S1) said, 'My father'.*

7c   & *Ø (S2) said, 'Here I am, my son'.*

7d   & *Ø (S2) said, 'See, the fire and the wood! & where [is] the lamb for a burnt offering?'*

8a   & **Abraham** *(S2) said, 'God will provide the lamb for a burnt offering, my son'.*

However, instances of NPs in context S1 are much more frequent in Biblical Hebrew stories than in comparable stories in Tyap and Koine Greek. This is illustrated by comparing passages in the three languages in which one participant performs most of the actions: Biblical Hebrew (appendix D), Tyap (appendix E), and Greek (Matthew 26:36–47).[18]

Table 15 indicates the number of clauses in each passage, the number of clauses that fit context S1, and the number of these in which an NP is used to refer to the subject. As the figures indicate, the percentage of NPs in context S1 is far higher in Biblical Hebrew than in the other two languages.

---

[15] See also Levinsohn 2006.

[16] The default encoding of reference to active participants in context S3 is also minimal whenever there is no ambiguity as to the referent (Steven Runge p.c.).

[17] On minimal reference to subjects in context S2, see Regt 1999:28–29.

[18] A much more extensive corpus would need to be examined to demonstrate that the differences in frequency between Hebrew and the other languages were statistically significant. However, I am satisfied that these passages are typical, as far as the points being made in this chapter are concerned. See also Callow's observation (1974:33), in connection with the frequency with which the name *Joseph* occurs in Genesis 42:6–9, that Hebrew is "rather unusual in the readiness with which it uses proper names to trace participants through a discourse".

8.3 NP references to active participants and story development in Biblical Hebrew

Table 15. Noun Phrases in context S1 in Hebrew, Tyap and Greek

Language	Total clauses	In context S1	NPs in S1	% NPs in S1
Hebrew	44	28	6	21%
Tyap	42	34	2	6%
Greek	17/26*	15/24*	0	0%

*The first figure indicates the number of independent clauses in the passage. The second figure includes participial clauses.

The reason for the higher number is that NPs are not used in Hebrew only to mark the beginning of a narrative unit or to highlight the action or speech concerned. In addition, I argue, they are found at places in a narrative where one might expect a **development marker** (DM – 6.5) to occur.[19]

Dooley and Levinsohn (2001:39) note that "changes in action ... when a story moves from reported conversation to nonspeech events ... are often marked" by the use of a DM such as *so* or *then*. For example, in the *New English Bible*, the transition from the reported conversation of Genesis 22:1c–2 to the resulting nonspeech events of 3 is marked by *so* (***So** Abraham rose early in the morning* ...).

1b & *the God tested Abraham*

1c & *Ø said to him, 'Abraham'.*

1d & *Ø said, 'Here I am'.*

2   & *Ø said, 'Take now your son, your only one whom you love, Isaac, & go into the land of Moriah & offer him there for a burnt offering on one of the mountains which I will say to you'.*

3a & ***Abraham** rose early in the morning*

It is common for DMs such as *so* and *then* to be mutually exclusive with the default way of conjoining clauses or sentences (whether a conjunction such as *and*, as in Greek, or the absence of any conjunction, as in Tyap). In Biblical Hebrew narratives, however, the norm is for every clause or sentence to begin with the same conjunction (*waw*). This means that the option of signalling a new development by selecting a particular conjunction is not available in Biblical Hebrew. The use of NPs to refer to active participants compensates for this.

Heimerdinger makes the following observation about the clauses of Genesis 22:1–6 in which Abraham is referred to by name: "they start a new scene or **open a new burst of closely related actions**" (1999:124; emphasis mine). In other words, they represent a new development in the story line. This is not indicated in Hebrew by a DM, however. Rather, it is implied by the 'redundant' use of an NP in context S1.[20]

The following chart shows how the presence of NP references to Abraham might lead us to divide 22:1–6 into five DUs (development units – represented by boxes).

1	& *Ø happened after these things & the God tested Abraham & Ø said to him, 'Abraham'.*
	& *Ø said, 'Here I am'.*
2	& *Ø said, 'Take now your son, your only one whom you love, Isaac, & go into the land of Moriah & offer him there for a burnt offering on one of the mountains which I will say to you'.*

---

[19] Andersen claims that "a seemingly redundant unnecessarily repeated subject noun serves to highlight the distinctiveness of an event" (1994:106). One of the functions of a DM is to indicate that the material concerned is distinctive (Levinsohn 2000:72), so Andersen is effectively making the same claim as the one presented here. See also Regt's (1999:20) statement that the references to David in 2 Samuel 11:8, 10 "mark off distinct stages of his actions". However, Regt goes on to explain the phenomenon in terms of highlighting; they "may show a crucial and climactic moment in the text, or indicate that what is about to be said is important or not expected" (p. 96). Since marked encoding is used cross-linguistically to highlight, this fails to explain the frequency of marked encoding in Hebrew.

[20] New developments are not indicated in Hebrew by distinct verb forms, either. Typically, only two basic verb forms are used in independent clauses to encode narrative events, and the choice between them is determined by constituent order. The default (*wyyqtl*) form is used when the clause begins with a verb. The *qtl* form is used when the clause begins with a point of departure or a focal constituent preposed for prominence (see 1b and 13c).

3	& ***Abraham*** rose early in the morning, & Ø saddled his ass, & Ø took two of his youths with him & Isaac his son, & Ø split wood for a burnt offering, & Ø rose up, & Ø went to the place which God had said to him.
4	Ø On third day & ***Abraham*** lifted up his eyes, & Ø saw the place from a distance.
5	& ***Abraham*** said to his young men, 'You stay here with the ass, & I & the boy will go on to that place, & we will worship & return to you'.
6	& ***Abraham*** took the wood of the burnt offering, & Ø laid [it] on Isaac his son, & Ø took in his hand the fire & the knife, & Ø went the two together.

Notice, in the above passage, that the reported conversation of 22:1–2 is grouped as a single DU. The conversation only represents a development in the story as it moves beyond the opening speeches to the instruction of 2 (see 7.5.2).

In contrast, the reported conversation of 22:7–9a extends over two DUs, as represented in the following. The highlighted speech of 8a represents a new development in the story (see above).

7	& *Isaac* spoke to Abraham his father, & Ø said, 'My father'.
	& Ø said, 'Here I am, my son'.
	& Ø said, 'See, the fire and the wood! & where [is] the lamb for a burnt offering?'

8a	& ***Abraham*** said, 'God will provide the lamb for a burnt offering, my son'.
8b	& Ø 3p-went on the two of them together,
9a	& Ø 3p-came to the place which God had said to him.

The above discussion might give the impression that, every time an NP reference occurs in context S1 or S2, a new DU will begin, even though an NP reference might already have been expected because of the presence of a discontinuity.[21] However, in languages that have DMs, the DM is not always used when there is a discontinuity (see 6.6c). For example, in the Tyap text, there is a discontinuity of time between 3b and 4, but the DM *kàn* is not used following the discontinuity until 6a.[22]

Research is needed in Biblical Hebrew in order to distinguish between NP references to active participants that are motivated by preceding discontinuities and those that are motivated by the beginning of a new DU.

8.3.2 Marked encoding of references to active participants in other contexts

NP references to active participants may be motivated by the presence of a new development not only in contexts S1 and S2, but also in other contexts. This section considers examples of NP references in the nonsubject contexts N1 (the referent occupies a nonsubject argument role in the current clause and in the previous clause or sentence) and N2 (the addressee of a reported speech was the speaker of the previous reported speech). It also notes the implications of referring, in the same clause, to **two** active participants with NPs (e.g. in contexts S1 and N1).

In the diagram below of Genesis 4:4b–6, 5b and 6 contain NP references to Cain, who was also involved in a nonsubject role in 5a. This suggests a division of the passage into DUs as follows:

4b	& the LORD *had favour on Abel & on his offering*
5a	& *on Cain & on his offering* Ø *did not have favour*.

5b	& it upset **Cain** (N1) very much, & his looks were downcast.

6–7	& the LORD said to **Cain** (N1), 'Why does it upset you & why are your looks downcast?'

---

[21] NP references to active participants for highlighting do not present a problem, because the highlighted action or speech will already be considered a new development.
[22] Elsewhere I argue that continuity and development "are *different* parameters" (Levinsohn 2000:77).

Sometimes, a single clause contains **two** NP references to active participants. Such is the case in 4:13: in the contexts S2 (Cain) and N2 (the LORD). The speech that is introduced in this way represents a change of direction in the reported conversation (to active participants probably increases the highlighting of this unexpected development:

9a	& the LORD said to Cain, 'Where is Abel your brother?'
9b	& Ø said [to-Ø], 'I don't know. Am I my brother's keeper?'
10	& Ø said [to-Ø], 'What have you done? The voice of the blood of your brother cries to me from the ground. (11) And now you are cursed more than the ground which opened its mouth to receive your brother's blood from your hand. (12) When you till the ground, it will not again give its strength to you. You shall be a vagabond and a fugitive on the earth.'

| 13 | & **Cain** (S2) said to **the LORD** (N2), 'My punishment is greater than I can bear. (14) Lo, you have driven me out from the face of the earth today, & I shall be hidden from your face, & I shall be a vagabond & a fugitive on the earth, & it will be that anyone who finds me shall kill me.' |

8.3.3 Conclusion

Statistics suggest that Biblical Hebrew uses a significantly greater number of NP references to active participants than Tyap and Koine Greek do. I have argued in this section that this increase compensates for the absence of a DM in Hebrew. Languages typically use increased encoding to refer to active participants when the subject remains the same for two reasons:
- to mark the beginning of a narrative unit, following a discontinuity, or
- to highlight the speech or action concerned.

Hebrew uses NP references to active participants not only in these contexts, but also in connection with new developments.[23]

8.3.4 Implication for translation

Translations tend to reproduce Hebrew's heavy encoding of reference to active participants. However, when such a form of reference does not follow a discontinuity or is not there to highlight a following speech or event, it would be better just to use a DM, if one exists in the receptor language. For a good example of this, see the *GNB* translation of Genesis 22:5, where *& said Abraham* has been rendered, *Then he said*.

Finally, a warning! If the receptor language uses marked encoding only following discontinuities or for highlighting, then a rendering of Genesis 22:5 which retains a nominal reference to Abraham would imply that his speech is highlighted, even though it is not highlighted in Hebrew.

Suggested reading

Chapters 16 and 18 of Dooley and Levinsohn 2001 relate to the topics covered in this chapter.

---

[23] In some Bantu languages, the 'salient' demonstrative set (see 9.2.1) is used to indicate that the actions performed by the referent represent a new development in the story. This is illustrated in the following extract from a folktale in Nyungwe [nyu] (Bantu N40, Mozambique). Each DU begins with a demonstrative (translated *that*) which marks the referent as the actor through whom the narrative develops.
  That man said, 'I'll go and return this afternoon'.
  (She) said, 'Fine, go!'
  That man ... walked and walked, then he climbed a tree that had bees.
  That.one began to cut that tree, he cut that tree, but those flies were few.

Appendix D: Chart for Biblical Hebrew: Genesis 21:33b–22:14

INTRO: introduction of participant; [PRE]: subject prior to verb; [to Ø]: implicit;
Ø, (3p): no overt reference other than 3rd person singular or plural inflection

Ref.	Conj	Preverbals	Subject	Context	Predicate
33b	&		Ø	S1	called there on name of the LORD God everlasting.
34	&		Abraham	S1	lived in the land of the Philistines many days.
1a	&		Ø	–	happened after these things
1b	&	the God	[PRE]	S4	tested Abraham
1c	&		Ø	S1	said to him, 'Abraham.'
1d	&		Ø	S2	said [to Ø], 'Here I am.'
2	&		Ø	S2	said [to Ø], 'Take your son, your only one whom you love, Isaac, & go into land of Moriah & offer him there for a burnt offering …'
3a	&		Abraham	S2	rose early in the morning
3b	&		Ø	S1	saddled his ass
3c	&		Ø	S1	took two of his youths with him & Isaac his son
3d	&		Ø	S1	split wood for a burnt offering
3e	&		Ø	S1	rose up
3f	&		Ø	S1	went to the place which the God had said to him.
4a	Ø	on third day &	Abraham	S1	lifted up his eyes
4b	&		Ø	S1	saw the place from a distance
5a	&		Abraham	S1	said to his young men, 'You stay here with the ass …'
6a	&		Abraham	S1	took the wood of the burnt offering
6b	&		Ø	S1	laid [it] on Isaac his son
6c	&		Ø	S1	took in his hand the fire & the knife
6d	&		(3P)	S1 +	went the two together
7a	&		Isaac	S4	spoke to Abraham his father
7b	&		Ø	S1	said [to Ø], 'My father.'
7c	&		Ø	S2	said [to Ø], 'Here I am, my son.'
7d	&		Ø	S2	said [to Ø], 'See, the fire & wood! & where [is] the lamb …?'
8a	&		Abraham	S2	said [to Ø], 'God will provide the lamb for a burnt offering …'
8b	&		(3P)	S1 +	went the two of them together
9a	&		(3P)	S1	came to the place which the God had said to him.
9b	&		Abraham	S4	built there the altar
9c	&		Ø	S1	arranged the wood
9d	&		Ø	S1	bound Isaac his son
9e	&		Ø	S1	laid him on the altar on wood
10a	&		Abraham	S1	stretched out his hand
10b	&		Ø	S1	took the knife to slay his son
11a	&		angel of the LORD	INTRO	called to him from the heavens
11b	&		Ø	S1	said [to Ø], 'Abraham, Abraham.'

Appendix D: Chart for Biblical Hebrew: Genesis 21:33b–22:14

Ref.	Conj	Preverbals	Subject	Context	Predicate
11c	&		Ø	S2	*said [to Ø], 'Here I am.'*
12	&		Ø	S2	*said [to Ø], 'Do not lay your hand on the boy …'*
13a	&		Abraham	S2	*lifted up his eyes*
13b	&		Ø	S1	*looked*
13c	&	behold a ram behind him [PRE]		INTRO	*was entangled in a thicket by its horns.*
13d	&		Abraham	S3	*went*
13e	&		Ø	S1	*took the ram*
13f	&		Ø	S1	*offered it for a burnt offering instead of his son*
14	&		Abraham	S1	*called the name of that place 'the LORD will see'*

Appendix E: Chart for Tyap

Extract from "The Healer and His Wife" (Follingstad 1994)
Preverbal particles: *si* 'thematic prominence'; *kàn* DM; *kìn* 'additive, nondevelopmental'

Ref.	Prenuclear constituents	Subject	Context	Particles		Predicate
1a		*Bashila*	S4			*was coming from grinding,*
1b		3s	S1	**si**	**kàn**	*heard the healer singing to their child [that he used to go and eat people]*
1c		3s	S1	**si**		*stood behind the room*
1d		3s	S1	**si**		*heard the song that 3s was singing.*
2a		*Bashila*	S1	**si**	**kìn**	*passed*
2b		3s	S1	**si**		*entered,*
2c		3s	S1	**si**		*returned*
2d		3s	S1	**si**		*kept quiet.*
3a		3s	S4	**si**		*took the child*
3b		3s	S1	**si**		*gave it to Bashila.*
4a	*It became morning,*	3s	S1	**si**		*got up,*
4b		3s	S1	**si**		*got up.*
5a	*When 3s (S1) got up,*	3s	S1	**si**		*left,*
5b		3s	S1	**si**		*again went to eat people.*
6a	*When 3s (S1) went to eat people,*					
		Bashila also	S4	**si**	**kàn**	*got up*
6b		3s	S1	**si**	**kìn**	*gathered her things*
6c		3s	S1	**si**		*fetched ashes*
6d		3s	S1	**si**		*added an egg*
6e		3s	S1	**si**		*put the things on her head*
6f		3s	S1	**si**		*caught the road.*
7a		3s	S1			*caught the road,*
7b		3s	S1			*went,*
7c		3s	S1			*went,*
7d		3s	S1			*went,*
7e		3s	S1	**si**	**kàn**	*looked*
7f		3s	S1	**si**		*saw the healer.*

Ref.	Prenuclear constituents	Subject	Context	Particles		Predicate
8		Healer also		si	kàn	saw her.
9		Healer	S1			said, 'What kind of woman looks like this?'
10a		3s	S1			walked,
10b		3s	S1			walked,
10c		3s	S1			walked,
10d		the woman	S4			was nearing him,
10e		3s	S1	si	kàn	rubbed the ashes on her face
10f		3s	S1	si	kàn	put the egg in her mouth.
11a		3s	S1	si		reached him,
11b		3s	S1	si	kàn	bit down on the egg
11c		3s	S1	si		bit down on it in her mouth
11d		the egg	S3	si	kàn	burst [all over her face].
12	There	3s	S4			said that the woman was not his wife, that 3s could pass.
13		The woman	S2	si	kìn	passed.

9

VIPs, Determiners, Directionals

This chapter covers three interrelated topics: participants who are the centre of attention for part or all of a narrative ("VIPs" – 9.1); common functions of different sets of determiners (a cover term for demonstratives such as *this* and *that* plus articles such as *a* and *the* – see Crystal 1997:112), including those that refer to local VIPs or to participants other than the VIP (9.2); and verbs such as *come* and *go* which are oriented with respect to a "deictic center" (Fillmore 1997 – 9.3).

9.1 VIPs

This section begins by describing two reference strategies in narratives: one in which the major participants are treated **equally**, and one in which one major participant (the VIP) is **favoured** over others (9.1.1). It then discusses the role of *other* in a reference strategy (9.1.2). Finally, it introduces a distinction between the **global** VIP and **local** VIPs (9.1.3).

9.1.1 Two reference strategies

When telling a story, authors may treat the major participants equally or make one of them the centre of attention. This is often reflected in the reference strategy that they choose.

Strategies for encoding and interpreting references to participants include the **sequential** ("look-back") and the **VIP** ones (Dooley and Levinsohn 2001:117–119).

a) In the **sequential** reference strategy (which was assumed in chapter 8), no referent (participant) has any kind of favoured status over any other. The following display applies the sequential strategy to the first few sentences of the Bekwarra folktale. Dog and Hare are referred to in the same way. In particular, they are referred to with pronouns only when the subject was the same as in the previous sentence:

	'Dog and Hare' with subject-oriented sequential strategy
1	One day **Hare** went and talked with Dog.
2	*He* told *him*, 'Fry one of your pups for us to eat!'
3	**Dog** refused.
4	**Hare** asked *him*, 'Why won't you fry it?'
5	**Dog** answered, '…'

b) In the **VIP** strategy, "one referent is distinguished from the rest ... and a special set of terms refer to it" (Grimes 1978:viii). Use of this strategy marks the participant concerned as **salient** (the centre of attention).

Narratives in the Kaba [ksp] (Nilo-Saharan, Central African Republic) language use this strategy. Unqualified nouns (i.e. nouns without a determiner) refer to the VIP. In contrast, references to all the other activated participants take a determiner.

The following display applies the Kaba strategy of identifying the VIP to the first few sentences of the Dog and Hare folktale. Dog is the VIP, and nominal references to Dog lack a determiner (-Ø indicates the absence of any determiner). In contrast, references to Hare take a determiner:

	'Dog and Hare' with an unqualified noun VIP strategy
1	One day **Hare-the** went and talked with **Dog-Ø**.
2	He told him, 'Fry one of your pups for us to eat!'
3	**Dog-Ø** refused.
4	**Hare-the** asked him, 'Why won't you fry it?'
5	**Dog-Ø** answered, '...'

9.1.2 The role of *other* in a reference strategy

One strategy for referring to two participants in turn involves the use of *other*. The way *other* is used depends on whether the sequential or VIP strategy is being employed.

a) In the **sequential** reference strategy, *other ... other* is employed as the author switches from one participant to the other.

The following applies this strategy to the first few sentences of the Dog and Hare story:

	'Dog and Hare' with subject-oriented sequential strategy and *other*
1	One day **Hare** went and talked with Dog.
2	He told him, 'Fry one of your pups for us to eat!'
3	**The other** refused.
4	**The other** asked him, 'Why won't you fry it?'
5	**The other** answered, '...'

b) In the **VIP** strategy, a default pronoun is used to refer to the VIP and *other* is used for references to the remaining participant(s).

This strategy has been observed in the C'Lela [dri] (Kainji, Nigeria) language. In such a language, references to Dog and Hare in the above passage might be encoded as follows:

	'Dog and Hare' with a VIP strategy and *other*
1	One day **Hare** went and talked with Dog.
2	He told him, 'Fry one of your pups for us to eat!'
3	**He** refused.
4	**The other** asked him, 'Why won't you fry it?'
5	**He** answered, '...'

9.1.3 Global and local VIPs

The VIP can be identified either on the **global** level (for the text as a whole, sometimes known as the **central character**) or on the **local** level (for a particular thematic grouping, sometimes called the **thematic referent**).

9.1 VIPs

In long narratives with a single global VIP (e.g. Jesus in the Gospels), the organisation of the individual episodes may be around the **other** participants with whom the VIP interacts. In other words, an episode may involve both the global VIP and a local VIP.

Even when using the sequential strategy of participant reference, there is a tendency to organise the material around different local VIPs in turn. This may be done, for example, by relating all the participants to him or her. Thus, in one episode involving a husband, wife and child, the local VIP may be the man, and the other participants are referred to as *his wife* and *his son*. In another episode, the local VIP may be the boy, and the other participants are referred to as *his father* and *his mother*.[1]

Note 1. Typically, less coding material is used to refer to the VIP than to other participants (see Marchese 1984). In Mambila, for example, the global VIP "is identified as little as possible once he is introduced ... Participants other than the main one [VIP] are re-identified by a noun every time they are mentioned" (with certain exceptions) (Perrin 1978:110–111). See below for an example from Goemai.

Note 2. Some narratives in a language may use the VIP strategy and others, the sequential one. See Levinsohn 1978:86–89 on this phenomenon in Inga.

Note 3. Often, the VIP strategy is NOT used in the **climactic** episode of a narrative, even when each preceding episode has been organised around a local VIP.

Note 4. Organisation around local VIPs appears to be more common in **oral** texts that in written ones.

The following is an English translation of an extract from a folktale in Goemai. Implicit references to the woman as subject imply that she is the VIP. The only time that an NP refers to her is in sentence 4, following a discontinuity of time. In contrast, all the references to the snake are explicit:

1 *Ø (She) returned and found that Snake really did come slithering out.*
2 *Snake was rising in anger towards her.*
3 *Ø (She) threw the liver at Snake, turned and went away.*
4 <u>*After three days,*</u> **the woman** *went there with the liver and again found Snake lying there.*
5 *Ø (She) threw the liver, turned and went back home, and came back another time.*
6 *Snake knew her.*
7 *Snake didn't rise in anger towards her.*
8 *Ø (She) threw the liver.*
9 *Snake didn't do anything to her.*

Review questions

1. How do the sequential and VIP reference strategies differ?
2. What is the difference between a global VIP and a local VIP?
3. Once activated, do references to the VIP typically employ more or less coding material than for other participants?[2]

---

[1] However, relating participants in this way does NOT guarantee that the participant who is the point of reference will be the local VIP. For example, following Exodus 2:16 (*The priest of Midian had seven daughters*), the events involve the daughters, not the father. Then, following Exodus 2:18 (*They returned to Reu'el their father*), the father takes the initiative.

[2] **Suggested answers**:
1. In the **sequential** reference strategy, no referent has any kind of favoured status over any other; they are treated equally. In the **VIP** strategy, one referent is made the centre of attention and a special set of terms refer to it.
2. A global VIP is identified for the text as a whole. A local VIP is identified for a particular thematic grouping.
3. Once activated, references to the VIP typically employ **less** coding material than for other participants.

9.2 Determiners

This section discusses how languages may use determiners and pronouns to mark which participants are currently salient and which are not (9.2.1). The determiner set selected to refer to salient participants often depends on whether the determiners in the language are person-oriented or distance-oriented (9.2.2). Section 9.2.3 notes other factors that may distinguish determiner sets in a language. Finally, section 9.2.4 considers why (definite) articles are not always used when referring to active participants. Appendix F in this chapter discusses the Greek demonstratives and shows that ONE of the pragmatic effects of using them is to identify the referent as salient (*houtos* 'this') or not salient (*ekeinos* 'that').

9.2.1 Thematic and athematic determiners

It is common for **determiners** and **pronouns** to be associated with references to VIPs. The following are some instances where such is the case.

- In folktales in a number of Amerindian languages of Brazil and Colombia, the only participant referred to with a **pronoun** is the VIP. At certain crucial points in folktales in the Kuo [xuo] (Adamawa, Chad) language, pronominal references to the VIP are with the pronoun for *you*!
- One determiner or pronoun set (**thematic**) may refer only to the local VIP, with another set (**athematic**) used for references to other participants, e.g. Sokoro [sok] (Chadic, Chad). Remember. The thematic set is often mistakenly called "emphatic" – see 4.6.1.)

    In Waunana [noa] (alt. Woun Meu; Chocó, Colombia and Panama), this distinction is taken a step further (see Binder 1977). One demonstrative set (*ma-*) is used for anaphoric references to the **global** VIP or main theme. A second set (*jã-*) is used for anaphoric references to **local** VIPs or themes.

    This is illustrated in the following extract from a text about how to buy and look after a pig. Anaphoric references to the pig (the main theme) take *ma-* (sent. 1), whereas anaphoric references to a local theme such as its ears take *jã-* (sent. 2):

1   *Look at the ears of the* (**ma-**) *pig!*
2   *If they* (**jã-**) *are bad ...*

    In addition to these two demonstrative sets, a third set (*ʔa-*) is used for anaphoric reference to **athematic** referents, and an **article** (*chi*) is used for anaphoric references to other participants.

    This is illustrated in the following extract from a text about how to make a canoe. Anaphoric references to the canoe (the main theme) take *ma-* (sent. 2). Anaphoric references to the tree (the secondary theme) take *jã-* (sents. 3–4) – until it looks more like a canoe than a log, when *ma-* is employed! Anaphoric references to the axe take the article *chi* (sent. 3). As for the river, the second reference in sentence 4 takes *ʔa-* to indicate that it is not thematic:

1   *I want to tell you about making a canoe.*
2   *To make it* (**ma-**), *a tree is selected and cut down with an axe.*
3   *That* (**jã-**) *tree is shaped with the* (**chi**) *axe.*
4   *It* (**jã-**) *is taken to the river, so that it can go on it* (**ʔa-**).

- The Tsuvadi language has an **athematic** pronominal prefix for subjects that are not thematic. The following sentences occur in an account of an incident involving thieves and an old woman. When the thieves as subject are thematic, reference to them is with the third-person plural prefix (3p). When they are not thematic, reference to them is with the athematic prefix *a-*:

1   (The thieves are thematic:)   *Then 3p-came, 3p-beat her, 3p-felt no pity for her.*
2   (The woman is thematic:)   *This old woman who is here ... **a**-felt no pity for her, **a**-beat her.*

9.2 Determiners 145

- In some languages (e.g. Kaba), references to the VIP are either with an unqualified noun or with a pronoun. In contrast, participants with whom the VIP interacts are referred to with a noun plus determiner (see 9.1.1). This is true even for proper names (see 9.2.4).
- In some languages in which an unqualified noun or pronoun is used to refer to the VIP, references to activated participants with whom the VIP interacts involve a noun plus a determiner when they are **salient**. They may then be thought of as **temporarily** displacing the VIP as the centre of attention. The determiner is commonly used also to refer to salient props (inanimate objects), once they have been activated.

   For example, a folktale in Herde concerns a woman whose husband does not love her or eat the food that she prepares for him. So she visits a fetish priest to ask for advice. He tells her, *Bring me three hairs from a live lion!* She succeeds, so he asks her how she succeeded. When she explains what she did, he tells her, *Do the same with your husband!* So she does so and her husband eats her food.

   Although various **props** feature in the story, the only ones that are marked with the determiner *na* are the lion hairs, because of their salience in the story.

   The two major **participants** in the story are the woman and the fetish priest. The determiner is never used to refer to the woman, who is the VIP. The determiner is used in connection with the fetish priest on the two occasions that he is temporarily salient because of the importance of his pronouncements for the development of the story (*Bring me three hairs from a live lion!* and *Do the same with your husband!*).[3]

- The same principle applies when **two major** participants interact throughout a story. In a folktale about Baboon and Crocodile in Nyungwe, neither animal is marked by a determiner when they are active. However, a **minor** participant who appears at one point in the story is marked with a particular determiner to indicate that he is temporarily salient because of the advice that he gives.

   The same observation applies to references to minor participants in Ekoti [eko] (Bantu P30, Mozambique). However, when a **major** participant is referred to with the same determiner, this indicates that the referent is temporarily LESS salient.

   If no VIP is identified in the story, then the determiner may occur frequently, to mark participants as salient each time they have a significant role to play.

9.2.2 Thematic determiners and orientation

Typically, the demonstratives described above as thematic/salient and athematic/not salient also have deictic-exophoric uses.[4] Anderson and Keenen (1985:282) distinguish two systems of demonstratives, which they describe as "person-oriented" versus "distance-oriented". Since both involve distance from one or more participants, I shall instead refer to them as people-oriented versus speaker-oriented.

- **People-oriented** demonstratives are oriented with respect to the distance from both the speaker and the addressee; e.g. *close to speaker, close to addressee, close to neither*.
- **Speaker-oriented** demonstratives are oriented only with respect to the distance from the speaker; e.g. *close to, intermediate from, far from the speaker*.[5]

In both instances, the distance involved may be spatial or temporal.

The demonstrative set chosen to refer to activated, salient participants varies with the language. It may be the **close to speaker** one (e.g. Koine Greek – see appendix F in this chapter), the **close**

---

[3] *Na* is also found at the end of subordinate clauses when what follows is particularly important; see 5.2.4 and 9.2.4.

[4] An exophoric reference is a direct reference "to the EXTRALINGUISTIC SITUATION accompanying an UTTERANCE" (Crystal 1997:143). In other words, the reference is to something in the real world, rather than in the discourse.

[5] Enfield (2003) claims that the demonstratives of Lao are not speaker-oriented. Rather, they should be viewed as "default" (with an "INDICATING function" – pp. 85–86) versus "marked" (one which "ENCODES not here" – p. 87). Enfield's article does not discuss their discourse-anaphoric use, but the general principle of one demonstrative being the default one is important.

to addressee one (e.g. Inga), or even the **far from speaker/close to neither** one (e.g. Ekoti and Nyungwe – 9.2.1).[6]

In some languages, however, deictic-exophoric orientation and salience are **separate parameters**. Such is the case in Mofu-Gudur (see Pohlig and Levinsohn 1994); the NP may consist of a noun followed by a deictic-exophoric demonstrative, followed by a "status" demonstrative.

Review questions

1. If a language is said to have a set of "emphatic pronouns", what should you check about its referents?
2. What is the difference between **people-oriented** and **speaker-oriented** demonstratives, according to Anderson and Keenen (1985)?[7]

9.2.3 Other distinctions signalled by determiners

The following distinctions were useful for distinguishing between determiner sets in Bafut (see also Mfonyam 2012):

- particular: *They arranged to meet on a certain day. On **that** day ...*
- deictic: *A: Where is it? B: **There** it is.*
- selective: *I want **that** book (not any of the others).*
- identity: *The next day they arrived at the town. That **same** day ...*
- unmarked (default).

"Selective" is one of Dik et al.'s categories of (prominent) **focus** (see 4.4). However, focus may be a separate parameter.

Another distinction between sets of determiners is **anaphoric-cataphoric**.[8] In Inga, for instance, if I say, *Do it like that!*, I have already shown you how to do it (*that* has anaphoric reference). If, in contrast, I say, *Do it like this!*, I am about to show you how to do it (*this* has cataphoric reference).

9.2.4 The (definite) article

"A definite referent is one which the speaker assumes that the hearer will be able to identify, i.e. to locate in his or her current mental representation" (Dooley and Levinsohn 2001:58).[9] It is "uniquely identifiable" (Gundel et al. 1993:275). It is not necessary to introduce a referent formally before using the definite article. For example:

> *We saw a house and went towards it. When we arrived at **the** door ...*

This is because, when an entity is introduced, other items that the culture associates with the entity are also **accessed**. Thus, when a reference is made in a Western culture to a *house*, the existence of its door, roof, windows, kitchen, etc., is also presupposed and, therefore, accessible.

Similarly, when reference is made in many African cultures to a *compound*, the existence of the people who live in the compound is presupposed and, therefore, accessible. An example of this is found

---

[6] Demonstratives that indicate that a referent is close to the speaker are called 'proximal'. Those that indicate that a referent is away from a 'deictic centre' are called 'distal'.

[7] **Suggested answers**:
1. If a language is said to have a set of "emphatic pronouns", you should check whether its primary function is to refer to local VIPs or themes. If so, it would be better to refer to it as a set as "thematic pronouns".
2. **People-oriented** demonstratives are oriented with respect to both the speaker and the addressee. **Speaker-oriented** demonstratives are oriented with respect to the distance from the speaker.

[8] An anaphoric reference is to "some previously expressed unit (the ANTECEDENT)" (Crystal 1997:19). Cataphoric reference is to "what is about to be expressed" (p. 55).

[9] Articles are determiners that do not have a deictic-exophoric usage. They are called **definite** only if there is also an overt **indefinite** article in the language.

in sentence 5 of the Cerma text below. Having referred to a compound, the storyteller can talk of *the people* without formally introducing them.

What is accessed is **culture specific**. In Biblical Jewish culture, for instance, mention of a town such as *Antioch in Pisidia* (Acts 13:14) accesses **the** *synagogue*, which in turn makes **the** *officials of the synagogue* accessible (15). Furthermore, in connection with *the Sabbath day*, **the** *reading of the law and the prophets* is also presupposed.

What is significant for translators is that readers of the receptor culture will not necessarily make the associations that the culture of the source text has presupposed.

Omission of the article when the referent is active and specific

In some languages, the article is sometimes omitted even though the referent is active and specific. The pragmatic effect of omitting the article is usually related to **prominence**.

In Koine Greek, for instance, the article may be omitted to give prominence to a referent or to a particularly significant action performed by that referent (Levinsohn 2000:155–166). This is illustrated from the conversation between Peter and Cornelius reported in Acts 10:25–43. The initial references in the speech orienters are to **the** *Peter* (25, 26) and **the** *Cornelius* (25, 30). However, Peter's climactic speech of 34ff. is introduced with a reference to *Ø Peter* (p. 157). The absence of the article has the effect of giving prominence to this speech, marking it as of particular significance.

Mfonyam (1994:202–203) reports a similar phenomenon in Bafut.

In Cerma, the article may be omitted when the referent is a major participant occupying an **active role**. In the following extract from a folktale about a singing fish, the major participants are the field owner and the fish. References to them do not take the article when they have an active role in the story (sents. 1, 3, 4). When the fish is an inactive object, however, it takes the article (sents. 1, 2, 6). The article is also used in sentence 5 to refer to the people of the compound, as they are minor participants.

1 *Field-owner-Ø he caught fish-**the** and put it in gourd.*
2 *In evening, he returned with fish-**the**.*
3 *When he arrived, he lifted out fish-Ø, saying that it sing.*
4 *Fish-Ø started to sing in compound.*
5 *People-**the** all went to listen.*
6 *It became day-**the**, he put fish-**the** in gourd, left, went to field.*

Just as the omission of an article may give prominence, so its **presence** may have the effect of **backgrounding** the information concerned. This is illustrated in the following extract from a folktale in Karai Karai. Prior to the extract, Rabbit (Ø) has persuaded the children of Hyena (Ø) to let him into the house and has told them that his name is *All of us*. When Hyena brings meat (sents. 1–2), a preliminary interaction between Hyena and her eldest child (3–4) precedes the theme-line interaction between Rabbit and Hyena's children (5ff.). The backgrounded status of this preliminary interaction is signalled by the use of the article in sentences 3 and 4.

1 *Rabbit-Ø sat in room of Hyena-Ø.*
2 *Then Hyena-Ø brought meat for children-her.*
3 *Then eldest of children-**the** asked Hyena-**the**, 'For all of us?'*
4 *Hyena-**the** said, 'Yes' and she left.*
5 *Rabbit-Ø said to children of Hyena-Ø, 'You heard what she said ...'*

Similarly, terminating a **subordinate clause** with an article or other determiner typically has the effect of backgrounding the event concerned with respect to what follows (see the last footnote of 9.2.1).

Review questions

1. If some references to activated participants include a determiner and others do not, name three factors that may lead to the **presence** of the determiner.
2. If the (definite) article is sometimes **omitted** even though the referent is active, what is the usual pragmatic effect?[10]

Application to the language you are analysing

Describe the system of determiners used, together with the deictic-exophoric and text-related functions of each. Which set of determiners or pronouns, if any, is used for thematic references? For athematic references?

9.3 Directional verbs and auxiliaries

The use of directionals (e.g. *come* and *go*) varies widely from language to language. Section 9.3.1 considers the points of orientation for directionals that different languages allow. In some languages, any movement between locations must be made explicit (9.3.2). Finally, section 9.3.3 notes common extended meanings of directionals.

9.3.1 Orientation

Suppose someone knocks at your door and you call something out as you go to open it to let them know that you are on your way. Which directional will you use? If you are an English speaker, you'll call out, *I'm coming*. If you are a Spanish speaker, however, you'll call out, *Ya voy* 'I'm **going**'.

In a language like English, the point of orientation or "deictic center" (Fillmore 1997) of *come* and *go* can be either the speaker or the addressee. In a language like Spanish, it can only be the speaker. In such languages, the reported speech of Luke 14:20 (*I have married a wife, and therefore I cannot* **come** – English and Greek) must be translated, *I cannot go*.[11]

As participants *come* and *go* in many languages, the point of orientation is the location of the global or local **VIP**. In the Greek of Luke, for example, tax collectors *come* to John to be baptised (Luke 3:12), and the disciples *go* from Jesus to enter a village of the Samaritans (Luke 9:52). In other languages (e.g. Inga), the point of orientation remains the location of the **author**.

When a VIP **changes locations**, the direction of movement may be related to a **fixed** location. Alternatively it may be related to the location of the **next theme-line events** involving the VIP.

In the Greek of Luke 1–4, the point of orientation for journeys by Jesus (and Mary – 1:39, 2:41, 44) is the town of Nazareth (e.g. Jesus *comes* to Nazareth – 2:51, 4:16; he *goes* from there – 4:30).

In Mark 1, in contrast, Jesus *comes* to the location of each set of theme-line events (e.g. from Galilee to be baptised by John – 1:9; into Galilee – 1:14; into the house of Simon and Andrew – 1:29; into all Galilee – 1:39). *Come* is used in Acts in a similar way, to bring Christian leaders to the location of each set of theme-line events.

The VIP may even *go* to a new location and *come* to it in successive sentences when the next set of theme-line events takes place at that location. In Oroko, for instance, successive sentences read, *Leopard* **went** *to the backyard. When he was* **coming** ...

---

[10] **Suggested answers:**
1. If some references to activated participants include a determiner and others do not, the determiner may be present:
- to indicate that the referent is not the VIP
- to indicate that the referent, though not the VIP, is salient
- to background the events performed by these participants.
2. If the (definite) article is sometimes omitted even though the referent is active, the pragmatic effect of omitting the article is usually related to **prominence**.

[11] For a fuller discussion of *come* and *go* in the Greek of Luke-Acts see Levinsohn 2001a.

9.3 Directional verbs and auxiliaries

The point of orientation for the story may also determine whether the **locative adverb** for *here* or for *there* is used. In Luke 15:13b (*and* **there** *he squandered his property in dissolute living*), the use of *ekei* 'there' indicates that the point of orientation for the parable is still the father's house, not the current location of the younger son. In the reported speech of 17–18, in contrast (*but* **here** *I am dying of hunger. I will get up and* **go** *to my father* ...), *hōde* 'here' is consistent with the point of orientation being the current location of the speaker.

9.3.2 Movement

If the performance of the next event involves movement over a distance, a directional auxiliary is obligatory in some languages (e.g. Mambila, Inga), whereas in other languages it is not (e.g. English, Greek). Examples:

*He hit him and [**went**] hid in the woods.*

*After leaving the synagogue he [**went**] entered Simon's house.* (Luke 4:38a)

9.3.3 Extended senses

Directional auxiliaries come to be used in extended senses. They most commonly express **tense** (*am going to*) and **aspect** ((*be*)***come*** – inchoative aspect – see Lichtenberk 1991). This is seen in sentence 7 of the Bekwarra text:

áng'-úbuhó	á-**bé**	ka	kpèrè	
that-of dog	s-came	then	was well	'Dog's then became well.'

We noted in 6.5 that, in some African languages, including Moroccan Arabic [ary] (Semitic, Morocco), *come* (or a marker derived from *come*) marks the **developments** that lead up to the climax of an episode. Such is the case in Kaansa [gna] (Gur, Burkina Faso). Kaansa also uses an *arrive* auxiliary in connection with events that result from the climax. This usage suggests that the author views the climax as the point of orientation for the events (see 9.3.1).

Application to the language you are analysing

1. Describe any devices that signal the point of orientation for part or all of your texts (e.g. *come* and *go* auxiliaries, locative adverbs such as *here* and *there*). Comment on any changes of orientation in connection with climax.

2. The following set of questions will help you determine the permitted centres of orientation for the language of verbs like *come* and *go* (see Levinsohn 2001a for fuller discussion).

2a. If the language has a verb like *come* that denotes motion toward the location of the speaker at **coding time** (the time of the speech act – e.g. *Please come in!*), can the same verb be used to denote:

- motion toward the location of the **addressee** at coding time (e.g. *I'm coming*)?
- motion toward the location of the speaker at **reference** time (the time that is being referred to in the sentence when that time is different from the coding time; e.g. *Please come there* at dawn!* [*where I'll be at the stated time])?
- motion toward the location of the **home base** of the speaker at reference time (e.g. *He came over to my place last night, but I wasn't home*)?
- motion that is **in the company of** the speaker (e.g. *Would you like to come [with me]?*)?

2b. Does the point of orientation in third-person narratives remain fixed or can it change? If it can change, what brings about the change (e.g. movement by the VIP)?

2c. When a third-person narrative involves a VIP, do other participants *come* and *go* with respect to the location of the VIP in the story? If not, what is the typical point of orientation in stories in which other participants interact with a VIP?

2d. When a third-person narrative describes movement by a VIP, what is the point of orientation to which this movement is related (e.g. the location of the first major event of the narrative, the location of the last events described, the location of the next theme-line events)?

3. If locative adverbs for *here* and *there* are ever oriented with respect to other than the current location of the speaker, then indicate the point of orientation to which they are related.

Suggested reading

Chapter 17 of Dooley and Levinsohn 2001 relates to the topics covered in this chapter. See also Levinsohn 2001a.

Appendix F: Demonstratives in Koine Greek

The core meaning of the demonstratives in Greek is NOT thematic or athematic.[12] The core meaning of *ekeinos* is 'distal' (not at the deictic centre) and the core meaning of *houtos* is 'proximal' (close to the deictic centre). Nevertheless, in certain contexts, a pragmatic effect of using *ekeinos* is to identify the referent as athematic. Conversely, a pragmatic effect of using *houtos* in certain contexts is to identify the referent as thematic. I consider the two demonstratives in turn.

Ekeinos 'that'. Because the core meaning of *ekeinos* is 'distal' (not at the deictic centre), **animate** participants in a narrative text who are designated with *ekeinos* are usually **athematic and not salient**.[13] In Acts 21:6, for instance, the theme line of the narrative concerns 'us', whereas *ekeinoi* 'those ones' refers to the people 'we' left behind. The preposing of *ekeinoi* switches attention temporarily from us to them, but the effect of using *ekeinoi* is to ensure that 'we' remain the centre of attention:

6a–b *We said farewell to one another. Then we went on board the ship,*

6c *and <u>those ones</u> (**ekeinoi**) returned home.*

In Mark 16:9–13, 19 *ekeinos* is used to refer to the participants with whom Jesus interacts following his resurrection. This ensures that Jesus remains the centre of attention throughout the passage.

9 *When he [Jesus] rose early on the first day of the week, he appeared first to Mary Magdalene, out of whom he had driven seven demons.*

10 *<u>That one</u> (**ekeinē**) went & told the ones who had been with him who were mourning and weeping.*

11 *<u>Those ones</u> (**ekeinoi**), on hearing that he was alive and had been seen by her, would not believe it.*

12 *<u>After these things</u> (**Meta tauta**), he appeared in a different form to two of them while they were walking in the country.*

13 *<u>Those ones</u> (**ekeinoi**) returned and reported it to the rest, but neither did they believe those ones (**ekeinois**) ...*

19 *The Lord Jesus, after speaking to them, was taken up into heaven and sat at the right hand of God.*

20 *<u>Those ones</u> (**ekeinoi**) went out and preached everywhere, with the Lord working with them ...*

The pragmatic effects of using *ekeinos* in a **temporal expression** vary with the context. For example:

- Use of *ekeinos* may imply the **same distal** time (past or future in relation to the time of speaking or writing) as that of the events just described. This is particularly clear when an earlier reference to time has just been made.
- Use of *ekeinos* may imply a **loose chronological relation** between episodes when there is a **discontinuity** in the theme line.[14]

Luke 4:2b illustrates the use of *ekeinos* to refer to the **same past** time as the one referred to in 2a:

2a ***for forty days*** *he was tempted by the devil.*

2b *and he ate nothing at all during those (**ekeinais**) days.*

For other references to 'those days' in the past, see Luke 9:36, Acts 7:41 and 9:37. For references to 'that [same] day' in the past, see Acts 2:41 and Acts 8:1.

Luke 21:23a illustrates the use of *ekeinos* to refer to the **same future** time as the one referred to in 22 (see below on the use of *hautai* 'these' in 22):

---

[12] For a fuller discussion of demonstratives in Koine Greek, including examples in non-narrative material, see Levinsohn 2009b.

[13] For a rare instance in which the referent of *ekeinos* is thematic, see 'that rest' in Hebrews 4:11.

[14] Examples of *houtos* in connection with references to past time are only found in Luke-Acts, so the following examples are taken from those two books.

22 *for these are **days of vengeance**, as a fulfillment of all that is written.*

23a *Woe to those who are pregnant and to those who are nursing infants in those (**ekeinais**) days!*

For other references to 'those days' in the future, see Luke 5:35 and Acts 2:18. For references to 'that day' in the future, see Luke 6:23, 17:31, 21:34, and 10:12 (referring to the last judgement, not to a time mentioned previously in the discourse).

Bauer (2000:301–302) cites Luke 2:1 as an example of the use of *ekeinos* "when the time cannot (or is not) to be given with exactness". The pragmatic effect of using the distal demonstrative is to imply a **discontinuity in the theme line** between the episodes so linked. The previous verse concerns Zechariah's son John, whereas the new episode leads up to the birth of Jesus:

1:80 *The child grew and became strong in spirit, and he was in the wilderness until the day he appeared publicly to Israel.*

2:1 *It came about in those days* (en tais hēmerais **ekeinais**) *that a decree went out from Emperor Augustus that all the world should be registered.*

Other instances of 'those days' cited by Bauer include Matthew 3:1 and Mark 8:1. For references to 'about that time' in connection with a discontinuity in the theme line, see Acts 12:1 and Acts 19:23.

Houtos 'this'. When the proximal demonstrative *houtos* is used in a **temporal expression** to refer to a past time,[15] the pragmatic effect is typically to imply **continuity in the theme line**, even when the chronological relation between the episodes is vague. This is illustrated in Luke 1:39. Mary is the thematic participant in both the preceding episode and the new one, and her decision to visit Elizabeth is prompted by the angel's words in 36, 'your relative Elizabeth in her old age has also conceived a son':

38 *Then the angel departed from her [Mary].*

39 *Mary set out in those (**tautais** 'these') days and went with haste to a Judean town in the hill country, (40) where she entered the house of Zechariah and greeted Elizabeth.*

For other references to 'these days' in connection with continuity in the theme line, see Luke 6:12, 23:7; Acts 1:15, Acts 6:1, Acts 11:27 and Acts 21:15.

Because the core meaning of *houtos* is 'proximal' (close to the deictic centre), **animate** participants in a narrative text who are designated with *houtos* are usually **thematic and salient**.[16] This is evident in Acts 10:36–43; the referent of each instance of *houtos* is Jesus Christ, who is the theme of the passage:[17]

36 *You know the message he sent to the people of Israel, preaching peace by Jesus Christ – <u>this one</u> (**houtos**) is Lord of all …*

40 *<u>this one</u> (**touton**) God raised on the third day …*

42 *and He commanded us to preach to the people and to testify that <u>this one</u> (**houtos**) is the one ordained by God as judge of the living and the dead.*

43 *<u>To this one</u> (**toutō**) all the prophets testify.*

---

[15] As befits a proximal demonstrative, *houtos* is also used in connection with references to the time of speaking. For references to 'these days', see Luke 24:18 and 21; Acts 1:5, 5:36 and 21:38. For references to 'this day', see Luke 19:42, Acts 2:29, 3:24, 23:1 and 26:22. See Luke 18:30 for a reference to 'this time'.

[16] *Houtos* is not a thematic demonstrative *per se*, as it is also used **cataphorically** (for referents that have yet to be stated) and **exophorically** (for referents found in the external world, rather than the discourse one). For a cataphoric instance of *houtos*, see Revelation 9:17: *And **this** was how I saw the horses in my vision: the riders wore breastplates …* (NRSV). For an exophoric instance of *houtos*, see John 2:19b: *Destroy **this** temple, and in three days I will raise it up.*

[17] The natural centre of attention in a speech involving the speaker is *ego* (in this case, *us* – 42). This is the probable reason for so explicitly identifying Jesus Christ as the thematic referent.

Appendix F: Demonstratives in Koine Greek

The referent of the proximal demonstrative may be the **theme-line event** or events that were mentioned immediately before. In Mark 16:12 (above), for instance, *meta tauta* 'after these things' refers to the theme-line events described in 9–11. See also the use of *hautai* 'these (days)' in Luke 21:22 (above).

Review questions

1. What is the core meaning of *ekeinos*? And of *houtos*?
2. When an animate participant in a narrative text is designated with *ekeinos*, is the referent usually thematic (the centre of attention) or athematic (not the centre of attention)?
3. When *houtos* is used in a temporal expression to refer to a past time, does this imply continuity or a discontinuity in the theme line?[18]

---

[18] **Suggested answers:**
1. The core meaning of *ekeinos* is 'distal' (not at the deictic centre). *Houtos* is 'proximal' (close to the deictic centre).
2. When an animate participant in a narrative text is designated with *ekeinos*, the referent is usually athematic.
3. The use of *houtos* in a temporal expression to refer to a past time implies continuity in the theme line.

Appendix G: Determiners in Languages of the Philippines

Although the ways that demonstratives are used in Philippine languages vary from one group to another, some generalisations can be made. Part of the variation stems from the fact that, when the usage is **spatial**, the basic distinction in some of the languages is a three-way one (proximal, near the addressee and distal), whereas in others it seems to be only a two-way one (proximal versus distal).

Proximal demonstratives may be used for cataphoric, exophoric or anaphoric reference. The anaphoric use tends to be restricted in narrative to introductory, parenthetical and concluding material. In non-narrative material, it gives **thematic prominence** to temporary or local themes.

In some of the languages, a **special** marker is used to track **thematic** material (e.g. in Sama Bangingih – see below). In others, the **close-to-addressee** demonstrative is used for the same purpose, e.g. in Kalagan [kqe] (Malayo-Polynesian, Philippines). In Sama Bangingih, in contrast, one anaphoric function of the close-to-addressee demonstrative is to track **'other' (nonthematic)** referents.

The following extract from a Sama Bangingih narrative illustrates how the thematic demonstrative *-in* and the close-to-addressee demonstrative *-u* differ when used anaphorically. In 2, the referents of *some* are others who leave the main party and go to Sangil Island, which is marked as another place (*-u*). In 3, in contrast, *some* is marked as thematic, as the referents are members of the main group who will eventually arrive at their current location:

1   *They travelled (in this direction) to Molukkas …*
2   *Now some-**u** travelled towards Sangil Island, and stayed there (**-u**) …*
3   *Then some-**in** proceeded to Cotabato.*

In most of the languages, the **distal** demonstrative is the default means of anaphoric reference when no prominence is given to the referent. In Sangil, however, the **absence** of any demonstrative is the default way of referring to established referents.

In Sama Bangingih narratives, the distal demonstrative *-è* may be attached to a reference to a participant who has been thematic, to anticipate a switch to a different thematic participant.

Some languages have '**emphatic**' long forms for concepts such as *particular, same, itself*. In Sama Bangingih, for example, *inaan* appears to be an emphatic form of the thematic demonstrative *-in* (e.g. *As long as that particular one* (**inaan**) *was chief, they would leave there*).

10

Subordinate Clauses, Especially Relative Clauses

This chapter addresses two major topics: whether the language being analysed allows brand-new information to be conveyed in prenuclear subordinate clauses (10.1) and the functions of relative clauses in the language (10.3). It also includes a brief discussion of information load (10.2).

10.1 Brand-new information and subordinate clauses

English permits the introduction of brand-new information in subordinate clauses, apparently without any significant restrictions. This is not true of all languages. For instance, Pope (1993:3) claims that it is unnatural for some languages "to convey new information" in (adverbial) subordinate clauses. She cites Acts 22:21 (*Go, **because I will send you far away to the Gentiles***) as an instance in which it would be unnatural to use a subordinate clause in the Waama [wwa] (Gur, Benin) language because the information being conveyed appears to be brand-new.

My own experience is that brand-new information may be presented in **postnuclear** subordinate clauses in most languages. It is common, however, to encounter severe restrictions on the introduction of brand-new information in **prenuclear** subordinate clauses in natural texts.

The following is a possible **Accessibility Scale** for determining what sorts of information are found in subordinate clauses in natural texts. Each category is illustrated below.[1]

- active information (examples in 1 below)
- immediately accessible information because of a schema (2)
- information which is accessible from a more removed context (3)
- brand-new (previously not accessed) information (4).

1a *They left to eat millet. After they had finished eating millet* … (Cerma)

1b (Matthew 2:15) … *and was there until the death of Herod* … (19) *When Herod died* …

2a *They decided to stop and return home. When they arrived there* … (Cerma)
    [In a travel schema, travelling to a destination leads to arriving there.]

2b *The hunter knifed the tiger. When the tiger saw the blood, it fled.* (Bakossi [bss], Bantu A, Cameroon)
    [In a hunting schema, knifing an animal leads to it bleeding.]

---

[1] Compare Lambrecht's (1994:165) "Topic Accessibility Scale". His categories are arranged so that the first are most acceptable and the last are least acceptable as topics: **active** – **accessible** – **unused** (i.e. identifiable yet inactive) – **brand-new anchored** (e.g. by a schema) – **brand-new unanchored**.

3   (Luke 3:22) *And a voice from heaven said, 'This is My Son.'*

   [*3:23–37 give a genealogy of Jesus/Joseph*]

   (4:3) *The devil said to him, 'If you are the Son of God ...'*

4a   (Matthew 4:12) *When he (Jesus) heard that John had been arrested ...*

4b   (Mark 2:14) *Jesus said to Levi, 'Follow me'. And he got up and followed him.*

   (15) *As he sat at dinner in Levi's house ...*[2]

Some apparently brand-new information may be accessible because it is judged to be **shared knowledge**. In (4a) above, for instance, Matthew might have assumed that the arrest of John the Baptist was common knowledge among his original readers.

Similarly, Matthew 3:7 (*When he [John] saw many Pharisees and Sadducees coming for baptism*) contains no brand-new information for the original readers who would know that *the people of Jerusalem* (3:5) included such classes of people. For later readers who did not share such knowledge, the clause concerned would contain brand-new information.

A further point to remember about prenuclear subordinate clauses is that they rarely occur in natural texts in some languages. For instance, the Bekwarra folktale contains only one prenuclear subordinate clause (sent. 27). Instead, spacers like *áná* background certain events in a sentence with respect to others (see 5.2.4).

Application to the language you are analysing

1. Indicate the function of prenuclear subordinate clauses. (They may only establish points of departure. Or they may also present events of secondary importance, as is the case with Greek participles.)
2. Indicate whether subordinate clauses can contain brand-new information. If they can, indicate any restrictions on the presentation of such information. (For example, they may only present brand-new information if they are postnuclear.)
3. Do the same restrictions apply to all types of prenuclear subordinate clauses (for example, to adverbial versus participial clauses, to subordinate clauses of time versus those of condition)?

10.2 Information load

Some languages tend to present only one or two "chunks" of brand-new information in each clause, especially in oral texts. For example, sentence 1 of the Bekwarra folktale is a single clause and communicates the fact that Dog and Hare entered an agreement, while sentence 2 specifies the nature of that agreement. This avoids a sentence such as *Once Dog and Hare made an agreement to fry their children and eat them* which communicates more than two chunks of brand-new information.

To determine what is the typical "information load" per clause (in other words, the number of chunks of new information introduced per clause) in natural texts in the language you are analysing, count subject, object, verb, location, etc. as one chunk each.

Table 16 (adapted from Headland 1975:3) illustrates how this is done. The extract is from Tunebo [tuf] (Chibchan, Colombia), which has OV constituent order. The locations *forest in* (sent. a), *river Sarari land* (sent. c) and the purpose *animal hunting* (sent. b) are each counted as one chunk. Columns three and four state the chunks of information that are brand-new, while the last column indicates the number of chunks of new information.

---

[2] In fact, neither of these prenuclear clauses is an adverbial subordinate clause in Greek. The underlined clause in Matthew 4:12 is participial, while the underlined clause in Mark 2:15 is the infinitival subject of *egeneto* 'happened'. See Levinsohn 2000:183ff. and 177ff. on the functions of such clauses.

10.2 Information load

Table 16. Information load in a Tunebo text

5.	Premain verb	Main verb	New nonverbal chunk	New verbal chunk	New chunks
a.	*Erara bowar ícara* there forest in	*bijacro* went	forest in	went	2
b.	*Ruwa yacay* animal hunting	*bijacro* went	animal hunting		1
c.	*Ri Sarari cajc* river Sarari land	*bijacro* went	river Sarari land		1
d.	*Cutiyi* Cutiyi	*bijacro* went	Cutiyi		1
e.	*Bowara ícara béyara* forest in having.gone	*iójacro* got.lost		got.lost	1

In the above extract, the maximum number of chunks of new information per clause was 2. Contrast a possible translation into English of the above extract as a single sentence: *Once there, he went hunting animals in the forest in the area of the river Sarari near Cutuyi, where he got lost.*[3]

Question

What are two text-related potential problems that may arise when translating Matthew 2:1 (*After Jesus was born in Bethlehem in Judea during the time of King Herod*) into a receptor language, according to the first two sections of this chapter?[4]

Application to the language you are analysing

1. What is the maximum number of chunks per clause that can convey new information in natural text?
2. What devices are used to spread new information over more than one clause (e.g. parallel clauses with the same subject and verb, *inclusio* structures[5])?

---

[3] Some languages typically use separate clauses when two constituents have the same grammatical role. Because *river Sarari land* and *Cutiyi* are both unmarked goals in Tunebo, it would be more natural in such languages to express the two goals in separate clauses, even though it would be acceptable to combine Tunebo sentences a–c into a single clause.

[4] **Suggested answer:**
Two text-related potential problems that may arise when translating Matthew 2:1a into a receptor language are:
1. It is a prenuclear subordinate clause in English, yet contains brand-new information (where Jesus was born and when).
2. It conveys more than one chunk of new information: *in Bethlehem in Judea* and *during the time of King Herod*. Greek uses a participle to encode the information of this clause. This backgrounds the information with respect to what follows in the sentence, so an equivalent backgrounding device should be used in the receptor language. If the language prefers only one chunk of new information to be introduced per clause, a possible rendering of this proposition might be: *Jesus was born in Bethlehem town. (This town is) in Judea land. At that time, the ruler of Judea was called Herod. After Jesus was born* ... (resumptive tail-head linkage, suggesting that what follows is significant – 3.2.3).

[5] *Inclusio* structures involve the bracketing of a unit by making a statement at the beginning, an approximation of which is repeated at the end (see Guthrie 1998:14).

10.3 Relative clauses

Section 10.1 noted some restrictions on the presentation of brand-new information in subordinate clauses. In the case of relative clauses, some languages are very particular about the types of information that they may convey – see 10.3.6. First, though, the terms used to talk about relative clauses are reviewed (10.3.1). Distinctions are made between restrictive and nonrestrictive clauses, and between certain subtypes of each (10.3.2–4). Some languages only allow a limited set of constituents to be relativised (10.3.5). Section 10.3.7 is devoted to relative clauses in selected passages in Biblical Hebrew. The chapter closes with some comments about how to render in receptor languages problematic relative clauses of the source languages.

10.3.1 Review of terminology

Relative clauses typically modify a head noun:[6]

    NP →   det + noun   [relative clause]

    e.g.   *the man*   *who arrived yesterday*

The following terms are commonly used in connection with relative clauses:

- **Head noun/NP**: the entity being modified by the relative clause.
- **Relative clause**: the clause that modifies the head noun.
- **Relativiser**: a particle or word in the relative clause that is substituted for the head noun (may be null [Ø]).
- **Relativised NP**: (the function of) the constituent which has been replaced by the relativiser.

The following sentence illustrates these terms. The head NP is *the basket*. The relative clause is enclosed in square brackets. The relativiser (in English) is *that*, which substitutes for the relativised NP *the basket* and introduces the relative clause in English.

                                            RELATIVISED NP

6 *Inside the basket*   *[he hung*   **the basket** *on a tree]*   *was the necklace.*

       HEAD NP   <- - - - - - - - - RELATIVE CLAUSE - - - - - - - - - ->

    *Inside **the basket***   *[**that***   *he hung*   -   *on a tree]*   *was the necklace.*
                         RELATIVISER

10.3.2 Restrictive and nonrestrictive relative clauses

Relative clauses are commonly divided into two types: restrictive and nonrestrictive.

Restrictive (identifying) relative clauses serve to delimit the potential referents (Comrie 1989:138).

7 *The man [who arrived yesterday] left this morning.*

Nonrestrictive relative clauses serve "merely to give the hearer an added piece of information about an already identified entity, but not to identify that entity" (Comrie 1989:138).

8 *Mr. Smith, [who had arrived only yesterday], left this morning.*

9 *Joseph of Arimathea, a respected member of the council, [who also himself was waiting expectantly for the Kingdom of God], went boldly to Pilate (Mark 15:43).*

Typologists maintain that all languages have restrictive relative clauses, and that some languages **only use relative clauses in a restrictive manner**. Pope (1993:2) claims that, using a relative clause

---

[6] In some languages, nominalised clauses function like relative clauses.

in Waama, *This Jesus, [who has been taken up from you into heaven]* ... (Acts 1:11) would therefore imply that the relative clause was identifying which Jesus the angels were talking about![7]

10.3.3 Types of restrictive relative clause

In some languages, different types of restrictive relative clauses are used, depending on whether the referent of the head noun has not previously been activated (10a) or has already been activated (10b). The following are successive sentences from a folktale in Kom [bkm] (Grassfields, Cameroon); the form of the two relative clauses is different in Kom:

10 a. *The bird settled on **a** rock [that was hidden in the grass].*
  b. *The elephant went to strike **the** bird [that had settled on the rock].*

Note: Relative clauses like (10b) above, which only recapitulate established information, are not clearly restrictive. However, typologists would not normally view them as nonrestrictive, either. They are typically used as a rhetorical device to slow down the story and thus highlight the next event to be described. See also examples (20)–(22) in 10.3.6.

Tadaksahak [dsq] (Nilo-Saharan, Mali) has three types of relative clause: two restrictive and one nonrestrictive. One type of restrictive relative clause is introduced with a relative pronoun (REL) and is used when the head is definite. The other type employs the 'gap' strategy[8] and is used when the head is indefinite. The nonrestrictive type is introduced with the complementiser (COMP) *sa*.

The following sentences illustrate the three types (see Christiansen and Levinsohn 2003:2):[9]

11 Restrictive with definite head: introduced with a relative pronoun

  Ci   na   imunaskon   [a**yo**ndo-zumbu   ʃali   daw]?
  who DET camel.riders REL.PL-go.down   NAME   LOC

  'Who are the camel riders [**who** dismounted at Rhali's (place)]?'

12 Restrictive with indefinite head: gap strategy

  a-gar   hamu   [Ø f-keni   aykaran   daw].
  3s-find meat   IMPF-lie   puppies   LOC

  'she (the lioness) found meat [**that** was lying next to the cubs].'

13 Nonrestrictive: introduced with complementiser sa

  A-b-ʃiʃken-an   ayn   nana   se,   [sa   ayn   man   Aminata].
  3s-IMPF-greet-ALLATIVE 3s.GEN mother   BEN   COMP   3s.GEN NAME   NAME

  'He greets his mother, [**whose** name is Aminata].'

10.3.4 Types of nonrestrictive relative clause

Nonrestrictive relative clauses are usually **descriptive** (e.g. (8) and (9) above). However, some may be **continuative**.

Continuative relative clauses typically describe an **event** that involves the referent of the relative pronoun and occurs subsequent to the previous event or situation in which the referent featured. The effect of using such a construction is to treat the information conveyed in the preceding clause as the

---

[7] In some languages, it is possible to use a relative clause within an *appositive* phrase to convey the same information (see [20] in 10.3.6); e.g. *This Jesus, the person [who has just been taken up from you into heaven]* ...

[8] The term "gap strategy" means "leave a gap at the position in the adjective clause where the relativised noun normally would occur in an independent clause" (Whaley 1997:262).

[9] The other abbreviations used in the Tadaksahak examples are as follows: BEN benefactive, DET determiner, GEN genitive, IMPF imperfective aspect, LOC locative, PL plural, 3s 3rd person singular.

ground for the information conveyed by the relative clause (Levinsohn 2000:191ff.). Typically, when a sentence contains such clauses, the final proposition is the one to which the sentence has been building.

The following Koine Greek example of continuative relative clauses is from Acts 7:44–46a:

14 a. *The tent of witness was with our fathers in the desert ...*
    b. ***which*** *also they brought in with Joshua when they dispossessed the nations*
    c. ***whom*** *God drove out before our fathers until the time of David*
    d. ***who*** *found favour before God and asked ...*

The following is the opening sentence of a text in Obolo (see Aaron 1999:89–90). If clause b is taken as a comment about the *male child* of clause a, then it is continuative:

15 a. *There was a certain male child*
    b. ***who*** *took (his bow and) arrows and entered the forest to look for birds (to shoot).*

Few languages use nonrestrictive relative clauses in a continuative manner. Instead, when they wish to background information within a sentence with respect to information conveyed later in the same sentence, they employ another of the devices described in 5.2.4.

Application to the language you are analysing

1. Indicate whether relative clauses can be used in a nonrestrictive sense. If they can, describe their function(s) (descriptive or continuative).
2. If the language uses more than one type of restrictive relative clause, distinguish their functions.

10.3.5 Which constituents may be relativised?

This section addresses the syntactic roles of the head noun in the relative clause. (Note: It is NOT asking in which constituents relative clauses may appear.)

English is somewhat unusual in allowing a broad range of constituents to be relativised (see Whaley 1997:263):

subject:	*the woman [that likes Mary]*	(from	*the woman likes Mary)*
direct object:	*the woman [(that) Mary likes]*	(from	*Mary likes the woman)*
adjunct:	*the woman [(that) Mary spoke with]*	(from	*Mary spoke with the woman)*
possessor:	*the woman [whose family Mary knows]*	(from	*Mary knows the family of the woman)*
comparative:	*the woman [that Mary is taller than]*	(from	*Mary is taller than the woman)*

Many languages permit the relativisation of only some of the above constituents. For example, **some languages relativise only subjects and direct objects**. Other languages also relativise spatial and temporal adjuncts, but not other adjuncts.

Certain languages "raise" adjuncts to direct object by affixing an "applicative" marker to the verb. For example, *Mary **with**-spoke the woman.*

Beware of the danger of creating forms that relativise other than these constituents, if they are not attested in natural texts!

Review question

Section 10.3.1 discussed example (6): *Inside the basket [that he had hung on a tree] was the necklace.* Which constituent has been relativised in this sentence?[10]

---

[10] The constituent that has been relativised in the sentence *Inside the basket [that he had hung on a tree] was the necklace* is the **object** (*the basket* is the object of *had hung*).

Application to the language you are analysing

Indicate which grammatical relations may be relativised (e.g. subject and direct object only).

10.3.6 Restrictions on the use of relative clauses in particular languages

Mona Perrin (p.c.) finds that, in many Central African languages, the use of relative clauses is always related in some sense to **prominence** (see also Beavon 1985), especially **thematic** salience (see 4.6).

Thus, relative clauses may be used in the **introduction** to a narrative to state information that is relevant to the development of its theme. Sentence (16) begins a folktale in Konzime [ozm] (Bantu A, Cameroon) (see Beavon 1985:49). The story concerns the problem that has to be addressed because Leopard is always killing other animals. In other words, the information conveyed in the relative clause is highly thematic.

16 *Leopard, the animal [that is always killing animals in the forest], was ...*

Similarly, relative clauses may be used in the **conclusion** of a narrative to reiterate its theme. This is illustrated from the conclusion to a folktale in Gude; the story has concerned what happened to the woman and her children, and the relative clause of (17) reiterates this theme.

17 *Thus was performed the thing [that happened to the woman and her children].*

Relative clauses may be used to highlight information that is thematically **salient** – i.e. significant for what follows. In the following extract from a Konzime folktale, for instance, the packet of elephant meat is a salient prop, and the place where it was placed is significant for the outcome of the story:

18 *He put the packet in the entrance, in the place [where the package of elephant meat was].*

In the following extract from a Kako (Bantu A, Cameroon) folktale, the relative clause states information that is significant for the outcome of the story. It occurs in the point of departure that establishes the **topic** about which the narrator comment is made:

19 *Nevertheless, the thing [that he picked up and threw there], he threw Tortoise.*

  (i.e. ... *concerning the thing [that he picked up and threw there], it was Tortoise that he threw.)*

In reported speeches, a relative clause may be found in the point of departure for the **climactic assertion** of the speech. This is illustrated from another Konzime folktale; the referent of the relative clause is thematically salient. In addition, the effect of using apposition and a relative clause in the point of departure is to slow down the speech and thus highlight the following assertion:

20 *This woman, the woman [who is here sitting down], it was she who gave me the (poisoned) pounded cassava.*

Relative clauses that redundantly identify the scope of a head noun modified by *all* or a negative equivalent serve to **intensify the inclusiveness** of the referent. This is illustrated by the following sentences from Konzime (21) and Bafut (22):

21 *Call all the animals [that are in the forest]! Call all the animals [that are in this world]!*
22 *(The chickens were looking for a volunteer to go to their owner and ask for water.)*

  They found no chicken [that was willing to stand before their master and ask for water].

Adjectival modifiers in Tadaksahak are introduced with a relative pronoun to give prominence to the **adjective**, rather than to the phrase as a whole. This is illustrated by the following pair of sentences (Christiansen and Levinsohn 2003:6):

23 a. *Taradaq   hincini   [ʒen-i].*
        NAME   goat   be.old-ADJECTIVISER
        'Taradaq is an old goat.'

    b. *Taradaq   hincini   [**ayo**   ʒen-i].*
        NAME   goat   REL   be.old-ADJECTIVISER
        'Taradaq is an **old** goat.'

Perrin's study found that relative clauses used in narrative in Central African languages are usually NOT found in clauses that describe theme-line events.[11] Thus, they occur in the introduction (16), conclusion (17) and background comments (19). If found in sentences that present events, they are often **right-dislocated** (18, 25) or **left-dislocated** (24), and so do not occur in the clause that actually describes the theme-line event.

Example (24) is from a Muan [moa] (Mande, Côte d'Ivoire) text:

24 *We went and, my father Zeiba, the place [where his field is], we arrived there.*

Example (25) involves the right dislocation of a relative clause which modifies the subject *these*. It is found in a folktale in Karai Karai:

25 *These (are) which kind of arrows, [that are like the embers from a bellows that never go dull]?*

One motivation for left-dislocating relative clauses in Tadaksahak is to give the referent extra focal prominence. This is achieved by following the relative clause with a thematic pronoun and the focus marker, as the following example illustrates (Christiansen and Levinsohn 2003:11).

26 [*Having been asked to which clan in particular he belongs, the speaker says:* 'I belong to all the Idaksahak …']

    meʃin   tawʃat   ayo,   sa   [a-f-tuwena   Ihanaqatan],
    but   clan   REL   COMP   3s-IMPF-PASSIVE.call   NAME

    anga   *ne-may*   *ayay*
    3s.THEMATIC   FOCUS-own   I

    '… but that clan, the one that is called "Ihanaqatan", it's **to it** that I belong.'

Restrictions on the use of relative clauses vary from language to language. Wiesmann (2000:72) finds that **brand-new** information is never given in a restrictive relative clause in Toussian, and the relative clause is never part of a focal constituent. In other languages, the head noun is established information, but the relative clause itself contains new information. Such is the case in the following example from Yemba [ybb] (Grassfields, Cameroon); the previous sentence had mentioned the message, but had not indicated its content:

27 *It is the message [that God loved us extraordinarily …]*

Now consider NPs in which neither the head noun nor the relative clause conveys established information. Perrin (p.c.) points out that, in an African language, the head noun of such NPs will be very **generic**. Often, it can only be *thing(s), person/people, time, place* or *manner*, with the relative clause specifying which thing, person, etc. is referred to. This is illustrated from a hortatory text in Herde – the head nouns are in bold:

---

[11] Eric Fields (p.c.) informs me that, in Kanuri [kau] (Nilo-Saharan, Nigeria), verbs used in relative clauses cannot have perfective aspect (see Hutchison 1981:218). This is consistent with relative clauses not being used to describe theme-line events.

28 a. *Then, at the beginning of the year you will think about **thing** [that you are going to do].*

   b. ***People** [who make sacrifices]: they exist; you will assemble them,*

      *then tell them **thing** [that they are to look out for in their district ...]*

   c. *Then **people** [who come with a problem]: you judge their problem well with justice.*

See also sentence 29 of the Bekwarra folktale: *ipì [àwo ó-ji kwom]* 'place where you ate'.

Question

The Bekwarra folktale also contains four instances of a nominalised constituent translated as 'child(ren)-eating agreement' (sents. 14, 20, 23, 27). If these constituents are the equivalent of relative clauses, how is their occurrence consistent with Perrin's assertion that relative clauses in Central African languages are always related in some sense to prominence, especially thematic prominence?[12]

Application to the language you are analysing

1. When relative clauses are used in a restrictive (identifying) sense, describe where they occur and what their function(s) are. (For example, they may usually not be found in clauses that describe theme-line events; they may always relate to thematic prominence.)
2. When relative clauses only recapitulate established information, what is their function? (For example, they may slow down the story and thus highlight the next event to be described.)

10.3.7 Relative clauses in Biblical Hebrew

If you are translating into an African language, the encouraging thing about relative clauses in Hebrew that begin with *'ašer* (hereafter, *'ašer*-clauses) is that their function is often very similar to that of relative clauses in many African languages. In other words, relative clauses in Biblical Hebrew are usually related to prominence, especially thematic prominence.

Prominence is conveyed by *'ašer*-clauses provided that they contain information which is not really needed to establish the identity of the referent. Some referents appear to be **thematically** prominent (e.g. Genesis 3:3, 11, 17b below); others are **intensified** by the *'ašer*-clause (3:1 below).[13]

This is illustrated in Genesis 3:1–22. Five *'ašer*-clauses are found in this passage, and just one of them occurs in the narrative superstructure. *More than all of the animals [that the* LORD *God made]* (1) intensifies *all* in the introduction to the story.

The other four *'ašer*-clauses in Genesis 3:1–22 occur in reported speeches.
- Three relate to the tree that God had commanded Adam and Eve not to eat – a prop that is thematically salient: 3:3, 3:11 (*From the tree [that I commanded you not to eat]: from it you ate?* – left-dislocated) and 3:17b (within a point of departure).
- In 3:12b *the woman [that you put with me]: she ...* is left-dislocated. The information in the *'ašer*-clause is redundant, and the rhetorical effect of introducing such information is to highlight the following assertion about her.

Similarly, only two *'ašer*-clauses are found in Genesis 3:23–4:16. Although one is in the narrative superstructure and the other in a reported speech, both relate to the same theme. Both occur in adjuncts:
- *(to work) the ground [from which he was taken]* (3:23)
- *from the ground [which opened its mouth to receive the blood of your brother from your hand]* (4:11).

---

[12] The theme of the Bekwarra folktale is the "child(ren)-eating agreement" that Dog and Hare had entered into. They therefore constitute an example of relative clauses being used for thematic prominence.

[13] Others again are used as a rhetorical device to slow down the story immediately before a significant development. This is illustrated by Exodus 1:15 (& *the king of Egypt said to the midwives of the Hebrews,* ['ašer *the name of the first: Beauty (Shiphrah) & the name of the second: Splendid (Pu'ah)]*). The instruction to kill all the male Hebrew babies immediately follows this sentence.

The information in this *'ašer*-clause is highly redundant, and the rhetorical effect is to slow the speech down immediately prior to the climactic assertion of 12, which also has *the ground* as its theme.[14]

Finally, Genesis 22:1–14 contains four *'ašer*-clauses, all of which relate to the same place *(one of the mountains I will tell you about* – 2; see also 3, 8, 14). Again, this place is thematically salient.

Notwithstanding the above three passages, *'ašer*-clauses are much more frequent in other chapters of Genesis (there are 13 in Genesis 7, for instance), and it is not obvious that their referents are always thematic or otherwise prominent. In 7:8, for instance, why is *that are unclean* an *'ašer*-clause, but *clean* is not, when both classes were mentioned in 7:2?

Note: The nominalised clause in 3:24 is glossed as a relative clause in the Hebrew-French interlinear (*l'épée [qui-tournoie pour-garder chemin-de arbre-de la-vie]*). However, the constituent is focal, and the referent is NOT established information.

The *NIV* uses some additional relative clauses:
- *her husband [who was with her]* (3:6) is punctuated as nonrestrictive
- *what is right* (4:7 – a headless relative clause)
- *whoever finds me* (4:14 – a headless relative clause)
- *anyone [who found him]* (4:15)

Application to the language you are analysing

Should any of these be rendered as relative clauses in the language?

10.3.8 Implications for translation

If it is not appropriate to use a relative clause in the receptor language to translate a relative clause in the source language, the following constructions may be appropriate:
- a nominalised form that does not involve a relative clause
  e.g. *When he arrived ... (The time [that he arrived])* might become *The time of his arrival ...*
- a comment with a referential point of departure
  e.g. *Joseph of Arimathea ... [who also himself was waiting expectantly for the Kingdom of God]* might become *Joseph of Arimathea ... He also, he was waiting ...*
- a marked focus structure
  e.g. *Praise God [who reigns on high]* might become *Praise God. It is he who reigns on high.*

---

[14] This may suggest that the author's primary concern in the passage is to explain why the earth that had been so fruitful has ceased to be so.

References

Aaron, Uche E. 1992. Reported speech in Obolo narrative discourse. In Shin Ja J. Hwang and William R. Merrifield (eds.), *Language in context: Essays for Robert E. Longacre*, 227–240. Dallas, TX: Summer Institute of Linguistics and the University of Texas at Arlington.

Aaron, Uche E. 1999. *Tense and aspect in Obolo grammar and discourse*. Summer Institute of Linguistics and the University of Texas at Arlington Publications in Linguistics 128. Dallas, TX.

Andersen, Francis I. 1994. Salience, implicature, ambiguity, and redundancy in clause-clause relationships in Biblical Hebrew. In Robert D. Bergen (ed.), *Biblical Hebrew and discourse linguistics*, 99–116. Dallas, TX: Summer Institute of Linguistics.

Anderson, Stephen R., and Edward Keenan. 1985. Deixis. In Timothy Shopen (ed.), *Language typology and syntactic description*, III.259–308. Cambridge: Cambridge University Press.

Andrews, Avery. 1985. The major functions of the noun phrase. In Timothy Shopen (ed.), *Language typology and syntactic description*, I.62–154. Cambridge: Cambridge University Press.

Andrews, Edna. 1990. *Markedness theory: The union of asymmetry and semiosis in language.* Durham, NC: Duke University Press.

Bailey, Nicholas Andrew. 2009. Thetic Constructions in Koine Greek with special attention to clauses with εἰμί 'be', γίνομαι 'occur', ἔρχομαι 'come', ἰδού/ἴδε 'behold', and complement clauses of ὁράω 'see'. PhD dissertation. Vrije Universiteit, Amsterdam. https://research.vu.nl/ws/portalfiles/portal/42185508/complete+dissertation.pdf.

Barjasteh Delforooz, Behrooz. 2010. Discourse features in Balochi of Sistan (Oral narratives). PhD dissertation. Studia Iranica Upsaliensia 15. Uppsala: Acta Universitatis Upsaliensis. http://uu.diva-portal.org/smash/record.jsf?searchId=2&pid=diva2:345413.

Beavon, Keith H. 1985. Two relativization strategies in Koozime discourse. *Journal of West African Languages* 15(1):31–56.

Beneš, Eduard. 1962. Die Verbstellung im Deutschen, von der Mitteilungsperspektive her betrachtet [The verb position in German, viewed from the communication perspective]. *Philologica Pragensia* 5:6–19.

Benton, Joseph. 1989. Clause- and sentence-level word order and discourse strategy in Chichicapan Zapotec oral narrative discourse. *OPTAT* 3(2):65–82.

Berthelette, John J. 2004. Information structure in narrative texts in Byali (a Gur language of Benin). MA thesis. University of North Dakota.

Bhat, D. N. S. 1999. *The prominence of tense, aspect and mood.* Studies in Language Companion Series 49. Amsterdam: John Benjamins.

Binder, Ronald. 1977. Thematic linkage in Waunana discourse. In Robert E. Longacre and Frances Woods (eds.), *Discourse grammar: Studies in indigenous languages of Colombia, Panama and Ecuador.* Summer Institute of Linguistics Publications in Linguistics and Related Fields 52(2), 159–190. Dallas, TX.

Blakemore, Diane. 1987. *Semantic constraints on relevance.* Oxford: Blackwell.
Blakemore, Diane. 2002. *Relevance and linguistic meaning: The semantics and pragmatics of discourse markers.* Cambridge Studies in Linguistics 99. Cambridge: Cambridge University Press.
Blass, Regina. 1990. *Relevance relations in discourse: A study with special reference to Sissala.* Cambridge Studies in Linguistics 55. Cambridge: Cambridge University Press. (See also *Notes on Linguistics* 48:8–20.)
Boutin, Michael E. 1988. Transitivity and discourse grounding in Banggi. Paper presented at International Symposium on Language and Linguistics, Bangkok, Thailand, August 1988.
Buth, Randall. 1999. Word order in the verbless clause: A generative-functional approach. In Cynthia L. Miller (ed.), *The verbless clause in Biblical Hebrew*, 79–108. Winona Lake, IN: Eisenbrauns.
Callow, Kathleen. 1974. *Discourse considerations in translating the Word of God.* Grand Rapids: Zondervan.
Carlson, Lauri. 1994. *'Well' in dialogue games: A discourse analysis of the interjection 'well' in idealized conversation.* Pragmatics and Beyond 5. Amsterdam: John Benjamins.
Chafe, Wallace L. 1976. Givenness, contrastiveness, definiteness, subjects, topics and point of view. In Charles N. Li (ed.), *Subject and topic*, 25–55. New York: Academic Press.
Chafe, Wallace L. 1987. Cognitive constraints on information flow. In Russell S. Tomlin (ed.), *Coherence and grounding in discourse*, 21–51. Amsterdam: John Benjamins.
Chafe, Wallace L. 1994. *Discourse, consciousness, and time: The flow and displacement of conscious experience in speaking and writing.* Chicago: University of Chicago Press.
Christiansen, Regula, and Stephen H. Levinsohn. 2003. Relative clauses in Tadaksahak. *SIL Electronic Working Papers* 2003-003. Dallas, TX: SIL International. https://www.sil.org/resources/archives/7885.
Comrie, Bernard. 1989. *Language universals and linguistic typology.* Second edition. Chicago: University of Chicago Press.
Coulthard, Malcolm. 1977. *An introduction to discourse analysis.* Applied Linguistics and Language Study. London: Longman.
Crozier, David H. 1984. A study in the discourse grammar of Cishingini. PhD dissertation. University of Ibadan, Nigeria.
Crystal, David. 1997. *A dictionary of linguistics and phonetics.* Fourth edition. Oxford: Basil Blackwell.
Delin, J. L. 1989. *The focus structure of it-clefts.* Research Report RP-25. Centre for Cognitive Science, University of Edinburgh.
Derbyshire, Desmond C. 1986. Topic continuity and OVS order in Hixkaryana. In Joel Sherzer and Greg Urban (eds.), *Native South American discourse*, 237–306. Berlin: Mouton de Gruyter.
Dik, Simon. 1989. *The theory of functional grammar. Part I: The structure of the clause.* Dordrecht: Foris.
Dik, Simon, Maria E. Hoffman, Jan R. de Jong, Sie Ing Djiang, Harry Stroomer, and Lourens de Vries. 1981. On the typology of focus phenomenon. In Teun Hoekstra, Harry van der Hulst, and Michael Moortgat (eds.), *Perspectives on functional grammar*, 41–74. Dordrecht: Foris.
Dooley, Robert A. 1989. Functional approaches to grammar: Implications for SIL training. Ms.
Dooley, Robert A. 1990. The positioning of non-pronominal clitics and particles in lowland South American languages. In Doris L. Payne (ed.), *Amazonian linguistics: Studies in lowland South American languages*, 457–483. Austin, TX: University of Texas Press.
Dooley, Robert A., and Stephen H. Levinsohn. 2001. *Analyzing discourse: A manual of basic concepts.* Dallas, TX: SIL International.
Dryer, Matthew S. 1997. On the six-way word order typology. *Studies in Language* 21(2):69–103.
Enfield, N. J. 2003. Demonstratives in space and interaction: Data from Lao speakers and implications for semantic analysis. *Language* 79(1):82–117.
Fanning, Buist M. 1990. *Verbal aspect in New Testament Greek.* Oxford Theological Monographs. Oxford: Clarendon Press.
Fast, Kara. 2008. Subordination, grounding and the packaging of information in Gojri. MA thesis. University of North Dakota.
Fillmore, Charles J. 1997. *Lectures on deixis.* CSLI Lecture Notes 65. Stanford, CA: Center for the Study of Language and Information.
Firbas, Jan. 1964. From comparative word-order studies. *BRNO Studies in English* 4:111–126.
Foley, William A., and Robert D. Van Valin Jr. 1984. *Functional syntax and universal grammar.* Cambridge Studies in Linguistics 38. Cambridge: Cambridge University Press.

Follingstad, Carl M. 1994. Thematic development and prominence in Tyap discourse. In Levinsohn 1994, 151–189.
Follingstad, Carl M. 1995. *Hinnēh* and focus function with application to Tyap. *Journal of Translation and Textlinguistics* 7(3):1–24.
Follingstad, Carl M. 2001. *Deictic viewpoint in Biblical Hebrew text: A syntagmatic and paradigmatic analysis of the particle* כִּי (*kî*). Journal of Translation and Textlinguistics. Dallas, TX: SIL International.
Fox, Barbara. 1987. Anaphora in popular written English narratives. In Russell S. Tomlin (ed.), *Coherence and grounding in discourse*, 157–174. Amsterdam: John Benjamins.
Garvin, Paul L. 1963. Czechoslovakia. In Thomas A. Sebeok (ed.), *Current trends in linguistics*, 1:499–522. The Hague: Mouton.
Gault, JoAnn. 1999. Thoughts concerning ergativity, subject and focus in Sama Bangingi'. In Elizabeth Zeitoun and Paul Jen-Kuei Li (eds.), *Papers of the Eighth International Conference on Austronesian Linguistics, Taipei, Taiwan*, Symposium Series of the Institute of Linguistics (Preparatory Office) Academia Sinica, I.393–422.
Givón, Talmy, ed. 1983. *Topic continuity in discourse*. Amsterdam: John Benjamins.
Givón, Talmy. 1984/1990. *Syntax: A functional-typological introduction*. 2 vols. Amsterdam: John Benjamins.
Green, Jay P., Sr. 1986. *The interlinear Bible: Hebrew-Greek-English*. Second edition. Lafayette, IN: Sovereign Grace Publishers.
Grimes, Joseph E. 1975. *The thread of discourse*. The Hague: Mouton.
Grimes, Joseph E., ed. 1978. *Papers on discourse*. Summer Institute of Linguistics Publications in Linguistics and Related Fields 51. Dallas, TX.
Gundel, Jeanette, Nancy Hedberg, and Ron Zacharski. 1993. Cognitive status and the form of referring expressions in discourse. *Language* 69:274–307.
Guthrie, George H. 1998. *The structure of Hebrews: A text-linguistic analysis*. Grand Rapids, MI: Baker Books.
Headland, Edna. 1975. Information load and layout in Tunebo. *Notes on Translation* 58:2–24.
Hedinger, Robert. 1984. Reported speech in Akoose. *Journal of West African Languages* 14(1):81–102.
Heimerdinger, Jean-Marc. 1999. *Topic, focus and foreground in Ancient Hebrew narratives*. Journal for the Study of the Old Testament: Supplement Series 295. Sheffield: Sheffield Academic Press.
Hopper, Paul J. 1979. Aspect and foregrounding in discourse. In Talmy Givón (ed.), *Syntax and semantics 12: Discourse and syntax*, 213–241. New York: Academic Press.
Hopper, Paul J., and Sandra A. Thompson. 1980. Transitivity in grammar and discourse. *Language* 56:251–299.
Hopper, Paul J., and Sandra A. Thompson. 1984. The discourse basis for lexical categories in universal grammar. *Language* 60:703–752.
Hutchison, John P. 1981. *The Kanuri language: A reference grammar*. Madison: University of Wisconsin.
Hwang, Shin Ja J. 1990. Foregrounding information in narrative. *Southwest Journal of Linguistics* 9(2):63–90.
Jackendoff, Ray S. 1972. *Semantic interpretation in generative grammar*. Studies in Linguistics Series 2. Cambridge, MA: The MIT Press.
Jarvis, Elisabeth. 1991. Tense and aspect in Podoko narrative and procedural discourse. In Stephen Anderson and Bernard Comrie (eds.), *Tense and aspect in eight languages of Cameroon*. Summer Institute of Linguistics and the University of Texas at Arlington Publications in Linguistics 99, 213–237. Dallas, TX.
Johnstone, Barbara. 1987. "He says ... so I said": Verb tense alternation and narrative depictions of authority in American English. *Linguistics* 25:33–52.
Kiss, Katalin É. 1998. Identificational focus versus information focus. *Language* 74(2):245–273.
König, Ekkehard. 1991. *The meaning of focus particles: A comparative perspective*. London: Routledge.
Koontz, Carol. 1978. Características del diálogo en el discurso narrativo teribe [Characteristics of dialogue in Teribe narrative discourse]. In Stephen H. Levinsohn (ed.), *Lenguas de Panamá, Tomo V: La estructura del diálogo en el discurso narrativo*, 29–61. Panamá: Instituto Nacional de Cultura, Dirección del Patrimonio Histórico e Instituto Lingüístico de Verano.

Koontz, Carol, and Joanne Anderson de Ostendorph. 1978. Los enlaces en el discurso teribe [Links in Teribe discourse]. In Stephen H. Levinsohn (ed.), *Lenguas de Panamá, Tomo IV: Estudios sobre el discurso*, 69–117. Panamá: Instituto Nacional de Cultura, Dirección del Patrimonio Histórico e Instituto Lingüístico de Verano.

Lambrecht, Knud. 1994. *Information structure and sentence form: Topic, focus, and the mental representation of discourse referents*. Cambridge Studies in Linguistics 71. New York: Cambridge University Press.

Lambrecht, Knud. 2000. When subjects behave like objects: An analysis of the merging of S and O in sentence-focus constructions across languages. *Studies in Language* 24(3):611–682.

Leech, Geoffrey N. 1983. *Principles of pragmatics*. Longman Linguistics Library 30. London: Longman.

Levinsohn, Stephen H. 1975. Functional sentence perspective in Inga (Quechuan). *Journal of Linguistics* 11:13–37.

Levinsohn, Stephen H. 1976. Progression and digression in Inga (Quechuan) discourse. *Forum Linguisticum* 1(2):122–147.

Levinsohn, Stephen H. 1978. Participant reference in Inga narrative discourse. In John Hinds (ed.), *Anaphora in discourse*, 69–135. Edmonton, Canada: Linguistic Research, Inc.

Levinsohn, Stephen H. 1992. Preposed and postposed adverbials in English. *1992 Work Papers of the Summer Institute of Linguistics, University of North Dakota Session*, 36:19–31.

Levinsohn, Stephen H., ed. 1994. *Discourse features of ten languages of West-Central Africa*. Summer Institute of Linguistics and the University of Texas at Arlington Publications in Linguistics 119. Dallas, TX.

Levinsohn, Stephen H. 2000. *Discourse features of New Testament Greek: A coursebook on the information structure of New Testament Greek*. Second edition. Dallas, TX: SIL International.

Levinsohn, Stephen H. 2001a. *Erchomai* and *poreuomai* in Luke-Acts: Two orientation strategies. *Notes on Translation* 15(3):13–30.

Levinsohn, Stephen H. 2001b. *Also*, *too* and *moreover* in a novel by Dorothy L. Sayers. *Work Papers of the Summer Institute of Linguistics, University of North Dakota Session 2001*. Vol. 45. https://commons.und.edu/sil-work-papers/vol45/iss1/1/.

Levinsohn, Stephen H. 2002. Towards a typology of additives. *AAP* 69:171–188. Institut für Afrikanistik, Köln, Germany.

Levinsohn, Stephen H. 2003. Some observations on the storyline status of gerunds in Koorete (Omotic). *Journal of Translation and Textlinguistics* 15:27–34.

Levinsohn, Stephen H. 2006. Towards a typology of story development marking (repeatedly naming the subject: The Hebrew equivalent of Greek Δέ). *Journal of Translation* 2(2):31–42.

Levinsohn, Stephen H. 2009a. Is ὅτι an interpretive use marker? In Stanley E. Porter and Matthew Brook O'Donnell (eds.), *The linguist as pedagogue: Trends in the teaching and linguistic analysis of the Greek New Testament*, 163–182. Sheffield, UK: Sheffield Phoenix Press.

Levinsohn, Stephen H. 2009b. Towards a unified linguistic description of οὗτος and ἐκεῖνος. In Stanley E. Porter and Matthew Brook O'Donnell (eds.), *The linguist as pedagogue: Trends in the teaching and linguistic analysis of the Greek New Testament*, 206–219. Sheffield, UK: Sheffield Phoenix Press.

Levinsohn, Stephen H. 2012. Further steps towards a typology of story development marking. Paper presented at Institutionen för lingvistik och filologi, Uppsala University, Sweden, June 2012.

Levinsohn, Stephen H. 2015. *Self-instruction materials on non-narrative discourse analysis*. Dallas, TX: SIL International.

Levinsohn, Stephen H., and Luis F. Avendaño, eds. 1982. *Parlocuna Leesunchi (Segunda cartilla de lectura en el Inga del Valle de Sibundoy)* [Let's read stories! (Second reading primer in Sibundoy Valley Inga)]. Lomalinda, Colombia: Editorial Townsend.

Li, Charles N. 1986. Direct speech and indirect speech: A functional study. In Florian Coulmas (ed.), *Direct and indirect speech*, 29–45. Berlin: Mouton de Gruyter.

Lichtenberk, Frantisek. 1991. Semantic change and heterosemy in grammaticalization. *Language* 67:475–509.

Longacre, Robert E. 1990. Storyline concerns and word order typologies in East and West Africa. *Studies in African Linguistics*, Supplement 10. Los Angeles, CA: James S. Coleman African Studies Center and Department of Linguistics, University of California at Los Angeles.

Longacre, Robert E. 1995. Left shifts in strongly VSO languages. In Pamela Downing and Michael Noonan (eds.), *Word order in discourse*, 331–354. Amsterdam: John Benjamins.

Longacre, Robert E. 1996. *The grammar of discourse*. Second edition. Topics in Language and Linguistics. New York: Plenum.

Longacre, Robert E., and Stephen H. Levinsohn. 1978. Field analysis of discourse. In Wolfgang U. Dressler (ed.), *Current trends in textlinguistics*, 103–122. Berlin: De Gruyter.

Loos, Eugene E. 1963. *Capanahua narrative structure*. Studies in Literature and Language 4. Austin, TX: University of Texas.

Lovelace, Christine Ann. 1992. Discourse grammar of Tsuvadi folktales. MA thesis. University of Texas at Arlington.

Lowe, Ivan. 1998. Why translators need to study the grammar of the receptor language. *Notes on Translation* 12(1):36–43.

Lowe, Ivan, and Ruth Hurlimann. 2002. Direct and indirect speech in Cerma narrative. In Tom Güldemann and Manfred von Roncador (eds.), *Reported discourse: A meeting ground for different linguistic domains*, 71–90. Amsterdam: John Benjamins.

Mann, William C., and Sandra A. Thompson. 1987. Rhetorical structure theory: A theory of text organization. In Livia Polanyi (ed.), *The structure of discourse*. Norwood, NJ: Ablex. Reprinted (1987) as report ISI/RS-87-190, Marina del Rey, CA: Information Sciences Institute, from which citations are taken. Reduced version published (1988) as Rhetorical structure theory: Toward a functional theory of text organization. *Text* 8:243–81.

Marchese, L. 1984. Pronouns and full nouns: A case of misrepresentation. *The Bible Translator* 35(2):234–235.

Mfonyam, Joseph Ngwa. 1994. Prominence in Bafut: Syntactic and pragmatic devices. In Levinsohn 1994, 191–210.

Mfonyam, Joseph Ngwa. 2012. Repetition and irritation emphasis in Bafut. *JWAL* 39(1):3–14.

Miguel López, Rodolfo N. 1998. *El carnero atrevido* [The daring ram]. Mexico: Instituto Lingüístico de Verano, A.C.

Morgan, David. 1994. Semantic constraints on relevance in Lobala discourse. In Levinsohn 1994, 125–149.

Olson, Clif. 2014. *Participant referencing in Gumawana narrative*. Data Papers on Papua New Guinea Languages. Vol. 60. Ukarumpa, PNG: SIL-PNG Academic Publications. http://www.sil.org/resources/archives/60504.

Oxford English Dictionary (OED). 1989. Second edition. 20 vols. Oxford: Oxford University Press. Continually updated at http://www.oed.com/.

Perrin, Mona. 1974. Direct and indirect speech in Mambila. *Journal of Linguistics* 10:27–37.

Perrin, Mona. 1978. Who's who in Mambila folk stories. In Joseph E. Grimes (ed.), *Papers on discourse*. Summer Institute of Linguistics Publications in Linguistics and Related Fields 51, 105–118. Dallas, TX.

Perrin, Mona. 1994. Rheme and focus in Mambila. In Levinsohn 1994, 231–241.

Perrin, Mona. n.d. *Aperçu des traits du discours* [Overview of discourse features]. Yaoundé, Cameroon: Société Internationale de Linguistique.

Pohlig, James N., and Stephen H. Levinsohn. 1994. Demonstrative adjectives in Mofu-Gudur folktales. In Levinsohn 1994, 53–90.

Pope, Kathrin. 1993. The use of subordinate clauses in Waama and how this affects translation. *Notes on Translation* 7(2):1–11.

Ramsey, Violeta. 1987. The functional distribution of preposed and postposed "if" and "when" clauses in written discourse. In Russell S. Tomlin (ed.), *Coherence and grounding in discourse*, 383–408. Amsterdam: Benjamins.

Reboul, Anne, and Jacques Moeschler. 1998. *Pragmatique du discours: De l'interprétation de l'énoncé à l'interprétation du discours* [Discourse pragmatics: From the interpretation of the utterance to the interpretation of the discourse]. Paris: Armand Colin.

Reed, Jeffrey T., and Ruth A. Reese. 1996. Verbal aspect, discourse prominence, and the letter of Jude. *Filología Neotestamentaria* 9:181–199.

Regt, Lénart J. de. 1999. *Participants in Old Testament texts and the translator: Reference devices and their rhetorical impact*. Studia Semitica Neerlandica 39. Assen, The Netherlands: Van Gorcum.

Roberts, John R. 1997. The syntax of discourse structure. *Notes on Translation* 11(2):15–34.

Sayers, Dorothy L. 1989. *The documents in the case*. Sevenoaks, Kent, England: Hodder & Stoughton Paperbacks.

Sayers, Dorothy L. 2018. *Lord Peter: A Collection of All the Lord Peter Wimsey Stories*. London: Hodder & Stoughton. First published 1972, New York: Harper & Row.

Schneider, Wolfgang. 1982. *Grammatik des Biblischen Hebräisch. Ein Lehrbuch* [Grammar of Biblical Hebrew. A textbook]. München: Claudius Verlag.

Sim, Ronald J. 2010. Lo and Behold! Revisiting Hebrew presentative particles. Paper presented at the Bible Translation 2010 (BT2010) Conference, Horsleys Green, England, 4–6 July 2010.

Speece, Richard F. 1989. Redundant clauses in Angave narratives. *Notes on Translation* 3(1):1–26.

Sperber, Dan, and Deirdre Wilson. 1995. *Relevance: Communication & cognition*. Second edition. Oxford: Blackwell.

Stanford, Ronald. 1967. The Bekwarra language of Nigeria: A grammatical description. PhD thesis. University of London, SOAS.

Taglicht, Josef. 1984. *Message and emphasis: On focus and scope in English*. English Language Series 15. London: Longman.

Thompson, Geoff. 1994. *Reporting*. Collins COBUILD English Guides 5. London: Harper & Collins.

Thompson, Sandra A. 1985. Grammar and written discourse: Initial versus final purpose clauses in English. *Text* 5:55–84.

Thompson, Sandra A., and Robert E. Longacre. 1985. Adverbial clauses. In Timothy Shopen (ed.), *Language typology and syntactic description*, 1:171–234. Cambridge: Cambridge University Press.

Vallejos Yopán, Rosa. 2009. The focus function(s) of =*pura* in Kokama-Kokamilla discourse. *IJAL* 75(3):399-432.

Van der Merwe, Christo H. J. 1999. The elusive Biblical Hebrew term ויהי (*wayyəhî*): A perspective in terms of its syntax, semantics and pragmatics in 1 Samuel. *Hebrew Studies* 40:83–114.

Van Otterloo, Roger. 1988. Towards an understanding of "lo" and "behold": Functions of *idou* and *ide* in the Greek New Testament. *Occasional Papers in Translation and Textlinguistics* 2(1):34–64.

Van Valin, Robert D., Jr. 2005. *Exploring the syntax-semantics interface*. Cambridge: Cambridge University Press.

Vendler, Zeno. 1967. *Linguistics in philosophy*. Ithaca: Cornell University Press.

Vries, Lourens de. 2005. Towards a typology of tail-head linkage in Papuan languages. *Studies in Language* 29(2):363–384.

Waugh, Linda R., and M. Monville-Burston. 1986. Aspect and discourse function: The French simple past in newspaper usage. *Language* 62:846–877.

Wenham, Gordon J. 1994. Genesis 16–50. *Word Biblical Commentary*. Vol. 2. Dallas, TX: Word Books.

Werth, Paul. 1984. *Focus, coherence and emphasis*. London: Croom Helm.

Whaley, Lindsay J. 1997. *Introduction to typology: The unity and diversity of language*. London: SAGE Publications.

Wiesmann, Hannes. 2000. Éléments du discours narratif dans les textes win (toussian du sud) [Elements of narrative discourse in Win texts (Southern Toussian)]. *Cahiers Voltaïques–Hors Série 2*. Bayreuth, Germany: Universität Bayreuth.

Wiesmann, Hannes. n.d. A propos du marqueur d'emploi interprétatif «nké» en Toussian [About the interpretive-use marker "nké" in Toussian]. Ms.

Zegarač, Vladimir. 1989. Relevance theory and the meaning of the English progressive. *University College London Working Papers in Linguistics* 1:19–31.

Questionnaire: Narrative Text Features

In each section, state the forms you are describing and indicate their functions.

Language:

Language family:

Linguist(s):

Texts used (originally oral, written, both?):

Date:

1 Variations in the order of clause constituents

1.1 Nuclear constituents (Subject Verb Object/Complement and possibly Indirect Object)

State the unmarked or most common order in narrative; in equative clauses (if different).

1.2 Preposing of nuclear and non-nuclear constituents

Describe the reasons for preposing constituents (e.g. to establish points of departure, to give prominence to focal constituents – see ch. 3). If there is more than one reason for preposing, indicate how they may be distinguished (e.g. by the presence of a pronominal trace if the point of departure is a nominal constituent, of a 'sentence topic/thematic' marker; cross-reference 2.1 if a 'focus' marker is used). If there is a difference between simple preposing and left dislocation (with a pronominal trace), then distinguish their functions.

1.3 Tail-head linkage

When tail-head linkage occurs, the aspect of the repeated verb is typically perfective, imperfective or completive.[1] Describe the function(s) in your texts of each of these types of tail-head linkage (e.g. maintain continuity in oral material, slow down the story or argument prior to a particularly important event or assertion, resume the theme line of the story or argument, introduce the next step of a procedure).

1.4 Postnuclear (peripheral) constituents

What is the maximum number of postnuclear constituents found in a clause in natural text?
    Indicate whether the order of postnuclear constituents is fixed, or whether there are special positions for constituents in 'unmarked focus' and for thematic/established information.

1.5 Postposing of subjects

If the subject is ever postposed, describe the reason(s) for doing so (e.g. to indicate that it is not the topic of a Topic-Comment structure and/or because the clause begins with a prominent nonsubject).[2] As appropriate, specify the different circumstances in which subject postposing is found (e.g. in relative clauses and in thetic and identificational structures).

---

[1] This is a special use of the term 'tail' which is distinct from that in 1.5.
[2] Many OV languages do not postpose constituents in written or well-edited oral texts.

1.6 Postposing of other constituents, including 'tails'

Describe the functions of postposing constituents (e.g. clarification, anticipation of a change of topic). If there is a difference between simple postposing and right dislocation (with a pronominal trace), then distinguish their functions. (See Dooley and Levinsohn 2001:70–71.)

2 Prominence

2.1 Focus

Describe the device(s) used to give prominence to focal constituents (e.g. preposing, postposing, focus marker, changes in the order of constituents that are not in focus).[3] Determine which of these devices are used for narrow focus, for contrastive focus, for emphatic focus, and to give prominence to the dominant focal element (DFE).

2.2 Thematic prominence

Describe the device(s) that are employed to give prominence to a point of departure.

2.3 Features of emphasis

Describe the device(s) that are employed to emphasise constituents or sentences.

3 Devices for backgrounding and highlighting sentences and clauses

3.1 Foreground events

Describe the unmarked way of presenting foreground events in a narrative (typically, with topic-comment articulation and the verb in the perfective [portray the event as a whole] aspect).[4]

3.2 Backgrounding events of secondary importance

Describe the devices that are used to background events in narrative. Distinguish their functions.
    Describe how flashbacks are encoded.

3.3 Highlighting

Describe the devices that are used to slow down a narrative immediately before a climax or significant development.
    Describe any other devices that give prominence to climactic sentences, significant developments, key assertions, etc. If the device is typically found in some genres but not in others (e.g. in reported conversation but not in the narrative superstructure), then note this fact.

4 Pragmatic connectives

4.1 Coordinating sentences

Which is the default way of coordinating sentences that present the main events of a narrative: by juxtaposing them or by means of a particular coordinating conjunction (specify which)?[5]
    What specific semantic or pragmatic relationships do the remaining ways of coordinating sentences signal?

---

[3] See chapter 4.
[4] See chapter 5.
[5] See chapter 6.

4.2 Coordinating clauses within a sentence

Which is the default way of coordinating clauses that describe successive events performed by the same subject: by juxtaposing them (i.e. by means of 'serial' verbs or predicates) or by means of a coordinating conjunction or repeated pronoun?

What are the effects of coordinating clauses in other ways?

4.3 Additives (markers of reinforcement and parallelism)

If more than one additive is found, distinguish their functions (e.g. parallelism with different subjects versus different predicates, similarity versus sameness, parallelism involving different constituents versus different propositions, linking propositions of unequal relevance).

What pragmatic effects does each additive convey (e.g. parallelism, confirmation, concession, grouping propositions together)?

What is the default position of each additive? What is its function when it occurs in other positions?

4.4 Countering markers

List any countering markers not covered in 4.1–4.2, and distinguish their functions.

Under what circumstances is the countering relation normally left implicit?

4.5 Markers of new information

Describe the (positive or negative) means used to indicate new developments in a narrative. If more than one means is used, then distinguish their functions.

4.6 Introducing nonevent material in narrative

If any connectives are used primarily to introduce nonevent material in a narrative (such as explanatory comments, summaries or morals), then list them and distinguish their functions.

4.7 Resumptives

Describe any markers or constructions not covered in 1.3 that are used to indicate the resumption of an earlier theme line.

4.8 Other coordinating connectives

Describe the functions of any coordinating connectives not covered in 4.1–4.7, indicating the semantic relationships between propositions that they signal.

Describe when such relationships are left implicit.

5 Reporting of conversation

5.1 Ways of reporting the speeches

Indicate which is the default way of reporting speech: direct, indirect or semidirect.[6]

Describe any other ways of reporting speeches, along with their functions.

What restrictions does the language place if the speaker or addressee is referred to in the reported speech (e.g. *He told me **you** have to go*, where *you* in English could refer either to the speaker or to the addressee)?

What restrictions does the language place on the embedding of a reported speech inside a reported speech? Are the restrictions more severe if the reported speaker or addressee is referred to in the embedded speech?

---

[6] See chapter 7.

5.2 Positions of the speech orienters

What is the normal position of the orienter relative to the speech being reported (prior to the speech, following the speech, both)?
    Is the orienter found in other positions? If so, describe when each is used.
    When is the orienter omitted completely: in oral material? in written material?

5.3 The relationship between successive speeches in a reported conversation

Is the default way of coordinating sentences (4.1) typically used also to link noninitial speeches of a reported conversation? If not, what means of coordination is typically used?

5.4 The status of reported speeches in the overall story

What is the default form of the orienter for noninitial speeches of a reported conversation (e.g. with the verb in the imperfective, without any speech verb)?
    Describe the function of each other form of the orienter (e.g. with the speech verb in the perfective, with a speech verb).

5.5 Changes of direction within a reported conversation

Describe the means of indicating a change of direction within a conversation (e.g. a verb such as *answer*).

5.6 Repetitions of speech orienters

Explain any repetitions of the same speech orienter in your texts.

5.7 Other observations about the speech orienters

Describe any other variation in the orienters in your texts (e.g. the function of each verb or particle used).

6 Participant reference

6.1 Activation of participants

Describe the different ways that MAJOR participants are activated (introduced) in your texts.[7] Distinguish introductions into a NEW mental representation from introductions into an EXISTING mental representation.
    Describe how MINOR participants are activated in the texts.
    Describe how the introduction of participants is HIGHLIGHTED (other than by tail-head linkage – 1.3).

6.2 Further reference to activated participants

Give the encoding scale for further reference to activated participants (see Dooley and Levinsohn 2001:127–128).
    State default encoding values for the following contexts involving activated **subjects** in the text (p. 132):
- S1: the subject is the same as in the previous sentence;
- S2: the subject was the addressee of the previous reported speech;
- S3: the subject had some other nonsubject role in the previous clause/sentence;
- S4: the subject was not involved in the previous clause/sentence.

---

[7] See chapters 8 and 9.

If a 'VIP strategy' (Dooley and Levinsohn 2001:119) is sometimes used, explain how this affects the default encodings.

Describe marked subject encodings and their discourse-pragmatic motivations (e.g. to mark the beginning of a narrative unit, to highlight the action or speech concerned).

[Present a similar scheme of default and marked encodings for references to activated nonsubjects.]

6.3 Determiners and pronouns

Describe the system of determiners used, together with the deictic-exophoric and text-related functions of each. Which set of determiners or pronouns, if any, is used for thematic references? For athematic references?

6.4 Point of orientation or centre of interest

1. Describe any devices that signal the point of orientation for part or all of your texts (e.g. *come* and *go* auxiliaries, locative adverbs such as *here* and *there*). Comment on any changes of orientation in connection with climax.
2. The following set of questions will help you determine the permitted centres of orientation for the language of verbs like *come* and *go* (see Levinsohn 2001 for fuller discussion).
    a. If the language has a verb like *come* that denotes motion toward the location of the speaker at **coding time** (the time of the speech act – e.g. *Please come in!*), can the same verb be used to denote:
        - motion toward the location of the **addressee** at coding time (e.g. *I'm just coming*)?
        - motion toward the location of the speaker at **reference** time (the time that is being referred to in the sentence when that time is different from coding time; e.g. *Please come there* at dawn!* [*where I'll be at the stated time])?
        - motion toward the location of the **home base** of the speaker at reference time (e.g. *He came over to my place last night, but I wasn't home*)?
        - motion that is **in the company of** the speaker (e.g. *Would you like to come [with me]?*)?
    b. Does the point of orientation in third-person narratives remain fixed or can it change? If it can change, what brings about the change (e.g. movement by the VIP)?
    c. When a third-person narrative involves a VIP, do other participants *come* and *go* with respect to the location of the VIP in the story? If not, what is the typical point of orientation in stories in which other participants interact with a VIP?
    d. When a third-person narrative describes movement by a VIP, what is the point of orientation to which this movement is related (e.g. the location of the first major event of the narrative, the location of the last events described, the location of the next theme-line events)?
3. If locative adverbs for *here* and *there* are ever oriented with respect to other than the current location of the speaker, then indicate the point of orientation to which they are related.

7 Subordination and given versus new information

7.1 New information and subordinate clauses

Indicate whether subordinate clauses (including relative clauses) can contain brand-new information.[8] If they can, indicate any restrictions on the presentation of such information in these clauses (e.g. if they contain brand-new information they have to be postnuclear – i.e. follow the clause to which they are subordinated –, or they have to be purpose clauses).

Indicate what types of information can be introduced in PRENUCLEAR subordinate clauses (e.g. only a point of departure at a discontinuity, information already given in the immediate context, information that is accessed by – implied by or expected from – the context).

---

[8] See chapter 10.

7.2 Relative clauses (including nominalisations)

Indicate which grammatical relations may be relativised (e.g. subject and direct object only).

When relative clauses are used in a RESTRICTIVE (identifying) sense, describe where they are found (e.g. usually off the event line or modifying a peripheral constituent, in narrative) and their function(s) (e.g. related to prominence – exemplify).

Indicate whether relative clauses can be used in a NONRESTRICTIVE (descriptive) sense. If they can, describe their function(s).

7.3 Information load

In natural text, what is the maximum number of constituents per sentence that can convey new information? (Count subject, object, verb, location, etc. as one constituent each.)

What devices are used to spread new information over more than one sentence (e.g. parallel sentences with the same subject and verb, *inclusio* structures)?[9]

---

[9] *Inclusio* structures involve the bracketing of a unit by making a statement at the beginning, an approximation of which is repeated at the end (see Guthrie 1998:14).

Index of Languages

Amharic [amh] 96
Arabic, Moroccan [ary] 102n23, 149
Arop-Lokep [apr] 88

Bafut [bfd] 64, 92, 95, 111, 146, 147, 161
Bakossi [bss] 155
Balochi of Sistan [bgn] 131
Bekwarra [bkv] 7, 9, 14, 15, 16–19, 24n2, 26, 28, 29, 32, 34, 35, 36–40, 41, 42, 43, 50, 54, 55, 71, 76, 81, 83, 88, 104, 105, 110, 111, 124, 130, 131, 141, 149, 156, 163
Bonggi [bdg] 73, 74
Bwamu [box] 90, 114

Cerma [cme] 77, 147, 155
Chadic 95
C'Lela [dri] 142

Dogosé/Khissé [dos] 63, 95, 96
Dungra Bhil [duh] 19–20, 56

Ekoti [eko] 145, 146
Engenni [enn] 54, 57
English [eng] 4, 6, 9, 12, 13, 26, 27, 31, 32, 34, 42n6, 43n, 44n8, 45, 48, 53, 54, 55, 56, 59, 61, 65, 66, 67, 71, 73, 76, 77, 82, 83, 84n26, 91, 92, 93, 96, 102, 109, 110, 112, 113, 119, 126, 148, 149, 155, 157, 158, 160, 173

French [fra] 5, 45, 55n4, 56, 64, 71, 74, 124n2 164

Goemai [ank] 111, 113, 143
Gojri [gju] 97n17, 102

Greek, Koine [grc] 2, 6, 26, 33, 44, 45, 47, 50n23, 51n25, 55, 56, 57, 58, 60, 62, 65, 66, 70, 71, 76, 78, 79, 80n22, 81n23, 84, 85, 87, 88, 89, 90, 91, 92, 93, 94, 96, 97, 101, 102, 105, 106, 107, 109, 110, 112, 113, 114, 115n, 116, 117, 118n, 120, 124, 125, 126, 127, 128, 130, 131, 132, 133, 135, 144, 145, 147, 148, 149, 151–153, 156, 157n4, 160
Guaraní, Mbyá [gun] 121n7
Guaymí [gym] 10
Gude [gde] 45, 72, 90, 95, 103, 104, 115, 116, 161
Gumawana [gvs] 44, 56, 62, 72, 75, 76, 77, 112, 113, 114, 115, 116

Hebrew, Biblical [hbo] 6, 8, 10, 48n17, 49n20, 51n24, 55, 57, 65, 71n4, 73n9, 80n21, 82, 84, 85, 87, 92, 93, 102, 110, 113, 117, 118, 120, 123, 125, 132, 133, 134, 135, 136, 158, 163–137, 164
Hebrew, Modern [heb] 125
Herde [hed] 75, 145, 162
Hixkaryána [hix] 114, 116, 128n8
Ho [hoc] 84

Inga, Highland [inb] 3, 9n1, 26, 58, 66, 70, 71, 73, 82, 92, 93, 102, 114, 143, 146, 148, 149
Inga, Jungle (Guayuyacu) [inj] 74, 80n22
Iten [etx] 114, 117

Kaansa [gna] 149
Kaba [ksp] 142, 145
Kako [kkj] 95, 161

Kalagan [kqe] 154
Kalinga, Lower Tanudon [kml] 51
Kambaata [ktb] 72
Kangri [xnr] 83
Kanuri [kau] 162n
Karai Karai [kai] 83, 117, 147, 162
Kenyang [ken] 95
Kera [ker] 95
Khoekhoe [naq] 67
Konso [kxc] 96
Konzime [ozm] 161
Koorete [kqy] 59, 60, 61, 64, 67, 100, 102, 106
Korean [kor] 113
Kouya [kyf] 61
Kuo [xuo] 144

Lobala [loq] 94
Longuda [lnu] 114

Makaa [mcp] 107
Mambila [mcu] 59, 60, 95, 117, 143, 149
Mbuko [mqb] 95
Mixtec, Southeastern Nochixtlán [mxy] 21, 126
Mofu-Gudur [mif] 119, 130, 146
Mono [mnh] 94
Muan [moa] 162

Ndyuka [djk] 62
Nyungwe [nyu] 135n, 145, 146

Obolo [ann] 59, 102n23, 160
Oroko [bdu] 75, 148

Podoko [pbi] 75, 81, 82

Shekacho [moy] 49
Sissala [sid] 92, 119n
Sokoro [sok] 144
Spanish [spa] 2, 9, 10, 45n11, 64, 148

Tadaksahak [dsq] 159, 161, 162
Teribe [tfr] 75, 119
Thai [tha] 73
Tombonuo [txa] 26
Toussian, Southern [wib] 119, 120, 124, 162
Tsuvadi [tvd] 48, 80, 144
Tula [tul] 51
Tunebo [tuf] 156, 157
Tyap [kcg] 92, 98, 99, 100, 102, 106, 115, 130, 131, 132, 133, 134, 135, 138–139

Waama [wwa] 155, 159
Waunana [noa] 144

Yemba [ybb] 162
Yoruba [yor] 65, 66, 102

Index of Scripture References

Old Testament

Genesis
  1:10 10
  2:17 65
  3:1–22 163
  3:3, 11, 17 163
  3:6, 24 164
  3:23–4:16 163
  4:1 57
  4:1–8 84
  4:3–4 92
  4:4 93
  4:4–6 134
  4:7, 14, 15 164
  7 164
  21:33–22:14 136
  22:1–2 133
  22:1–6 133
  22:1–14 132, 164
  22:5 135
  22:7 6
  22:8 118
  39:7 124
  42:6–9 132n18

Exodus
  1:15 163n13
  2:16, 18 143

Exodus, continued
  4:6 85
  7:7 51n24
  8:1 112
  10:25 93

Numbers
  5:21 118

Deuteronomy
  4:26 56

Ruth
  1:1 125n3

1 Samuel
  17:35 82

2 Samuel
  11:8, 10 133n19

1 Kings
  20:21 80n21
  21:12–13 73n9

Jeremiah
  30:18–21 113

New Testament

Matthew
  1:20 60, 126
  2:1 126, 157
  2:9 85
  2:15 155
  3:1 152
  3:7 156
  4:3–11 118
  4:6, 7 121
  4:12 156
  5:22 62
  6:2 43
  6:12–14 49
  6:13 96
  6:14 43
  6:15 43, 45
  7:28 31
  9:1–8 105
  10:2 27
  14:8 112
  19:6 27
  25:15 31
  26:36–47 132

Mark
  1 148
  1:9 148
  1:14 148
  1:29 148
  1:39 148
  2:14–15 156
  6:14 125
  6:17 30, 47
  8:1 152
  12:38 48
  13:21 89
  15:43 158
  16:9–13 151
  16:12 153
  16:19 151

Luke
  1–4 148
  1:11 26, 27, 56
  1:30–38 116
  1:39 148, 152
  1:52 97
  2:1 152
  2:1–7 101, 106
  2:19 96
  2:36–37 47, 129
  2:36–38 79
  2:41 148

Luke, continued
  2:41–42 79
  2:42–43 76
  2:44 148
  2:51 148
  3:12 148
  3:22 156
  3:23–37 156
  4:2 151
  4:3 156
  4:16 148
  4:30 148
  4:31–33 125
  4:33 56
  4:38 125, 149
  5:27 124
  5:29 125
  5:35 152
  6:12 152
  6:23 152
  7:1 49
  7:40 113
  9:37 151
  9:52 148
  10:12 152
  13:10 124
  13:14 124
  14:20 148
  15:11 25, 124
  15:11–13 30
  15:11–32 128
  15:12 129
  15:13 41, 42, 129, 149
  15:14 84, 129
  15:15–16 129
  15:20 81n23
  15:21–22 113
  15:22–24 130
  16:24–31 116
  17:31 152
  18:16 96, 97
  18:30 152n15
  19:1–10 10
  19:42 152n15
  21:22 153
  21:23 151
  21:34 152
  22:40–41 48
  23:7 152
  23:9 72
  24:15 78
  24:18, 21 152n15

John
  1:21 112
  2:19 152n16
  4:7 124
  4:17 120
  4:20 120
  4:51 120
  6:18 91, 93
  8:12 116
  8:31 80
  10:1–7 120
  11:4–6 106–107
  15:4 44
  20:31 70

Acts
  1:5 152n15
  1:11 159
  1:15 152
  2:18 152
  2:29 152n15
  2:41 151
  3:24 152n15
  4:1 49, 126
  5:2 129
  5:7 26, 106
  5:19 125, 126
  5:21 51
  5:25 124
  5:36 152n15
  6:1 152
  7:41 151
  7:44–46 160
  8:1 151
  8:9 125n4
  9:10 56, 118n, 124
  9:10–14 117
  9:11 112
  9:13 117
  9:36 26, 28, 43
  9:36–43 29, 30
  9:37 84, 151
  10:1 29, 30, 125
  10:3–4 113
  10:4 116, 118n
  10:25–43 147
  10:36–43 152
  11:27 152
  12:1 152
  12:5 31
  12:14 110
  13:14 147
  14:26 43
  16:14 125n4

Acts, continued
  16:36 6
  19:13–14 82
  19:14 31, 81
  19:23 152
  20:6 45, 50
  21:6 151
  21:15 152
  21:16 90
  21:18 91
  21:38 152n15
  22:21 155
  23:11 152n15
  26:22 152n15

Romans
  8:17–18 89
  11:30 46, 51n24

1 Corinthians
  2:10 92, 93
  8:1 45
  11:25 51

Galatians
  1:13–2:14 69
  2:11 65
  3:2 66
  5:7 62

Ephesians
  6:21 44

Philippians
  1:18 94

1 Timothy
  4:7–8 88
  4:8 97

Philemon
  14 6

Hebrews
  4:11 151n13

James
  2:2 47
  2:18 58

Revelation
  1:18 112
  3:16 44
  5:3 82
  5:8 49
  9:17 152n16
  12:15 55

Stephen H. Levinsohn is a senior linguistics consultant with SIL International. He has a doctorate in Linguistic Sciences from the University of Reading, England, on the topic, "Relationships Between Constituents Beyond the Clause in the Acts of the Apostles" (1980), parts of which were published in 1987 by the Society of Biblical Literature under the title *Textual Connections in Acts* (1987). He and his wife, Nessie, became members of SIL International in 1965. They worked with the Inga (Quechuan) people in Colombia from 1968 to 1997. Since 1997 Stephen has run "Discourse for Translation" workshops in 20 countries for linguist-translators working with over 400 languages. National and expatriate participants in the workshops first learn how to analyse texts in the languages they are studying (the receptor languages), while learning how the source languages handle the same discourse tasks. They then apply their discoveries to draft translations into the receptor languages.

Academic website
sil.org/biography/stephen-levinsohn

Works by this author in SIL Language & Culture Archives
sil.org/resources/search/contributor/levinsohn-stephen-h

Works by this author in Google Scholar
scholar.google.com/citations?user=RpsBdtsAAAAJ&hl=en

www.ingramcontent.com/pod-product-compliance
Lightning Source LLC
Chambersburg PA
CBHW080924300426
44115CB00018B/2936